HERE AT LAST in paperback—with several all-new chapters and dramatic new revelations—is the number one *New York Times* bestseller that warned America that the Clinton White House was for sale, its security system a disaster, and its staff irredeemably corrupt.

As one of only two FBI agents posted at the White House, Gary Aldrich's job was to protect the President from danger and scandal by performing security checks on White House appointees. But when Bill Clinton came into office the new administration deliberately dismantled that security system—for one simple scandalous reason: Too many people hired by the Clintons could not meet the required ethical standards.

One driving force: First Lady Hillary Rodham Clinton, who usurped control of domestic policy and hiring decisions. As Aldrich shows, Mrs. Clinton and her aides destroyed the careers and reputations of longtime non-political White House employees to open "slots" for their Arkansas friends, no matter how unqualified or corrupt.

New appointees ran roughshod over White House tradition, common decency, and even federal law. Aldrich and members of the permanent White House staff were repeatedly shocked to discover drug use, rampant theft, open gay/lesbian sex, and—perhaps most alarming—widespread access to classified materials by personnel without security clearances.

When Agent Aldrich, unable to enforce the law from within, decided to blow the whistle, he was viciously denounced by the Clintons and their allies in the media. But the months that followed saw the White House being opened up—for a price—to convicted felons, foreign agents trying to buy changes in U.S. foreign policy, and even foreign governments illegally funding the Clintons' reelection campaign.

Now Gary Aldrich completes his story, with shocking new revelations, including the Clintons' sadly successful attempt to turn parts of the FBI into their own personal political police force.

Aldrich takes on his critics and shows how even his most controversial allegations—from the First Lady's pornographic Christmas tree, to President Clinton eluding the Secret Service to make alleged secret liaisons—could have been verified had the media been as interested in ferreting out the truth as they are in defending the Clintons.

Unlimited Access sheds new light on such White House scandals as "Nannygate," "Travelgate," "Filegate," and the mysterious death of Vince Foster—whose true motive for committing suicide was revealed to Aldrich by the now disgraced Craig Livingstone, then White House Security Director and a key-player in the "Filegate" scandal.

Throughout *Unlimited Access*, Aldrich relies on eyewitness testimony: his own and that of other White House insiders. He concludes with a mock FBI "background report" on the President and First Lady—a report that will surely be deeply disturbing to every loyal, law-abiding American.

To Lucas

UNLIMITED ACCESS

An FBI Agent Inside
the Clinton White House

Best Wishes

GARY ALDRICH

Gary Aldrich

REGNERY PUBLISHING, INC.
WASHINGTON, D.C.

Library of Congress Cataloging-in-Publication Data

Aldrich, Gary Warren.
   Unlimited access : an FBI agent inside the Clinton White House / Gary Warren Aldrich.
      p. cm.
   Includes index.
   ISBN 0-89526-454-4 (acid-free paper)
   1. Presidents—United States—Staff—Selection and appointment.
2. United States—Officials and employees—Selection and appointment. 3. Employee screening—United States. 4. United States—Politics and government—1989– I. Title.
JK518.A63 1996
353.001'325—dc20   95-26817
                                                       CIP

Published in the United States by
Regnery Publishing, Inc.
An Eagle Publishing Company
One Massachusetts Avenue, NW
Washington, DC 20001

Distributed to the trade by
National Book Network
4720-A Boston Way
Lanham, MD 20706

Printed on acid-free paper.
Manufactured in the United States of America

10 9 8 7 6 5

Books are available in quantity for promotional or premium use. Write to Director of Special Sales, Regnery Publishing, Inc., One Massachusetts Avenue, NW, Washington, DC 20001, for information on discounts and terms or call (202) 216-0600.

To my wife, Nina, who understands better than anyone what this means to me and knows the risks but gave me support to continue on, even in the face of tremendous odds. For my children, who had to settle for less time with dad so that I could finish this book. To all my family and friends, for what they've endured and for the endless joy and support they bring me.

Contents

About the Quotes

I've set off each chapter with a quote from Saul Alinsky's *Rules for Radicals: A Practical Primer for Realistic Radicals* (hereinafter called *Rules for Radicals*) and *George Washington's Rules of Civility and Decent Behaviour in Company and Conversation* (hereinafter called *George Washington's Rules of Civility and Decent Behaviour*), because each presents a competing view of the world—the latter a collection of appropriate ethical and moral behavior, and the former, in stark contrast, a lack thereof.

Saul Alinsky's view seems to me to convey the adjustable ethics and moral relativism of the Clintons and their associates, while sharing their vague but constant ends. George Washington's view is what I think most people expect from those who work in the White House, and rightly so. Without ethical men and women in government, the pomp and circumstance is a sham and power is merely abused.

Foreword: "One Who Dared"
BY MICHAEL REAGAN

Some very powerful people tried to keep this book out of your hands—and they nearly succeeded.

When Gary Aldrich submitted a manuscript copy of *Unlimited Access* to his former bosses at the FBI for review (as required by law), the Bureau's general counsel turned right around and sent it straight to the Clinton White House. There it was read with great interest—and even greater alarm. Panicked at the thought of so much ugly truth coming out in an election year, the Clinton forces leaped into action, turning the FBI into a truth-suppression arm of the White House.

At White House behest, the FBI held *Unlimited Access* hostage, forcing Gary Aldrich to spend his book advance, his life savings, and more on attorney fees, trying to pry his book out of the Bureau's clutches. If the Clinton administration could keep the book bottled up with legal maneuvering, Gary would eventually be forced to give up—and the truth contained in these pages would remain buried forever.

The strategy nearly worked—but at the eleventh hour, the Southeastern Legal Foundation provided a team of attorneys to take on the power of government attorneys and win the release of the book. But getting *Unlimited Access* off the press and into the stores was only the beginning of the battle.

As the book went into release, the White House strong-armed its friends in the media to keep Gary Aldrich off the air. Some shows that had planned to interview him—including CNN's *Larry King Live*, NBC's *Dateline*, and ABC's *Nightline*—abruptly canceled his appearance. Gary was virtually blackballed from network airwaves. One of the few shows that bucked the ban was the David Brinkley show on ABC—but there, Gary faced a hostile grilling, as well as being jeered as a "pathological liar" by the likes of George Stephanopoulos.

Gary Aldrich stayed in the kitchen and endured the heat. Day after day, he withstood what the Apostle Paul called the "wickedness of men who suppress the truth." Most of all, Gary Aldrich persevered, trusting in the strength of the U.S. Constitution and the biblical promise that "you will know the truth, and the truth will set you free."

Gary went directly to the people through our republic's newest and most vibrant source of truth—hundreds of radio talk shows across the country, including my own national show. His radio appearances fired up a listening public that was eager and hungry for truth. Information from *Unlimited Access*, as well as corroborating evidence from other sources, ricocheted all over the Internet as the public deliberately bypassed the information bottleneck of the dominant liberal media.

As *Unlimited Access* jumped onto the bestseller lists, the Clinton camp discovered that its attempt to suppress the book had only piqued public curiosity. Once people had a chance to read Gary Aldrich's book for themselves, an amazing phenomenon occurred: The book was passed from the original buyer to neighbors, co-workers, friends, and family members. Many bought extra copies to give away. It is reported that a single copy of *Unlimited Access* often circulated like a chain letter, being read by thirty or more people. Public libraries put eager readers on waiting lists, while at bookstores it was not unusual to see a hundred or more customers waiting in line to buy a copy.

Unlimited Access was eagerly snatched up, read, and believed— because the story in this book rings true. It is meticulously documented. It is one piece of the vast, sordid puzzle of the Clinton scandals. Gary Aldrich's piece of the puzzle meshes perfectly with so many other pieces unearthed by Ambrose Evans-Pritchard (*The Secret Life of Bill Clinton*), Christopher Ruddy, R. Emmett Tyrrell (*Boy Clinton* and *The American Spectator*), James Stewart (*Blood Sport*), Terry Reed (*Compromised*), Elizabeth Drew (*On the Edge: The Clinton Presidency*), Reed Irvine (chairman, Accuracy in Media), Mark Levin (president, Landmark Legal Foundation), and others.

But there's one big difference between Gary's piece of the puzzle and all those other pieces, as important as they are: *Unlimited Access* is the only *insider's* account of the Clinton White House. As a result, *Unlimited Access* has become the "bible," the "rosetta stone" that must be read in order to understand what the Clinton administration and the Clinton culture are all about. Gary's book is the basic, required textbook for anyone who wants to know what these refugees from the radical '60s are trying to impose on America at the brink of the new millennium. Any political or media "expert," "pundit," or "talking head" who hasn't delved into *Unlimited Access* doesn't know jack about Bill and Hill.

Every day, more pieces of the puzzle emerge, confirming the careful accuracy of Gary Aldrich's story. Some of the most important pieces of the Clinton web of scandal are still to be uncovered. Many pieces have certainly been shredded. But there is more than enough evidence to know that something has gone terribly wrong over at 1600 Pennsylvania Avenue.

Gary Aldrich's primary responsibility at the White House was security. He was entrusted with one of the most sensitive assignments in the entire FBI apparatus because he had *earned* that trust. Ironically, Gary Aldrich had passed security checks, background checks, and character checks that the president himself could not pass. Gary's job was to ensure the trustworthiness of those who worked in the White House, because the security of the White House is inseparable from the security of the United States of America.

When my dad was president of the United States, I got a close-up look at how White House security works. You might think that I, as the son of Ronald Reagan, could just walk into the White House anytime I wanted, no problem. Well, you'd be wrong! Before my wife Colleen and I could enter the White House for the first time, we had to give the Secret Service a lot of information, including a driver's license number, Social Security number, date of birth, and mother's maiden name. That information was handed over to the FBI for a detailed background check.

And that's the way it should be. The Secret Service and the FBI were doing exactly what they were supposed to do—exactly what Gary Aldrich was brought in to do. But when the Clintons took over, Gary Aldrich could no longer do the job he was sworn to do. Instead, he was forced to watch helplessly as the entire White House security system broke down.

He saw seasoned White House professionals replaced by political operatives such as Craig Livingstone and Patsy Thomasson. Livingstone, hired as personnel security chief, was a former bar bouncer and political dirty trickster. Thomasson, a former associate of convicted drug dealer Dan Lasater, worked at the White House without a security clearance—and she was in charge of drug testing!

When Gary Aldrich went public with his story, he was jeered by the Clinton administration and the media. They said he made it all up. But as events unfolded, we began to catch a glimpse of the kind of people passing through the gates of the Clinton White House: Grigori Loutchanski, a known arms and drug smuggler; convicted Cuban drug godfather Jorge Cabrera; Wang Jun, a Chinese gunrunner linked to a huge shipment of AK-47 machine guns intended for American street gangs; Roger Tamraz, a fugitive wanted by Interpol; John Huang, Johnny Chung, and other probable agents of unfriendly foreign powers; and so on.

Do you think any of these unsavory types would have gotten past the front gate if they had undergone the same security check that was given the son of Ronald Reagan? Hardly. But criminals and spies were escorted right into the corridors of American power, hauling bales and bags and armloads of cash. These events prove what some of us have known all along: Gary Aldrich told the truth.

The day Bill Clinton took office in 1993, he promised to give us "the most ethical administration in the history of the republic." But Gary Aldrich saw a very different administration than the one Clinton promised. He tried to warn the American people—but his voice was drowned out by the idiotic blare of network news, which treats elections as horse-races rather than contests of governing principles.

So the self-righteous, self-proclaimed "most ethical administration in the history of the republic" was returned to power, where it has continued to spew forth its vomit of scandals, shreddings, denials, obfuscations, smokescreens, stonewalls, obstructions, sex, lies, and videotapes. The Clinton White House has produced more fired, disgraced, convicted, jailed, and ethically clouded officials than any other administration in history: Webster Hubbell, Roger C. Altman, David Watkins, Henry Cisneros, William Kennedy III, Anthony Marseca, Craig Livingstone, Bernard Nussbaum, Bruce Lindsey, Harold Ickes, Ira Magaziner, Ron Brown, Mike Espy, Hazel O'Leary, Josh Steiner, and so on!

Most importantly, Gary Aldrich has put his finger on the reason for all this sordid behavior within a single administration: This White House has a completely amoral worldview. When Gary starts each chapter with contrasting quotations from Saul Alinsky's *Rules for Radicals* and *George Washington's Rules of Civility and Decent Behavior*, he draws a clear line of demarcation between two competing philosophies of governance:

Reagan-Bush Administrations	Clinton Administration
Conservative respect for values, virtues, and tradition	Liberal "no rules" attitude and scorn for tradition
Substance and reality	Style and image
Sense of responsibility	Attitude of entitlement
Principles of duty, honor, country	Pragmatism of the moment
Desire to serve	Lust for power
Core principles	Strategy of the day
Truth is absolute	Truth is relative
Accountability	Arrogance

We see this contrast on virtually every page of *Unlimited Access*, but it truly smacks us in the face when Gary quotes the man who personifies everything wrong in the Clinton White House, Filegate operative Craig Livingstone: "Don't you know that truth is relative?" he asks on page 134. "Truth is whatever you want it to be."

Long before Bill and Hillary Clinton came to Washington, their philosophy of governance was laid out by Niccolo Machiavelli (1469-1527), an Italian political philosopher who advocated complete amorality, ruthlessness, cunning, deception, and the systematic ruin of all opposition in the pursuit of power. When you read the words of Machiavelli, you almost believe he wrote them to describe the 42nd president of the United States: "Everyone sees what you appear to be, few know what you are; and those few dare not oppose the opinion of the many."

The Clintons are not who they appear to be—and those who dare expose the truth usually pay a price. An old Arabian proverb says, "He who tells the truth should have one foot in the stirrup." Well, Gary Aldrich knew there would be a price to pay for telling the truth. He had seen the ruthless attempt to destroy White House travel office director Billy Dale for no more reason than to install Clinton cronies in Dale's place. He had seen the White House and the dominant media collude to discredit and destroy whistleblowers such as Whitewater witness Jean Lewis of the Resolution Trust Corporation, and John Libonati and Jeffrey Undercoffer—two Secret Service agents who were criminally investigated by the Clinton Treasury Department because they told the truth about Filegate.

So Gary Aldrich was under no illusions. He knew that the vast machinery of a corrupted government and a co-opted press would be unleashed against him if he told the truth. But that didn't stop him. He stood tall, he told the truth, he persevered, he paid the price. That kind of integrity is the mark of a great human being. That kind of courage is the mark of a great American.

Those in the Clinton circle—influenced as they seem to be by the philosophies of Alinsky and Machiavelli—failed to reckon with the power of a single honest and courageous career FBI agent. In vivid contrast to the Clinton philosophy, Gary Aldrich's personal and professional philosophy is grounded in the lives and words of our founding fathers—people of integrity and principle such as George Washington, who persevered through trials of fiery war and icy winters to create a new nation; and George Mason and Patrick Henry, who largely framed our precious Bill of Rights, including the right of free speech.

Unlimited Access is an important historical document. It is an eyewitness account of secrets that were meant to remain forever hidden—a glimpse of the ugly, wretched things that infest the dank, dark underside of the rock of our democracy. It is crucial that these truths, as ugly as they are, be aired out in the light of day, because the effects of this corruption radiate out into the nation and into the world. It is becoming increasingly clear that White House corruption has had a disturbing affect on both foreign and domestic policy. So this is no small matter, no tempest in a Teapot Dome. The security of our republic is on the line.

Truth has a way of snowballing. A time is coming when the world will see the Clinton White House as the most brazenly corrupt administration in history. The verdict on Bill Clinton may come as a result of Congressman Bob Barr's move to impeach President Clinton, or the verdict may have to await future historians. Whether the Clinton scandals achieve critical mass in the public consciousness soon or sometime down the road, we know that history will ultimately deal harshly with William Jefferson Clinton.

The good news of *Unlimited Access* is that the actors in this sordid drama all tried so hard to keep the truth out of your hands. That can only mean one thing: Those people are scared to death of you. They fear your power—the power of "We the People." They think the government belongs to them; we know it still belongs to us. They temporarily hold an office, but "We the People" hold the power. We will not allow the White House, the people's house, to be turned into a den of thieves.

That is the reason for our hope and optimism for the future: We believe in the sound character and common goodness of the American people. Ronald Reagan once said, "A state is nothing more than a reflection of its citizens; the more decent the citizens, the more decent the state." So let's live worthily, and let's demand that our government live up to its people.

I urge you to read this book, and buy extra copies and give it to friends. Spread the word, spread the truth.

Then write, call, or e-mail your elected representatives, and demand that they hold this White House accountable for the security of our nation and the integrity of our government. Demand legislation that restores the security apparatus of the White House. Write your local newspaper and call a radio talk show or two. Serve notice that Americans will no longer accept the sorry spectacle of White House security being handed over to a bar bouncer and the moll of a convicted drug dealer. Let the world know that Americans will no longer tolerate this kind of sleaze and corruption in the people's house. The American people deserve—and demand—much better than this.

Thank you, Gary Aldrich, for standing tall and telling the truth. Thank you for *Unlimited Access*. You sounded the alarm.

The rest is up to us.

Michael Reagan
Author, *Making Waves* and
The City On A Hill

Introduction

Printed on my FBI credentials, now punched through with the word "retired" and mounted on a plaque hanging on my library wall, are the following words:

> Gary Aldrich is a regularly appointed Special Agent of the Federal Bureau of Investigation, United States Department of Justice, and as such is charged with the duty of investigating violations of the laws of the United States, collecting evidence in cases in which the United States is or may be a party in interest, and performing other duties imposed upon him by law.

Special agents of the FBI are trained to find truth, document truth, and present it to a judge, to a jury, or even to the counsel of the president of the United States.

In the many assignments that I was privileged to have over the course of a twenty-six-year career with the FBI, I would often come across a *special* kind of truth. Everyone has experienced moments of great clarity when we see or hear evidence that is irrefutable. Judges have a name for it—they call it prima facie evidence, facts that are indisputable and require no explanation. Water is wet, fire burns, con men con.

When I was a young agent in Los Angeles, my prosecutor partner was an assistant U.S. attorney, fresh from Stanford University Law School. We had a bribery case to take to trial. We needed to prove that a Department of Housing and Urban Development (HUD) inspector took bribes from contractors so they could pocket money earmarked for home repairs that they never made—repairs paid for with taxpayer dollars.

Our evidence, frankly, was weak, but the crimes were especially heinous, because when the "repaired" roof leaked like a sieve or when the electrical outlet shorted out or when the furnace didn't work, the poor couldn't afford to make the repairs. When they walked away from their defective homes, because they had been defrauded and could not repair them, they walked away from their small chance to have the American Dream. Their credit could be destroyed by a mortgage foreclosure and eventual bankruptcy. Their neighborhoods, full of similarly defrauded people, would disintegrate, and disintegrating neighborhoods were breeding grounds for serious crime.

It was a hard case to prove because the bribes were paid in cash, and the HUD inspector—I'll call him Raymond—never put the money in a bank. Of course Raymond denied the bribes and blamed the contractors for not doing the work. He claimed that, if there was a fraud, it was the contractor's fault because the contractor encouraged him to sign forms without seeing the completed construction. If he was guilty of anything, it was of being too nice or regrettably lazy. You could fire a lazy inspector, but you couldn't put him in jail.

The inspector was very slick in his defense. In the end only one contractor had the guts to testify for the government, and he was on the witness stand.

He had some serious problems in his past, including alcoholism and divorce, and the defense attorney took him apart, destroying his credibility. The assistant U.S. attorney and I were worried. The defense attorney's withering attack on our witness's character meant we might lose the case. Our witness was now "on trial," and he was unraveling. But the defense attorney, not knowing when to quit, asked, "Mr. Smith, you didn't pay any bribes, did you? You're making all of this up, aren't you, to save your own skin? You don't seem to remember much of anything, do you? You were drunk all of the time. Your wife threw you out of the house. In short, you were a mess, weren't you?"

"Well, actually now that you ask, there is this one thing . . . ," Smith began.

The defense attorney, sensing danger, tried to cut him off. "Never mind, Mr. Smith, I think the jury has heard enough of your lies. We all know what your answer is going to be. No further questions, your honor."

The prosecutor stood up. He had a hunch our witness had something important to say. "Wait a minute, your honor, I think we are entitled to hear Mr. Smith's answer, don't you?"

The judge concurred. "Go ahead, Mr. Smith, you can finish your answer."

Smith looked alarmed. "Judge, if I tell it, I gotta use some, well, bad language, and I don't feel right about that." He looked over at the jury.

The judge smiled at Smith. "Mr. Smith, I am sure that this Los Angeles jury has probably already heard whatever words you might need to use." All eyes turned to the jury. They nodded.

"Well, your honor, there was this one thing. Raymond always made us come to his office to pay the bribes. He insisted that it had to be in his office because it was safe there. Behind his desk, where he sat when we paid him, was this *big* mounted moosehead. Well, when Raymond looked into the envelope to count the hundred dollar bills, he would always laugh. He'd point up at the moosehead behind his desk and say, "If that f---ing moosehead could talk, we'd all go to jail!"

There it was. The moosehead truth. The MHT. The guilty look on Raymond's face said the rest. It was all over.

The jury came back inside of thirty minutes with guilty verdicts on all counts.

I've always remembered that trial and the discovery of the MHT, and in every case I handled thereafter, I searched for the moosehead truth. In twenty years of criminal investigations, in very complex and confusing trials—some lasting months—I achieved scores of convictions and suffered only one acquittal. It was a good career, a winning career, thanks in large part to Raymond's stuffed moosehead.

In this book I hope to help the reader find the moosehead truth about the Clintons, their friends, and their political agenda, an agenda that I conclude is at odds with the Constitution I had been sworn to uphold.

Still, I know there will be some readers who will say that this book shouldn't come from me; that, in my position, I should keep quiet.

Some will say that I should trust the system and rely on Congress to blow the whistle on the White House. But I believe that Congress knows even more about what went on at the White House than I did. Yet with the exception of the efforts of a few individual congressmen, Congress's actions have been timid.

Or some readers will say that I should have left the job of informing the public to the media, to investigative journalists. But in good conscience I couldn't do that, because no one in the media was reporting the administration I *saw* every day. It was an administration where many little things—like the evidence police officers drop into small plastic bags during the investigation of a crime scene—added up to something big.

As a trained investigator, an FBI special agent for a quarter of a century, I noticed first the "character profiling" things about the new Clinton administration—clothes, demeanor, the sort of language people used. And these were troubling indicators. But I quickly discovered more serious problems. These included an apparent total disregard for honesty, integrity, or even cooperating with me, with the FBI, so that I could do my job of proving the good character of new employees. It wasn't long before I found evidence not only of real criminal activity, but of the willful endangerment of the president, the White House staff, and national security.

I entered the White House thinking I had landed a nice, white-collar job—and it was at first. I never had any intention of writing a book about my time in the White House, and even now I feel somewhat uncomfortable about it. I'm sure high-ranking people I respect from the Bush administration would have liked to talk me out of it. Given all the hard work and, frankly, the pain and distress this book has caused me and my family, I almost wish I was talked out of it.

The FBI certainly did its best to talk me out of it. I tried in good faith to have this book cleared by the FBI, but the bureau's unreasonable strictures on the public's right to know made that impossible. So I say here at the outset that this book is going to press without the bureau's written permission: I feel that strongly about it. My conscience compelled me to write this book.

When Bill Clinton was elected, I *wanted* to believe that he'd make a fine president. I obviously deeply admired the many fine people I knew in the Bush administration, but I was basically apolitical. I was an FBI agent, not a campaign worker.

But what I was seeing at the White House each and every day was not evidence of what I had hoped for. There was no evidence of Georgetown-, Oxford-, and Yale-educated brilliance, or even that this would be a folksy, moderate, southern Democrat administration.

I left the Clinton White House thinking that I'd spent more than two years back on the streets, fighting a new mafia—this one from Arkansas. And I thought the American people had a right to know about it.

Chapter One

MEETING THE CLINTON ADMINISTRATION

Rules for Radicals: "The ninth rule of the ethics of means and ends is that any effective means is automatically judged by the opposition as being unethical."

George Washington's Rules of Civility and Decent Behaviour: "Associate yourself with men of good quality, if you esteem your own reputation; for it is better to be alone than in bad company."

I returned to the White House on Monday, 25 January. I didn't attend the inauguration on the twentieth because I wasn't required to, and I knew it would be a traffic nightmare. The inauguration was on a Wednesday. I watched it on TV and took a few days off to get ready for the enormous workload I knew was ahead.

Driving in on I-66, I was thinking of the changes I might see at the White House: different faces, new friends, a whole new administration to get to know.

For more than three decades the FBI, the Secret Service, and the president's counsels had worked as a team to "clear" the hundreds of new staff members who come with a new president. It is a comprehensive and effective security system that has been perfected by six

5

different presidents to protect national security, the president, the taxpayer, and the White House itself.

This clearance process is accomplished through a lengthy FBI background investigation to document the good character of each and every White House staff member, from the chief of staff right down to the most obscure messenger located far from the Oval Office. In addition, the FBI clears all of the cabinet secretary positions, working with the U.S. Senate in the confirmation process.

As part of the permanent two-man FBI post in the White House, I was a key player in the SPIN Unit (or Special Inquiry Unit) team responsible for investigating the backgrounds of executive branch employees and federal judges. My partner in the White House post, Special Agent Dennis Sculimbrene, and I were particularly responsible for anyone who would work in the White House complex. That meant for anyone who might harm or embarrass the president or compromise White House—indeed, national—security.

Our work was all about access. In order to get our job done we needed unlimited access to the White House grounds, buildings, and office space, and to its several thousand permanent and political employees.

Every one of the staff in the White House Office would be new, which meant hundreds of background investigations. There was also the Executive Office of the President, a collection of semipermanent agencies within the White House, including the Office of Management and Budget (OMB) and the National Security Council (NSC). And though most of the civil servants in the permanent White House staff would remain in place, they too had to be re-cleared every five years.

I spent more than two years in the Bush White House. Each month my partner and I were responsible for up to fifty investigations apiece. Each investigation was thorough, requiring at least seven interviews at the White House, two record checks, and a letter-perfect ten-page report for the White House counsel.

We could never anticipate how long an interview would last. Many of these people were meeting an FBI agent for the first time. Many were being asked questions that nobody had ever asked them before. People going through an FBI investigation might be very afraid, and many had good reason to fear us.

That's because many a hopeful staffer had made it all the way to the FBI interview, only to be discovered as a liar. Some lies—or some behavior openly confessed—justified barring a staffer from the White House.

An FBI background investigation is more extensive than any other —save perhaps one conducted by the CIA. For lower level employees, we investigate the past fifteen years of their lives. For more senior employees, we investigate their entire adult lives—including all former employers and employment records. We also review college transcripts, interview representative professors, and investigate other material related to education. We also investigate any accusation or record of criminal wrongdoing and interview neighbors, friends, and associates of a potential employee.

There were very few limits—though some have lately, and wrongly, been imposed—on what we could, or were even obligated, to investigate. If we found character problems, we would often go beyond investigating the basics—like credit reports—to looking into phone logs, medical records, and other detailed reports that would help us decide whether a character problem would "wash out" or whether it was an indelible stain that the White House counsel needed to be aware of in order to protect the president and the presidency.

Up to one hundred agents could be assigned to a case, and interviews could be conducted worldwide. An FBI background investigation is no small undertaking. That's because it's so important.

The standards to which White House employees were held were certainly not unreasonable. The standards were well thought out and legal.

There are four key elements to a background investigation: *character, associates, reputation*, and *loyalty*, or CARL.

- *Character*—Good traits include honesty, integrity, work ethic, attitude, demeanor, and bearing. A bad character would be determined by finding that someone is dishonest, lacks integrity, is lazy, has been found guilty of criminal conduct, and so forth.
- *Associates*—An individual is assessed by the company he keeps. If a person is a doctor by day, he shouldn't hang out with drug traffickers by night. If a person is an FBI agent by day, he shouldn't socialize with criminals at night. If a man is married, he shouldn't spend his social time with single women.

- *Reputation*—Most people make an enemy or two in the course of their lives, but if the overall impression of those who know a candidate is negative, additional investigation is needed to determine why.
- *Loyalty*—When I first became an FBI agent, this meant loyalty to the United States, to the flag, and to the Constitution. Today, staffers often misinterpret it as loyalty to the president.

The FBI also investigates an applicant's *dangerousness* and *suitability*.

- *Dangerousness*—The Secret Service is haunted by memories of the Kennedy assassination and other assassination attempts, and they take every precaution—not just with the outside world, but also with White House staff—to protect the president. The only way to predict human behavior—including possible dangerous behavior—is to know past behavior. Background investigations have always been the best available tool. Although FBI background investigations may be imperfect, they're the best means we have.
- *Suitability*—Suitability includes verifying U.S. citizenship, education, skills, experience, and other factors that help predict whether a particular individual has the "right stuff" to be a government employee—paid out of your hard-earned taxpayer dollars. Finding evidence of an applicant's "suitability" was another part of our job.

The end result of all our work was the protection of the reputation and credibility of the president. With the arrival of a new administration, my assignment was to discover and document character flaws present in the new staff, if any, and to report them to the president—actually to the president's counsel through the SPIN Unit—though I knew from my days working in the Bush administration that the president often already knew the findings of the SPIN reports.

In the past I had been aware of the careful way new people were selected. Nobody wanted to recommend the wrong people, because if they "crashed and burned" it would reflect badly not only on them, but on the president as well.

But we were already off to a bad start. There were about seventy days between the election and the inauguration—sufficient time to complete a large number of SPIN cases. But for some reason, there weren't many cases coming in.

The only big influx of cases had been at Christmas, when numerous cabinet-level and other appointments were dumped into the system *after these appointments had already been made public*—the reverse of normal procedure. Some of these cases—which included cabinet choices such as Zoe Baird, Les Aspin, Warren Christopher, Bruce Babbitt, Alice Rivlin, Mike Espy, and Robert Woolsey—required the completion of a hundred or more items of investigation, including anywhere from thirty-five to fifty complex personal interviews each (more than six hundred total). We were ordered to complete these investigations and type our reports letter-perfect in an average of only four calendar days!

A fairly routine process became a crisis. Our first problem was that these people needed to be located so they could be interviewed. But it was Christmastime and, having received their invitation to the ball, many of the new big players were off to their ski chalet or to the islands. FBI investigation? Oh, yeah, I forgot.

And persons who knew them well—character witnesses—had to be found and interviewed. Where were *these* people during the holidays?

All of this chaos was so unnecessary and it eventually caused the administration so much trouble that there seemed to be only three possible explanations, all very disturbing.

The administration was being managed by people so disorganized that they could not conform to basic procedures essential to the administration's own effectiveness.

Or key people in the administration had simply decided that the security procedures were not important and were taking a "so what" attitude toward possible scandal, embarrassment, or worse.

Or key people in the administration were so actively hostile to the background investigation process that they wanted to guarantee we wouldn't have enough time to perform adequate checks and follow up on allegations. This might be because some people in the administration had serious matters to hide. Or it might simply be because people in the administration were instinctively hostile to authority figures of all types and to all those regular procedures, customs, and standards by which high-level organizations, whether in the White House or the corporate board room, avoid even the appearance of impropriety, scandal, or just loose practices. Like the Clintons, I'd lived through the 1960s and I knew there were a lot of people who still thought like that—who thought it was oppressive to have to wear a tie, show up to work on time, restrain their bad language or raw emotions, or even obey the law. As an FBI agent, I knew *that* often spelled trouble. People who were hostile to the normal, law-abiding world and its standards were often also hostile to normal, law-abiding morality and ethics. And those were the sort of people who might bring embarrassment to the White House.

But whatever the reason, this sudden dumping of names into the SPIN process put us investigators in an impossible situation, and the unavoidable aftermath was not long in coming. Clinton's inauguration coincided with his withdrawal of Zoe Baird as his nominee for the slot of attorney general (AG). It seemed she'd employed an illegal alien as a nanny and had not paid the appropriate taxes.

Needless to say, that was not an auspicious beginning.

Looking back on it now, there were other warning signs. Some were comical. I remember a funny story told to me by Tony Benedi, former deputy director of Scheduling, for the Bush administration. Mel Lukins, deputy director of the Bush Advance Office, confirmed the story.

Just before the inauguration in January 1993, Tony and Mel went to the Capitol to meet with personal representatives of President-elect Clinton to ensure a smooth transition of responsibilities after the Oath of Office was administered. Dressed in their usual impeccable suits, Tony and Mel waited and waited. They began to get a little nervous, because three rough-looking characters had arrived and were hanging around, eyeballing them. Were they about to be mugged? The trio looked like bikers, with earrings and ponytails, jeans that were torn or dirty, and faded sweatshirts or Levi jackets. Tony thought they might be there to erect bleachers or do some other construction. He walked over to them.

"Guys," Tony began, "we're supposed to meet a few folks from the Clinton administration. Have you run into any guys who might be the Clinton Advance Team?"

One of them gave Tony a dirty look. "*We're* the Clinton Advance Team."

(Later, another friend of mine remarked how the Secret Service's attention was captured by a Clinton Advance Team member wearing a red Lenin lapel pin.)

Other warning signs were more ominous. The Clintons, for instance, had been late for their own inauguration. A case of jitters or understandable last-minute fussing?

No, not according to extremely reliable sources who have spoken to me and who, for obvious reasons, must remain anonymous. One of the reasons the Clintons were late was because Vice President Gore had just found out that the West Wing office usually reserved for the vice president was instead going to be occupied by the first lady.

Network news cameras, trained on Blair House the morning of the inauguration, recorded a glimpse of the president and first lady screaming at each other. Sources I consider very reliable affirm that Clinton told Hillary that if she didn't back off from her plans to unseat Gore, Gore would go public with his anger and perhaps resign. Hillary shouted at him that as far as she was concerned, they had a deal—a deal that dated back to the campaign, when Lloyd Cutler had convinced her to stand by Clinton despite the allegations that he'd had an affair with Gennifer Flowers. The matter had already been decided, she said, and she had no intention of backing off; Gore was bluffing.

The Clintons arrived a half hour late at the White House Residence to join President and Barbara Bush. They also established an odd precedent. No first couple–elect had ever brought friends with them for the traditional tea with the retiring president and first lady in the Blue Room before the motorcade journey to the Capitol for the swearing-in ceremony. But for some indiscernible reason, the Clintons brought along their friends Harry Thomason and his wife.

After taking the oath, Bill and Hillary Clinton were taken to a holding room in the Capitol building. Minutes passed while everyone waited for Bill and Hillary to emerge to commence the inaugural festivities. A Capitol Hill police officer was ordered to inform the Clintons that everyone was ready and waiting.

The policeman knocked and opened the door of the holding room. He immediately shut it, beating a hasty retreat. Hillary Clinton was screaming at her husband in what was described as "uncontrolled and unbridled fury." Apparently, the matter of office space was *not* settled.

The Capitol Hill police and the Secret Service quickly conferred about intervening if it appeared the president's life might be threatened by the first lady! The question before them was, "How much physical abuse is too much physical abuse?"

I reached the intersection of 17th Street and F and angled my FBI car into the government parking area. A parking space near the White House was a major perk, and I knew it. I looked up at the west side of the Old Executive Office Building (OEOB). It looked the same as the last time I saw it, days ago, just before the Bush administration ended.

The same uniformed Secret Service guard was still standing in the same guard shack, and I watched a few permanent staff members hurrying in and out of the gate. Everything looked the same to me, but then, why would I expect anything to be different? Except for a change of political party and a new president, this was *the White House.*

I checked over the visor for my blue White House pass and slipped the chain with the pass around my neck. I needed the pass to get through the electronic gate, and although everyone knew me, wearing the pass at all times set a good example to those who were not so concerned about security.

As I approached the uniformed, armed Secret Service guard, he smiled and waved a greeting. Then he rolled his eyes and pointed behind him, shaking his head. There wasn't anyone there, so I had to assume he was referring to the new Clinton people inside.

What was he trying to tell me? The Secret Service has a blood oath to never, ever criticize a president or his staff. I didn't stop to ask, but turned up the drive and headed to the canteen for my usual morning coffee-to-go. I passed through the electrically operated double doors and walked down the hallway to the northwest corner of the building and looked around. Still, there was nothing that caught my attention. Everything seemed the same.

But when I entered the canteen, things changed—dramatically. All my sensors went up, like a police officer's at a crime scene. It almost looked like one. It was my first glimpse of the Clinton administration and, boy, was it different from the buttoned-down Bush administration. The canteen, which was usually spotless, was a mess. Napkins were scattered like windblown Kleenex, and somebody had spilled coffee on the floor. Instead of wiping it up, people had simply tracked through it, making a muddy trail. I took some napkins and tried to mop up the mess before someone fell and got hurt.

I looked around. I saw a shaggy-haired, middle-aged guy over in the corner in a loud, checkered, polyester, double-knit suit and badly scuffed shoes. The woman next to me was dressed like a cocktail waitress. Her shirt was tight and ended at her midriff; her skirt was short, and she wasn't wearing any hose. Between the two of them, I almost wondered if I'd walked into *Hooters* by mistake.

I looked around some more. There was a girl wearing a peasant blouse and a guy dressed in jeans. I remember thinking, "Is this how they dress at offices in Arkansas?" Having friends and family in the South, I found that hard to believe.

I shook my head and gave the cashier fifty-five cents for my large coffee. "Good morning, Bernice. How are you feeling?" Bernice was an older black woman suffering from an illness that had forced her to miss a lot of work.

"I'm fine, Mr. Aldrich, I'm fine." I was glad to hear it. She was a nice woman. Besides, if she left I would have another investigation on my hands to help "clear" a new cashier.

I grabbed my coffee and headed for the elevator, a few steps down from the canteen. I hoped that what I'd just seen was an anomaly, but when I got to the elevator my day didn't get any better.

There was a small crowd of Clinton people waiting right up against the elevator door, like kids crowding the window of a candy shop. They had the same "unfinished" look as the crowd in the canteen, but then I noticed they were staring at *me*. I guess *I* looked out of place in *their* group.

The elevator arrived, and the Clinton crowd rushed it like animals at feeding time, without giving people a chance to get off. People pushed, shoved, grunted, bumped, and swore, trying to sort it out. The men didn't give any deference at all to the women, who were giving as good as they got. It looked like a sale day at Macy's—or worse. I held back until the dust settled, and then I got on.

On the way up, two Clinton staffers loudly shared their deepest, most personal, and, frankly, intensely negative thoughts about their new supervisor. I wondered how they knew that I, or someone else in the elevator, wasn't a good friend of the supervisor. Someone behind me sneezed a big wet one. I made a mental note to check the back of my coat.

I got off the elevator at the fifth floor and unlocked the door to room 532, the FBI Liaison Office. I was the first in. I flicked on the lights and walked over to my desk.

The FBI Liaison Office had become comfortable to me over the past two-and-a-half years, and I always felt good about coming to work. After all, who wouldn't want to work at the White House? It might not be as exciting as chasing the mafia, but I'd wiretapped the mob and chased drug dealers and all the rest. Been there, done that.

Dennis and I had furnished the office with some old, heavy, refinished oak desks, leather chairs, a couch, and a coffee table. It was nice, but not as nice as the offices over in the West Wing. On our walls were framed "jumbo" prints taken during the Reagan and Bush administrations. Dennis and I had received these pictures as a token of thanks for our good work. But they weren't ours to keep. The jumbos were the property of the White House, and I expected the Clinton administration would make us take them down.

We had three windows facing north, south, and west. I could look down 17th Street to Constitution Avenue. I would often hear the sirens and see the motorcycles as the president's or vice president's motorcade passed by. Sometimes it was a king or a queen visiting the president.

As a rule, FBI agents didn't get office space with inspiring views. My last view, from our office at Buzzard's Point in southwest Washington, looked down on the Anacostia River. We saw old tires and other garbage floating by. Sometimes dead bodies would surface near the docks, and we would watch as the police pulled them out. It was a grim location, and catching federal felons was grim work.

In 1985, I had arrived in Washington full of ambition and optimism, and then I saw the FBI office at Buzzard's Point. My special agent in charge (SAC), Douglas Gow, was fresh from Houston and had also been looking forward to something less shabby. He put me in charge of an office survey to recommend ways to make our work environment better.

My report concluded that, basically, such an effort was hopeless. The place was a dump, located in a dumpy neighborhood. Gow's subordinate, Assistant SAC Dave Binney, read my conclusions, initialed my report, and sent it to the "no-action" file. Binney might as well have thrown it in the wastebasket. Dave said, "You should see New York. This is much better!"

Maybe I'd had my fill of roughing it, and I didn't apologize for feeling that I wanted something a little nicer in my last years with the bureau. You couldn't get much better than the White House. I considered myself especially lucky to be selected for the assignment.

There was always an enormous amount of work for us to complete, but I didn't mind the extra work since it meant spending my last years away from criminals, victims, and defense attorneys . . . and Buzzard's Point.

As I sat drinking my coffee, I wondered whether the people downstairs were temporary volunteers. There were always volunteers working at the White House. That had to be it.

I went through my messages. One was from the new assistant to the president for Management and Administration, David Watkins, a personal friend of President Clinton's who had held a top spot on the campaign. I needed to reach Watkins for two reasons. The first was that I had to interview him. I also needed to meet him to establish a liaison between his office and ours.

During the Bush administration two key offices were involved in the FBI's operations at the White House. One was the Counsel's Office, and the other was the Office of Administration, or OA. The Counsel's Office was the heart of our SPIN investigations conducted for the president. The Counsel's Office ordered the investigations and reviewed the results. They were in daily contact with our office and the bureau. For thirty years this system had been used to clear White House personnel.

The other important contact for us was in Watkins's office. FBI agents normally had a liaison relationship with the OA's director. The OA ran the Personnel Office and supplied logistical support for FBI operations at the White House. In fact, Bush's director, Paul Bateman, had assigned us our office space. So Dennis and I would be harshly criticized if we did not establish a good relationship with David Watkins.

I called the OA front office in the West Wing and spoke to Clarissa Cerda, who answered the secretary's phone. Her voice had an edge to it; she was quick to point out that she was a *deputy* to Mr. Watkins, *not* a secretary, and while it was not her job to take messages, she would try to get him to call me. She sounded hostile. It was a little early, it seemed to me, to be so upset, but a lot of Clinton staffers appeared to be suffering from irrational gloom at the outset of the administration.

Watkins returned my call promptly, and he was friendly. Actually, *overly* friendly. The exact opposite of Cerda. I thought, "What is this guy up to?" He was *too* nice, *too* cooperative, *too* friendly.

Sure, it was a quick first impression. I did not make much of it then, and, except for my experiences of the next two and a half years, I wouldn't mention it now. But remember, I had been in the bureau for more than twenty years. And though it might sound funny, any good agent will tell you that one of our basic investigative tools is observing how people we deal with react to dealing with an FBI agent. Except for longtime friends or fellow law enforcement investigators, *very* few people talk or act normal around agents. Even good, honest citizens are apt to be a little nervous. Crooks are apt to get violent or to shamelessly deny everything, figuring a well-paid attorney will set them free. And then there are guys like Watkins who are just so "damn glad to see ya." Well, nobody is just "damn glad to see" the FBI. I'd been in the office only an hour, had talked to Watkins for just a couple minutes, and already I was getting—in a small way—the same sort of signals I'd picked up while chasing professional con men, white-collar criminals, and even some rougher types.

As I hung up the phone, the General Services Administration (GSA) cleaning lady came in. She looked worried, not her usual self. A problem at home? Perhaps a child who didn't return last night? Crime touched these women more than most others. They'd told me stories that would make the average yuppie's hair stand on end.

When she finished her work, I followed her out and closed and locked the door behind me. I took the quick way to Watkins's office, which was located about one hundred yards east, over in the prestigious West Wing.

There were several routes to the West Wing, but no matter which way I went, the walk took about five minutes. I could use the elevator or walk down the steps. I could go by the Indian Treaty Room or by the Vice President's Office. I could go around the building and pass by the Executive Clerk's Office and the Travel Office. I could find variety in routine, if I wanted to.

While I walked, I noticed other oddly dressed new personnel. By their numbers, I was beginning to realize that I was not looking at volunteers at all. These people *were* the new Clinton administration. I saw jeans, T-shirts, and sweatshirts; men with earrings and ponytails; and every manner of footwear except normal dress shoes.

One young lady was dressed entirely in black—black pants, black T-shirt, black shoes, even black lipstick. She was the only one I saw wearing business shoes. But they were men's shoes—big, black wingtips.

As I left the OEOB and crossed the West Executive parking lot, I glanced at the cars. Same cars, same drivers. That was something of a relief. One constant in a sea of change. During the campaign the Clintons had criticized the "limousines" used by the "preppie" Bush administration. Clinton's people had said they intended to get rid of the limos, which weren't limos at all, just dark-colored, full-size American sedans. Later, the Clintons *did* get rid of them. They bought new ones to replace the year-old models.

I passed under the canopy of the West Wing basement entrance and went through the double doors. The Secret Service guard was the same man I had said goodbye to the previous week. The West Wing walls were bare. Where a dozen jumbos of George and Barbara Bush had hung on the walls, there were only darkened spots and nail holes. The hallways looked stark and barren.

I stepped through the doors of the West Wing and entered the outer office of the OA. I saw two young women at desks. One of the women was Cerda, the not-a-secretary. She didn't look like she was having a good day. I introduced myself and told her why I was there. She motioned me in the direction of Watkins's office. Thanks. I knew where it was.

On my way to his office I passed the other not-a-secretary and introduced myself. She was Catherine Cornelius. I found out that she and Cerda were deputies to David Watkins.

Watkins was a tall, slender man in his early forties. I noticed he was not wearing his jacket. Not a big deal, but in the Bush administration, if you were about to meet someone for the first time, you wore your coat. It was a sign of respect, a touch of class I appreciated after Buzzard's Point.

The first thing that struck me about Watkins was his blinding, fluorescent pink tie with a complex geometric design. Later, as I got to know Watkins better, I realized that the loud ties, which never seemed to match anything he wore, were his trademark.

Watkins was oppressively friendly, like a used car salesman hot to make a sale. I half-expected him to hug me.

Before I met Watkins, I had interviewed thousands of people, and every so often I came across someone who would set off alarm bells. It didn't happen often, and it hadn't happened for a long time. But when the old alarm went off, I paid attention. I was paying attention now.

I began my interview of Watkins. I can't tell you the substance of the interview because of Privacy Act restrictions, but I can say that instead of answering my questions directly, Watkins used words or phrases that could have a double meaning. He acted as though I were trying to trap him or trick him. In short, he was behaving as if he were guilty—but guilty of what?

I was trained to "turn up the heat" when an individual was trying to hide something. I shifted my style, bearing down a bit more, and asking more pointed questions, ones that could not be dodged so easily. I needed to establish the good character of someone Watkins knew well. He became more and more evasive. I turned up the heat even higher. And then, I reached the limit.

He felt I crossed the line. I knew the mentality; I had seen it before. I thought, "Here it comes," and sure enough, Watkins reminded me that he was a close personal friend of Bill and Hillary Clinton, and I had better back off! He looked as though he were about to explode, and I learned later that Watkins had a hair-trigger temper. I excused myself and said I'd be back. He calmed down a little, and I made my exit.

The White House staff had an obligation to cooperate with the FBI, and it was clearly to their advantage to do so. If an individual refused to answer my questions, I would simply report their failure to cooperate to the bureau, who would in turn call the Counsel's Office. To maintain the security program and the FBI's credibility, the Counsel's Office would then order the individual to cooperate—at least it did in the Bush administration.

If a staff member still refused to cooperate with the FBI, it would be grounds for dismissal. This seemingly harsh approach was the only way the SPIN investigations could have any credibility. It wouldn't take too many refused interviews before the word would get around to the rest of the staff, and then we would have little or no effectiveness. Reporting staffers for failure to cooperate was rarely necessary since, in the Bush administration, they had been so well screened and had little to hide. The Bush people, including the president, understood that the purpose of the SPIN investigations was not to disrupt, impede, or embarrass the administration, but was just the opposite—to help the president do his job effectively.

I thought Dennis might get along better with Watkins than I had. I made a mental note to suggest that Dennis meet him and perhaps become our liaison contact. I didn't want to repeat my risk of being hugged.

Back in my office, I placed a few phone calls, made some notes of my Watkins interview, and waited for Dennis to arrive. He walked through the door shortly before noon. He had stopped by the SPIN office at Tyson's Corner, Virginia, before coming down.

Dennis was a White House veteran. He'd spent most of his FBI career assigned to Washington, where he became a friend to senators, congressmen, and chiefs of staff, and was an expert on White House politics and protocol. His reputation had been forged first on Capitol Hill, then at the White House over the course of nearly fifteen years. He had worked under three administrations—Carter, Reagan, and Bush.

By the time I ended my partnership with Scully (Dennis's nickname), I had handled more than two thousand White House staff investigations in the Bush and Clinton administrations and had conducted as many as ten thousand interviews.

Dennis looked agitated. "I tell you, Gary, this is going to be a challenge. I don't know about you, but I'm having a heck of a time getting these Clinton people to grant interviews. I call people up, tell them who I am and what I need to do, and they tell me they're too busy to talk to the FBI!"

Too busy to talk to the FBI? How did they expect to get permanent passes to the White House or security clearances so they could read classified material? Even during the Gulf War, people in the Bush administration worked us into their schedule.

Our SPIN cases had short deadlines, and there were hundreds of cases to complete. The temporary passes that were issued by the Secret Service ran out in ninety days. By my calculations, we would have to complete several cases every day if we were to avoid a problem with the Secret Service and Counsel's Office. There wasn't any time to chase staff who considered themselves "too busy."

"Gary, I think we're in for some real trouble," Dennis warned. "With Bush, we were dealing with straight arrows. I don't think that's going to be the case here. Just look at Zoe Baird and her husband—two rich yuppies screwing over two ignorant illegal aliens, while she's making over $500,000 a year. And they wanted her to be the AG [attorney general]—an AG who doesn't know or doesn't care that she's violating federal law. These are the sort of people we're dealing with, Gary. And if that's true for the AG, just think of the rest of the administration."

Dennis was right, that was a bad sign. But I was optimistic that things would get straightened out.

The day wound down, and Dennis went out to try to conduct some interviews over in the West Wing. I finished my paperwork and started to clear my desk. I turned on the radio to listen for the traffic report. Instead, I heard that the president had made his wife, Hillary, director of the Clinton administration Health Care Task Force.

Chapter Two

SPIN

Rules for Radicals: "We must first see the world as it is and not what we would like it to be. We must see the world as all political realists have, in terms of 'what men do and not what they ought to do,' as Machiavelli and others have put it."

George Washington's Rules of Civility and Decent Behaviour: "They that are in dignity or in office have in all places precedency; but whilst they are young, they ought to respect those that are their equals in birth or other qualities, though they have no public charge."

After coming to the White House in the summer of 1990, I quickly realized that the White House consisted of three distinct realities. First, the White House is history and tradition, a representation of America's culture, standards, and customs.

The White House is also a location—a mansion, with office buildings and grounds, at 1600 Pennsylvania Avenue in Washington, D.C.

The White House also includes the Old Executive Office Building (OEOB). The FBI Liaison Office is in the OEOB adjacent to the White House, but there is really no way to separate the two locations. The president's senior staff is shoe-horned into postage stamp–size offices in the West Wing. Everyone else spills over into the OEOB.

Like everywhere else, location means a lot at the White House, and your office space is a sign to others of where you stand in the pecking order. One of those cramped little offices in the West Wing is best. First floor of the OEOB, east side, facing the West Wing is next best. But even fifth floor, west side, facing 17th Street, next to the Law Library is not bad, considering that there are hundreds more offices over in the New Executive Office Building (NEOB), which isn't even located on the White House grounds.

The OEOB takes up the entire block from Pennsylvania Avenue on the north, 17th Street on the west, and E Street on the south, and it can't be missed. It's as if this huge granite structure had been air-lifted straight from old Europe. At night, numerous spotlights give it a truly royal appearance.

Ordinary citizens cannot enter the White House or any buildings of the complex without an invitation, an escort, *and* a security check. The White House is guarded by the Uniform Division of the Secret Service. It is surrounded by a high, wrought-iron security fence and has the latest in security devices to catch the occasional nutcase or stray cat that might wander onto the grounds.

The OEOB halls are long and poorly lit. The floors are made of two kinds of polished marble, shipped from Italy. The quarries are shut down now, so when a tile is broken it shows. The new ones just aren't the same.

The government must have made some small town in Italy very wealthy, because the same marble tiles are used in the huge Treasury Building that flanks the White House on the east side. The marble is white and jet black. If you look closely at the tiles, you'll see fossilized shells captured there for all time.

The ceilings are high, and the trim around the doors and columns is ornate. The trim looks like carved wood but is really plaster. When a piece breaks, or gets waterlogged from a leaking roof, GSA artists make repairs so that you can't tell it was ever damaged. The White House is that kind of place—immaculate.

But by far the most important reality at the White House is the people. As an FBI agent, my job was to help maintain the high quality of White House personnel. Each administration has hundreds of political appointees. But in terms of numbers, they are far fewer than the permanent staff who work from one presidency to the next.

The political appointees filled vacancies ranging from support slots that paid about $25,000 to start, to special assistants to the president, who made more than $100,000. They could keep those jobs as long as their candidate held office.

But many of the permanent staff could expect to work at the White House for twenty years or more. The permanent staff could, however, be fired or transferred if they did not measure up, and they were investigated every five years by the FBI to ensure their continuing good character.

Other nonpolitical employees were detailees from an agency that loaned them to the White House. Some had one- or two-year assignments. Others had open-ended terms and could stay as long as they wanted or until some high-level political appointee got angry with them.

Everyone knew that coming to the White House would mean hard work, long hours, and tough times. Kids' soccer, Cub Scouts, and PTA were all back-burnered. But at the end, one had the reward of having worked there. After all, this was the federal government's equivalent of Mecca. This was the fountain, the source of all power. This was the White House, and to go there was to reach the top.

The permanent staff embraced the White House as if it were their home. The GSA gardener trimmed the hedge just so. The flower shop employee placed the roses just right. The file clerk checked twice to see that every file was complete and properly put away. The Marine Guard kept his shoes gleaming. The Old Guard, in their Revolutionary War uniforms, played their fife and drums, marching with backs so straight, faces so serious. Working at the White House could be one long celebration of excellence—a continuous Fourth of July.

One of the finest White House managers was Phil Larsen, head of Personnel for the Office of Administration. But at the end of the first full week of the new Clinton administration, Phil called to say goodbye. He had submitted his resignation to David Watkins, and he was being careful about what he was saying over the phone. Why?

Larsen would tell me only that he didn't like what was going on, and "I'm out of here."

Larsen's staff on the fourth floor of the New Executive Office Building was a pleasure to work with. As part of my FBI SPIN investigations, I often went there to examine the personnel files, and his staff went out of their way to help me track down documents. Larsen, who'd been hired by President Carter, was well respected and admired for the diversity he'd brought to his office. It wasn't a diversity for diversity's sake, either. All of his employees had merit and were of good character, I knew that, because I'd investigated them.

Now Larsen was leaving. What had happened? Months later, when Congress's investigators, the General Accounting Office, stormed the White House to examine the files of the Office of Personnel, I found out about some of what must have been on Larsen's mind. It seems that on January 20, 1993, when hundreds of Clinton people came to the White House to work, many didn't have a job. Hundreds were instructed to come, or somebody told them, "Okay, come in, maybe we'll have something for you to do," but they weren't official U.S. government employees, so they couldn't get paid.

They hadn't filled out forms, they hadn't submitted resumes, there wasn't even any proof that they were U.S. citizens!

It eventually dawned on the Clinton administration that they had to be given appointments. David Watkins supervised Larsen. Did he call Larsen and indicate that Larsen should draw up the "appropriate" documents? It would have been illegal. Larsen admitted to me later that he was worried Watkins would order him to do it, but Larsen told me that he resigned chiefly because Watkins wanted him to create false numbers to conform with Clinton's promised 25 percent staff cuts. "I just could not be a party to that kind of thing," Larsen told me later.

Watkins didn't seem to care what was legal or illegal, honest or dishonest. After Larsen's departure, Watkins immediately reorganized the Personnel Office, with the result that one of the best-run government offices became one of the least helpful.

But there was more fallout from Larsen's departure than that. Under Watkins, the Clinton staffers not only got paid, but according to a GAO investigative report dated September 9, 1993, some of the more enterprising Clinton staffers actually double-dipped.

Every new administration is afforded a taxpayer-sponsored transition period, overseen by the General Services Administration. From the election of a president until the inauguration, office space, supporting equipment (like phones and computers), and even salaries are furnished to the incoming administration at taxpayer's expense.

Apparently, the Clinton campaign selected twenty-five staffers to work in the transition office. Later, however, but still during the transition period, these transition staffers also became White House staffers collecting White House salaries. These twenty-five had no problem paying their bills, since they were now collecting two taxpayer-financed paychecks. Some were caught by the GAO audit and forced to pay the money back. But as late as September 1993, nine months after the inauguration, they still refused to reimburse the government and resisted official notice that they had committed what amounted to fraud against the government... a federal felony.

Under any other administration, if a "Suzy Brown" working at the

Department of Labor or some other government office had been caught knowingly taking salaries from separate government coffers, she would not only have been fired, she would also likely have been subjected to an FBI criminal investigation. But as regards these White House employees who should have been held to the highest standards, the Clinton administration said that it had failed to notice the abuse because it was "too busy," and the Clinton double-dippers were held to be blameless. David Watkins was the senior manager of the Personnel Department. If he was too busy to handle personnel matters, just exactly what was he doing?

The GAO report also detailed how many new Clinton staffers failed to provide financial reports to the White House Counsel's Office, as required by law. These staffers were the "big fish," the ones making $85,000 or more a year. As a result, $200 fines were assessed against each one of them. But did they even know they had to file these reports? Telling them about this federal law was the responsibility of the Counsel's Office, under the leadership of Bernard Nussbaum, Vince Foster, and Bill Kennedy. Were they "too busy" as well?

Altogether, more than two hundred Clinton White House staffers came to work on 20 January, and many worked and worked for weeks, some for months, without any salary, any medical coverage, or any other employee benefits. Nor did they have any legal right to work in the White House, review classified material, or do anything else as government employees.

At the beginning of the administration, the White House was inundated by *hundreds* of uncleared personnel entering as "volunteers" or Health Care Task Force members working on Hillary Clinton's Health Care Plan.

Soon Secret Service ran out of temporary access passes and converted other passes into *something* that could be hung around the necks of these employees—whoever they were. No requests for investigating their backgrounds had yet been filed with the FBI. And that was a serious problem—based perhaps on a serious misunderstanding. Clinton staffers and volunteers behaved as if they had a "right" to work in the White House, independent of their being investigated by the FBI and being cleared by the Counsel's Office and the Secret Service. When the Secret Service tried to screen people as they came through the gates, Clinton staffers often responded angrily—with shouts and insults, as if the Secret Service was there only to harass them, not to protect the president.

Given the apparent breakdown in the usual process of clearing employees, I remember asking my partner Dennis whether the Clinton administration was going to retain George Saunders, a retired FBI agent who had been advising the White House on security for thirty years.

"Well," Dennis said, "I spoke to Jane last week, and she didn't know. She doesn't think they even know about George yet, or even what he did for the other administrations."

Jane was Jane Dannenhauer, director of the White House Counsel's Office of Security. Jane was the main liaison between the White House and FBI headquarters, and she had been at this work since the Reagan administration. As a political appointee, she would eventually have to leave, but she had agreed to stay on to show the new administration how the security system worked.

Jane typified the Reagan and Bush administrations' approach to security. They "scrubbed" their people *before* they came to the White House, *before* they were submitted to the FBI for background checks. Both wanted personnel who were squeaky clean, and if any appointee sneaked through and was later found out to have lied, they'd immediately be handed a cardboard box, told to put their personal belongings in it, ordered to hand over their pass, and then escorted out the building.

But so far, the only people being escorted out of the Clinton White House were would-be attorney generals. Less than a month into the administration, history repeated itself. On 4 February the president announced that the new attorney general nominee would be Kimba Wood, a federal judge working in a New York district. The very next day her nomination was withdrawn. It appeared that, like Zoe Baird, Kimba Wood had employed an illegal immigrant as a nanny. Unlike Zoe Baird, Wood and her husband *had* paid the appropriate employment taxes.

But Wood's problems actually went deeper than that. It was later reported that Wood had indulged in a rather un-attorney general–like affair, neatly documented in a diary by her then-lover, New York financier Frank Richardson. Perhaps more worrying for the Clinton administration was that Judge Wood—a former Playboy Bunny— might be "exposed" by *Playboy* magazine.

So to its credit and to the Department of Justice's relief, the Clinton administration pulled Wood's name. But how much better it would have been for all involved if the entire episode had been avoided by the simple use of an FBI investigation conducted *before* Wood was announced!

So far I had handled a grand total of twelve SPIN investigations involving senior White House staffers and had probably met and interviewed about sixty or so of the more senior staffers. In the twelve cases I had handled, I realized that the Clintons and their transition team staff were paying even less attention to how they were staffing the White House. In addition, I experienced the new phenomenon of White House employees, that is, the Clinton staff, trying to avoid being interviewed by the FBI. They were not cooperative.

My calls were not returned. Appointments finally made were canceled, or in some cases the persons to be interviewed never came to my office, as had been arranged. Some even failed to show up at their own offices at a prearranged time.

When I finally located these persons and asked them why they didn't keep their appointments, their excuses were at least consistent, "I was too busy to come."

"Well, why didn't you call or have your secretary call me?"

The answer would be, "I forgot," or "I didn't have time," or "I did call, and nobody answered your phone."

"Why didn't you leave a message on the machine?"

"I didn't want to."

"Why not?"

"I didn't want to."

Some enterprising dodgers did return our calls—but at 10:30 P.M. or at midnight, when they knew full well we wouldn't be there. Their messages would be, "I'm returning your call," and that was it. They wouldn't offer any clues as to how, where, or when we might interview them.

They were playing a game, but I could think of no good reason to play games with them. *They* needed *me* to get their White House clearance. Or did they? Had someone told them that clearances were not a problem? Had someone told them, "Don't sweat the FBI, we've got it covered"? There had to be something to explain their lack of concern and cooperation.

Dennis was more willing to play cat and mouse than I was. In one case, Dennis was having difficulty interviewing Isabel Tapia, the president's director of advance. Finally, he decided to lurk outside her doorway. When he saw Tapia enter her office, he ran to a phone and called, only to be told she wasn't in. So he waited at the office door, and when she came out, he "pounced." Clearly annoyed, she reluctantly allowed the interview. I refused to play those games.

Dennis and I made countless complaints and wrote many memos to the FBI about the failure of Clinton's staffers to cooperate. When cases started to get behind, our supervisor finally responded, urging us to "be aggressive, within the bounds of professionalism." In other words, "the FBI can't help you guys. But get it done."

David Watkins was a good example of what we were up against. Watkins was an FOB, or "Friend of Bill," a person who had been hand-picked for his job at the White House by the president. He was also a good example of the "quality" of staff that Bill and Hillary Clinton deemed suitable. Watkins was a long-time close personal friend of the Clintons, and the FBI SPIN was supposed to establish the good character of Watkins so that he could obtain a security clearance and obtain permanent access to the White House.

Before long, Watkins was identified in the mainstream media as a Clinton Campaign official who had been accused of sexual harassment in 1992 at about the same time Bill Clinton's alleged affair with Gennifer Flowers surfaced. It was also reported that the victim of the harassment, an accountant from Little Rock, was illegally given $37,000 of campaign funds to keep her mouth shut. The media reported that all parties signed a document crafted by Chris Varney, Clinton's campaign counsel and also a good friend of the Clintons, affirming that they would keep silent about the incident. Varney was now working in the White House as Cabinet Secretary, a very high level position. I approached Varney about the matter and she told me I "shouldn't worry about it." Shouldn't worry about it? That was my job—to worry about serious allegations that involved White House staff.

I told Varney I didn't think a legal document signed in Little Rock, involving what was clearly a civil matter, could or should prevent the FBI from completing a background investigation. Varney disagreed.

I called my headquarters and reported the failure of cooperation. I wrote a memorandum about the allegation and the circumstances, along with a request that the FBI SPIN Unit chief, James Bourke, call the White House Counsel's Office and insist that the relevant parties submit to interviews so I could do my job. I waited and waited. Nothing happened. Later, when I asked my immediate supervisor about my request, he told me the case was to be closed without the interviews.

The FBI had several options, including a strong request to the White House Counsel's Office to order persons with knowledge of any allegations against any White House staffer under investigation to submit to interview, and provide relevant information. I knew that without such cooperation beween the FBI and White House Counsel, SPINs would have little effectiveness, and FBI agents at the White House would have little or no power to obtain the kind of testimony that enables us to do our jobs. Of course Watkins went on to cause enormous damage to the reputation of the presidency with his ham-fisted, ill-thought-out personnel decisions, including the firing of the Travel Office staff, ordered by Hillary Clinton.

Watkins was finally given the "boot" when he used the president's multi-million-dollar helicopter, Marine-One, as a golf cart, and the military crew as caddies. Dennis and I could see all of this kind of collateral damage coming, and that was the *reason* we were there—to surface the "David Watkins" types and enable the president the means to deny such troubling persons access, *before* they had a chance to self-destruct. We were powerless to stop it.

Other examples of high level staff with dubious character were all around the White House. A good example is one of President Clinton's closest political friends. He was typical of many of the Clinton crowd. Young or old, man or woman—too many people in the Clinton White House couldn't control their tempers or their tongues.

This particular man worked at the White House for almost a year before we were finally "allowed" to conduct his background investigation. Over the months, I had noticed that this staffer's dress, demeanor, and bearing never rose above the level of unacceptable. He was frequently sloppy, often arrogant, always disagreeable, and had a reputation for being very inconsiderate. Like so many in the Clinton administration, including the president and, sadly, the first lady, this staffer was not able to express his thoughts or make a point without the use of obscene language and rage. The rage was more important to me from an investigative standpoint. There were reports that he had fits of raging fury when crossed. He used violent, coarse language as a "sludge hammer" to bully people. His office was in the West Wing, not far from the Oval Office, hardly a place to "lose it."

Because he held a high-level position, it was necessary to interview senior staff, including Mack McLarty. I had already interviewed other senior staff about him. They agreed he had a reputation for using four-letter words and screaming at people, but, of course, *they themselves* had never heard any of his tirades.

Only one individual thought his behavior was any "big deal" and this person was not a member of the Clinton inner circle. The Clinton friends were amused and puzzled that I would be asking about a staffer's obnoxious and rhetorically violent behavior. It was telling to me that they thought this staffer's behavior was normal.

I met McLarty in his West Wing office, just doors down from the Oval Office. McLarty was an unusual man. He was highly polished in his manner and dress, but when he opened his mouth, out rolled one of the heaviest southern accents I had ever heard.

McLarty's physical appearance was also unusual. There was a uni-sex quality to the Clinton staff that set it far apart from the Bush administration. It was the shape of their bodies. In the Clinton administration, the broad-shouldered, pants-wearing women and the pear-shaped, bowling-pin men blurred distinctions between the sexes. I was used to athletic types, physically fit persons who took pride in body image and good health. Arnold Schwarzenegger had called the Clinton friends "girlie men" during the campaign in 1992. I now knew what he was getting at.

"Mr. McLarty, this particular staffer seems to have an unusual way of expressing his thoughts, and I wonder if I could ask you about that."

"I'm not sure I understand your meaning, Gary."

"Well, in the many interviews that I have conducted there seems to be a common observation and complaint about him. They say he yells and swears at everybody—at staff, on the phone, everybody. And a lot of his screaming is obscene, according to the persons I have interviewed. Can you comment on that?"

"Now, uh, now, uh, Gary, I can't really see how this is the proper business of the FBI. After all, history tells us that virtually all of the presidents used foul language. Kennedy, Johnson, certainly Nixon, Reagan, and Bush. They have all used, uh, locker room jargon, so I don't see how that is a proper area of inquiry in an FBI investigation. Besides, he's a young man, and it's true that he has some, let's say, rough edges, but he'll mature. We think he's a diamond in the rough."

"Mr. McLarty, I'm glad you asked me how this might be part of an FBI investigation and why it might matter. Sir, let me first say that I worked for more than two years in the Bush White House. It *may* be true that President Bush swore, I don't know. I never heard him swear, and I never heard anyone claim that he did. In fact, President Bush was known for trying to *avoid* using coarse language, reverting to 'gosh' and 'darn' and 'heck' and the like. So I can't confirm that President Bush ever used objectionable words, here, in the White House. I guess it's possible. And, sir, you left out President Carter."

I watched for his reaction. There was none, so I continued, "Mr. McLarty, there is the issue of loss of emotional control, sir. This man works in close proximity to the president, and he can't seem to moderate his anger. He can't seem to control his emotions. That doesn't necessarily mean he's dangerous, but loss of emotional control, fits of rage, may be warning signs of a bigger problem. Sometimes rage can be attributed to an emotional disturbance, and sometimes rage is an indication of illegal drug use. Cocaine, for example, can cause fits of rage in many people. Do you understand now why I would ask these questions, sir?"

"Well, there is no question of any illegal drug use here. None at all. No, that's not possible. He's just highly emotional, highly excitable. We like those qualities here, you see? Passion, drive, commitment. Those aren't negative qualities to us. They're qualities that define the president."

"Mr. McLarty, as to the coarseness of language, sir, I'm not talking about President Clinton's behavior. I'm talking about a member of the president's staff, sir, and you see, it's one thing for President Clinton to scream or swear, sir. He's the president, and he can do just about anything he pleases, everyone knows that. But does that give license to anyone on your staff to act in the same manner?"

"No, no, no. I didn't mean that. It's just that . . . I don't see how such behavior impacts on a security clearance, and so what if somebody screams or swears around here? It gets pretty intense sometimes."

"Sir, I will be happy to answer that question. First of all, this *is* the White House, and there are a whole lot of people who think this is a special place that possesses an air of history, tradition, restrained power, and muted emotion. People who work here generally are considered a cut above, a finer lot, if you will, and not taken to screaming and ranting. There is a perception that the White House is made up of persons of proper manners and respect, if not for the White House, then at least respect for their fellow White House co-workers, and respect for the president and the presidency.

"This man has several permanent female staff members working near him as support employees, and they are decent people. One I know is very religious. He also has several very young women sitting just outside of his office, and I know they are decent and are probably embarrassed by his behavior. I know that, because I know their backgrounds; I conducted their background investigations. By all indications, sir, these women are not motorcycle mamas. I guess what I am trying to say, sir, is that they probably resent being forced to listen to his out-of-control screaming, his explosive temper, his vulgarity, his disrespectful attitude to religion, and his obscene references to biological, scatological, and sexual acts and perversions, all of which seem to be an important part of this man's vocabulary.

"Sir, I guess I'm asking you if you have received any formal complaints yet, because if you haven't, you probably will soon, sir, since this kind of behavior is lately seen as sexual harassment in most government agencies, most businesses that I am aware of, sir. And this is the White House, where I seriously doubt the standard is expected to be any lower."

"I don't think that's an issue here. I recommend him without reservation as a promising young man. Is there anything else?"

Well, I guess that was that. McLarty didn't seem to care much for *my* "passion, drive, commitment" to maintain White House standards of civility, if not security.

"No, sir," I said. As I walked out I recall thinking, "Man, this place has fallen so far, so fast."

The Clinton crowd justified their behavior by their power—and the limits of their power and behavior were, in their own eyes, nonexistent.

I returned to my office and waited for a call from headquarters that would instruct me to pack my belongings and leave the White House immediately.

But, of course, the call never came. It might have been better for me if it had.

Chapter Three

SO WHAT?
(PART ONE)

Rules for Radicals: "The tenth rule of the ethics of means and ends is
that you do what you can do with what you have and clothe it with
moral garments."

George Washington's Rules of Civility and Decent Behaviour: "Put not
off your clothes in the presence of others, nor go out your chamber
half dressed."

One morning I went downstairs to check in with my friend Frank
Posey, "Frank the Framer," and his partner Roland. Frank was an ex-
Coast Guard serviceman and trained carpenter now responsible for
framing photos and documents for the White House.

As a testimony to his fine work, his walls were lined with personally signed photographs of Reagan, Bush, their chiefs of staff, and
other senior officials ranging from cabinet secretaries to directors of
agencies.

"There he is. Mr. FBI. Where have you been hiding, my friend?"

"Hi ya, Frank. Hi, Roland. How are you guys doing? Busy?"

"Are we busy? Man, don't ask. Look at this!"

Frank pointed to a huge stack of unmounted jumbos of the president. I walked over and flipped one right-side up so that I could have
a look. It was a very good portrait of Bill Clinton.

"Do you have to mount all these?"

"Yeah, sure, and of course it all has to be done *yesterday* as usual."

I asked Frank to save one for the FBI Office, if he came up with any extras.

Frank seemed pleased to be a part of the new administration. If I had to guess, Frank was a Democrat, but he had nothing but praise for Presidents Reagan and Bush.

I looked down through the stack. "Where is Al Gore? I don't see any of the vice president."

Frank grinned. He pointed over to another part of his shop where there was another stack of pictures. "Take a look at those."

I walked over and flipped one right-side up. But it wasn't Al Gore, it was Hillary Clinton. "Frank, seriously, don't you have any of the vice president?"

"Nope. Not a one. These all have to be framed right away—and then we have to hang them, *together.*"

In the weeks that followed the inauguration, almost every office received a giant picture of Bill and Hillary Clinton. But in offices that had some connection to Hillary Clinton, there were few if any pictures of the president. Al Gore *did* get some jumbos, but they were restricted almost entirely to the vice president's offices.

In all of the administrations that I had been a part of, going back to Nixon, the president's and the *vice president's* pictures hung side by side in federal buildings and in American embassies.

Certainly, some offices with special ties to the first lady might have a picture or two of her; and in the Bush White House the East Wing had many pictures of Barbara Bush because the East Wing was the first lady's domain.

But to have *no* picture of the vice president sent an obvious message. Al Gore was just a pretty face.

As it turned out, Vice President Gore *did* get the office space usually reserved for the vice president in the White House.

The vice president also has possession of three offices on Capitol Hill. One of the offices is located in the Dirksen Building and is rarely used by the vice president. Veep staffers who could not or did not want to work at the White House were often stationed here to deal with matters that overlapped with the vice president's responsibility as president of the Senate. Part of this office space had been made available as a courtesy to the FBI for more than a decade. During the Bush administration, FBI Agent Greg Schwarz was so trusted that the staff even gave him his own door key. Gore, however, kicked Schwarz out of the office.

I called Greg when I learned he had been evicted. Gore staffers, he told me, had complained that they "didn't want to be in the same room with an FBI agent" and that they "couldn't imagine sharing office space with a fed." Why not?

Soon the mystery was solved. It appears that Al and Tipper Gore decided to reward their "incredibly hardworking staff" after the inauguration by inviting them to a Grateful Dead concert. The Gores were described by a Gore spokesperson as dedicated "Deadheads."

As an FBI agent, I knew the parking lots of Grateful Dead concerts were notorious open-air drug markets and that the band itself and its followers were an entrenched part of the "drug culture."

Perhaps I was naive, but given Tipper Gore's history as a critic of offensive rock-and-roll lyrics and given the fact that both Bill Clinton and Al Gore posed as moderate New Democrats from the conservative South, I hadn't expected this sort of animosity to the FBI or this sort of openness to what pundits still call, perhaps over optimistically, "the counterculture."

I was disappointed when I discovered that the vice president's staff was not much different than the Clinton staff. They too had serious character flaws which were reflective of counterculture roots, including a casual attitude about the use of illegal drugs. Indeed, many Gore staffers had radical political attitudes. Gore speechwriter Robert Lehrman was one such example.

Talking to Lehrman one day, I noticed a book about crime on his shelf. His name was on the jacket as a coauthor. Before joining Gore, Lehrman had been a speechwriter for David Bonior and had also worked for then-Senator Lloyd Bentsen. Lehrman moved on from Bentsen's office after writing an explicit novel about teenage sexual experiences.

Lehrman told me that the teen novel was really a how-to book for young teens, instructing them in the proper techniques of lovemaking. He was very proud of the book, but it had caused a firestorm of protest among Bentsen's constituents in Texas, and that had made Lehrman a liability to the senator.

I asked him about his book on crime—a subject more up my alley than a how-to sex manual for teens. He loaned it to me with a warning that I might disagree with his findings. I read it with interest and found it hard to imagine how anyone in law enforcement *couldn't* disagree with his analysis.

Lehrman and his coauthor had put together a fairly comprehensive history of crime and the various theories of punishment. His conclusions were unusual, to say the least. For example, Lehrman suggested that the crime rate would probably go down if we released *all* convicted criminals—murderers, rapists, child molesters—from prison. His reasoning? The longer someone is incarcerated, the angrier they become so that when they get out they're worse than before.

Lehrman's book was a signal to me that the times at the White House were a-changin'.

The new White House director of security was Craig Livingstone. Craig had no experience in security issues. His only qualifications were that he was a thirty-something friend of the Clintons and was built like an overweight bouncer. And his Washington career had opened with a bang. Federal employees were trying to find more than $150,000 worth of equipment lost or stolen from the inauguration—equipment that had been in the charge of Craig Livingstone. Further warning bells had gone off when Associate Counsel William Kennedy had asked me what the FBI thought of Craig's replacing Jane Dannenhauer and asked me in particular what the FBI would think if there were "character issues in his background." I responded gingerly, saying it was a post that should be filled with someone squeaky clean, before Kennedy cut me off: "I guess I see your point, but it doesn't matter. It's a done deal. Hillary wants him."

During one of my first meetings with Craig, he asked me to brief a new class of White House interns. Livingstone confessed his briefing for the first batch had not been serious enough and that they had had trouble with them. But this time Livingstone hoped that lectures from the FBI, the Secret Service, and the Metropolitan Police Department would impress the new interns to keep their noses clean.

I asked him what sort of trouble he'd had, and he told me that if I repeated what he was about to say, he would know it. The intern problems were a closely held secret known by only four people: Livingstone, the president, the first lady, and Mack McLarty.

I said, "Okay, fire away." I couldn't wait to hear this.

It seemed that when the first group of interns came, they had several problems "adjusting" to working in the White House. For one thing, they routinely violated the Clintons' dress code. *That* got my attention. The first "serious" violation occurred when a well-endowed young lady had trouble keeping her breasts from tumbling out of her blouse. She had become something of a legend around the White House before some female staffers complained about her. But I'd already heard about this one. What else?

The second dress-code violation was observed by none other than Hillary Rodham Clinton. It seemed that while crossing the West Executive Drive parking area on her way to the OEOB, the first lady caught sight of a young lady's bare behind. The young lady, wearing a very short skirt and nothing beneath, had bent over.

A friend of mine, who must remain anonymous, saw the incident and swears that the young lady turned to the first lady and smiled.

According to Craig Livingstone, Hillary immediately called Mack McLarty and ordered him to ensure that in the future, all White House staff wore underwear! McLarty then called Craig and passed the order down to him, confessing that he wasn't sure how one would go about "briefing" staff members or interns on the necessity of wearing underwear.

Craig asked me for suggestions, but I couldn't stop laughing.

But there were also more serious problems, Craig said. Hillary had complained that interns and staff members were "stalking" her. She ordered that Craig ensure that no one looked at her, followed her, or tried to talk to her as she made her rounds. So Craig wanted me to hammer home that interns must remain fully clothed, wear underwear, and *not look upon* the first lady.

After I stopped laughing, I told Craig that I was not an FBI spokesperson authorized to brief White House interns but that I was able to talk about SPINs and employment opportunities at the FBI. He asked me if I could talk about standards at the same time. I told him I thought I could.

At my first intern briefing, I was surprised to hear Craig stress in his presentation, which lasted about half an hour, that the interns should "have fun." But wasn't that lack of seriousness the problem I was supposed to address? These students weren't at the White House for spring break. They were here to work and earn course credit. My jaw fell when he closed with, "And I know what some of you guys are going to do, but don't get caught. I mean, I'm not asking you to become a narc or anything, but go easy on 'that kind of thing.' "

He could be talking only about drug use. So in my own remarks I warned that "what you do can surely come back to haunt you"—a message I thought they needed to hear.

Each semester until I retired I participated in the briefing of new interns, maybe two hundred or so, who would assemble in Room 450 of the OEOB. Room 450 was a theater used mostly by the president. For the better part of a day the interns would learn about how the White House operated.

At my last intern briefing, Craig was clearly tired. His message had changed to, "Stay out of trouble, period." It seemed that, as director of security, Livingstone was growing old fast. If he didn't watch out, he'd become one of us—a "Mormon" or a "straight," which is what Clinton staffers called FBI agents, the Secret Service, and former Bush employees. Of course, Craig had more problems with his interns than the Bush administration had had with theirs.

The Bush and Clinton interns came, obviously, from different pools of applicants. Trouble with the Bush interns was generally limited to using White House stationery for personal letters or making long-distance phone calls. In the Clinton administration, we had a major problem with interns walking off with laptop computers. At least one of these interns was caught by a video surveillance camera. After many denials, he eventually confessed, but only to make a counter-accusation—that he had been set up because he was a member of a minority group.

The cultural changes in the political staff of the White House were stark and often depressing, for the FBI, the Secret Service, and the permanent staff.

One evening, when Dennis was manning the office, GSA Supervising Carpenter Woody DiGuiseppe stomped in, visibly angry, and said, "Dennis, I'm here to lodge a serious complaint against the Clinton administration."

"Woody, as I've told you before, our role here is very limited."

"Yeah, I know, I know. But, Dennis, I know I trust you, and I don't know about these Clinton people. I'm not even sure of George Saun-

ders anymore—who does he work for, anyway? If you can't do anything about this, you'll know who to pass it on to, right?"

"Well, yes, Woody, I suppose. What is it?"

"Look. My guys have to be able to do their work around here, but
if the Clinton staff won't let 'em, then how are they going to do it? I
had two guys sent down to the first floor to do some work last night,
and they couldn't do the job. Do you know *why* they couldn't do
their job, Dennis?"

Woody was shaking with anger. "They couldn't do their job
because they walked into a locked office and found two Clinton
staffers doing their thing on a desk! That's why!"

"Woody, Woody, Woody, calm down, my friend. Let's have a reality check here. Yes, I know it's the White House, Woody, but there's
been sex here before, and there will be sex in offices here long after
we're gone. I don't like it, and you don't like it, and it's disgusting,
but it's not an issue for the FBI, unless there is some kind of extramarital affair going on, so. . . ."

"Look, Dennis, you don't understand. It was *two guys doing it!*"

Dennis told me he had to stop and think for a moment to digest
what Woody had just told him. "Are you sure, Woody?"

"Yes, I'm sure. These workers of mine are two of my best, my most
reliable, and Dennis, they are very religious guys. They're real angry
right now, and I don't know what they'll do. What if they go to the
press or something? I don't know what to tell them."

"Well, look Woody, let's think before we run off with this. We've
never had anything like *this* before. I still don't think it's an issue for
us, not unless there was a security issue involved. Maybe we could get
them on misuse of government property."

"Woody, I suggest you make it a matter of record by getting your
guys to write a memorandum. Send it to the GSA front office. Let
them deal with it."

Dennis had tried to stay cool, but even this FBI veteran was shocked.
Later, leaving out the identities of Woody and the men who were
offended, he retold the story to a group of permanent staff members.
They didn't so much as blink.

One of the female staffers said, "Big deal. You think that's something? Last week I went down to the ladies room on the ground
floor—you know the ones that have the shower stalls for joggers to
use? Well, anyway, I walked in the door and heard the shower run-

ning, and as I turned the corner I noticed two forms in the shower stall, together. They were both women, and they were *really* going at it! One was standing and the other one was on her knees, and you can guess the rest!"

"What? This can't be happening!" Dennis exclaimed. "This is the White House. Don't these people have any shame?"

"No, they don't seem to, Dennis. They saw me come in, but they didn't even break stride. I thought you FBI guys were here to prevent that kind of thing from happening! Aren't you guys doing your jobs? And what happened to the Secret Service?"

The Clinton staff may have been "too busy" to talk to the FBI, but they didn't seem particularly diligent in their work habits. I'd often walk into offices and find the new staffers with their feet on the desk, newspapers spread out in front of them, making personal phone calls—some obviously long distance—on the taxpayers' dime.

Staff would gather in the hallways and chat as though they were in a college dorm. I also noticed the hallways were becoming cluttered with boxes, office equipment, and furniture. We were well into the new administration, but they were apparently still in the process of moving in.

Melba was our office's GSA cleaning lady. She was almost always cheerful, but for the past several weeks she'd seemed sad or depressed.

"Melba, I don't mean to pry, but is there something wrong, something I can help you with?"

Melba thought for a moment, and a worried look crossed her face before she blurted, "Mr. Aldrich, sir, no harm intended, but these new people are terrible! Every day we go into their offices and clean up after them, and the very next day it's as if we had never been there before. They're messy people, Mr. Aldrich. These people are sloppy. Some are real slobs, sir! They throw garbage on the floor, or they throw cups of coffee and miss the waste can and it splashes all over the wall. And *they* don't clean it up!

"It's as if they don't care, Mr. Aldrich, and I hate to say this, and you must never repeat this as long as I'm here, but sir, President Bush's people were much neater *and* much nicer to us. And that's the God's honest truth, sir.

"And Mr. Aldrich, you know that recycle program that President Bush started? Well, the soda cans, plastic coffee cups, white papers, and such are supposed to be separated, put into containers that are marked for each. Then, we're supposed to empty them downstairs. Sir, they are throwing everything into one box, or the wrong box, paying no mind to it, and then we have to go through each box and sort their mess out. You would think that these smart people would know how to read instructions plainly written on the side of a box, sir. But I've said too much."

Melba looked uneasy, but I reassured her that I wouldn't "rat" on her to the Clintons. But I did think it was ironic that the supposedly "green" Clinton administration was not "environmentally friendly."

It wasn't long before Melba told me she was taking early retirement. She didn't want to go, but she couldn't bear to stay; watching the White House deteriorate was just too hard.

One of the Clinton staffers who might have pushed Melba into early retirement was George Stephanopoulos.

Stephanopoulos had taken over the big office that had been used by President Bush's press secretary, Marlin Fitzwater. Clinton's press secretary was Dee Dee Myers, but Dee Dee was stuck over in a small corner office. Why had Dee Dee been relegated to third-class office space?

It turned out that the answer was Hillary Clinton. She insisted on having office space in the West Wing and took an office next door to the Counsel's Office. This changed the entire West Wing floor plan and led to a series of "musical chairs" moves. When the music stopped, Dee Dee Myers was out.

I had an appointment with Stephanopoulos. He kept me waiting for half an hour. When I was finally allowed into his office, it was a mess. There was a half-eaten sandwich on a paper plate that was on the coffee table. Potato chips littered the rug. Newspapers were strewn all over the room, and work papers had been balled up and thrown around. A birthday cake that had been given to him on 10 February—nine days ago—was still sitting on an end table. A vase of wilted red roses was nearby. Tired birthday balloons limped along the floor. There were doodads and coffee mugs, and what looked like trash, sitting in boxes in the middle of the room. I noticed that he had to walk around the boxes to get from the door to his desk. This was day 29 of the administration.

Stephanopoulos made no effort to greet me or to be friendly. He was clearly annoyed, which seemed to be the usual mood of Clinton staffers when they met the FBI. It was a hard attitude to swallow, especially after the graciousness of the Bush people.

Stephanopoulos looked younger than his thirty-two years. He had a boyish tilt to his head. His hair was obviously something he was proud of. He must have spent hours each morning in front of a mirror with a brush, a hair dryer, and hair spray, working hard to perfect the "fluff" and "cascade" over his forehead.

I completed my interview with Stephanopoulos very quickly. I can't tell you what this particular interview was about, but he was knowledgeable about someone who needed to be interviewed.

I cannot claim that his answers were deceptive, but they were not terribly informative, either. He never uttered one syllable more than he had to in order to cover himself.

Before I retired from the White House, I would interview Stephanopoulos several more times. His office never got any neater, though the cake and balloons eventually disappeared.

I remember during one press conference early in the administration, Stephanopoulos was seen blowing a big, pink bubble gum bubble that ended up hiding half of his face. Bubble gum, blown by the director of communications during a presidential press conference—that was one reason the media started talking about the Clinton administration as being a bunch of kids. The Reagan and Bush administrations had had plenty of twenty- and thirty-something staffers, too, but none of whom behaved like this. It wasn't a matter of age; it was a matter of maturity.

I doubt if anyone would rank Dee Dee Myers as any more mature than Stephanopoulos. I know that in the interviews I had with Dee Dee, I didn't particularly care for her casual and immature attitude. And sometimes, neither did the press.

One day when they were bearing down on her, she lost it. Stomping out of the press room, she headed for her office, cursing, "eat sh-t and die!" Cursing in the Clinton White House was not unusual. Cursing at the press might sometimes be appropriate, but not if they could quote you. It was the beginning of the end for Dee Dee.

For almost a year she refused to fill out the forms that would allow the FBI to conduct a SPIN investigation. It became a matter of contention with Craig Livingstone, and he mentioned it in a senior staff meeting attended by Dee Dee and the president. Craig said, "Dee Dee, just how do you plan to answer Dan Rather or Brit Hume when they ask you why you don't have a security clearance?" Dee Dee gave him a flip answer, and President Clinton didn't bat an eye.

One day, I sat outside Dee Dee's office and watched as she put down the phone and picked up the West Wing mess menu. She knew I'd spent the past thirty minutes sitting there, waiting to interview her per our appointment. But it was amazing how many "important" matters could come up, like reading the lunch menu, that might interfere with an FBI background investigation. She finally gave me eye contact and motioned for me to come into her office. As usual, she, like so many Clinton staffers, gave me only half of her attention, shuffling some papers or stacking paper clips, which was supposed to be a clear message about how important she thought my visit was. If she thought the interview was nonsense, who could blame her? The president evidently hadn't disabused her of that idea.

I dragged as much information as I could out of her. When we were done, Dee Dee relaxed somewhat. "Well," she said, "I guess I'll have to fill out those silly forms one of these days, so that you guys can do my investigation."

"You haven't filled out the forms, yet? Do you have them? Have you been told to fill them out?"

"Well, yes, I do, but as you know we have been *so* busy around here. These forms are long and complicated. I haven't had the time. I'll get to it, I promise." She grinned somewhat sheepishly.

"Look, Miss Myers, I have no power to force you to fill out the forms, but without them the FBI cannot investigate you. And if we can't investigate you, you won't have a security clearance or a permanent pass. The fact is, people like you make protecting the president and our national security that much harder."

"Look, *Gary,* I said I'd fill out the forms, okay?!"

I didn't wait around to be told to "eat sh-t and die."

I went back to my office, wrote my report, and faxed it to FBI headquarters and my immediate supervisor. Here was a senior White House employee in clear violation of all known security regulations. In her position, Myers was seeing and hearing highly classified, very sensitive information on a daily basis, and yet her background had never been investigated.

And she couldn't even claim to be an old Arkansas "Friend of Bill." Dee Dee was a valley girl from California who had come late to the Clinton machine. The closest thing to a SPIN investigation Myers had ever experienced was having grown up in the San Fernando Valley next door to an FBI agent.

I filed my report, and the FBI ignored it.

With the coming of the new administration, Marty Black, a wonderful, polite, calm, and competent executive secretary, was assigned to work for Phil Lader, the Clinton management guru and father of the annual "Renaissance Weekend."

I needed to interview Lader. After days and days of unreturned phone calls and missed appointments, I complained to Marty and told her that FBI headquarters was harassing me because I couldn't close the case without interviewing Lader. Marty shocked me when she let loose with, "Gary, just tell your FBI headquarters that it is very hard to make and keep appointments, or do other normal things, when you are *so f---ing smart!*

"You see, Gary, when you are *brilliant* like Lader and the rest of these Clinton people are, you don't have to follow the rules that all of us mere idiots follow!"

I did eventually get the interview with Lader. He was *so* slick that I almost slid out the door after we talked.

Like David Watkins, Mack McLarty, and others close to the president and first lady, he made me think, "Here's another guy I shouldn't turn my back on." Marty retired soon after my meeting with Lader. She told me, "I just can't take these Clinton people any more." I was sorry to see her go.

One of President Clinton's first major reforms at the White House was to replace the "antique and old-fashioned" phone system. No one had ever complained about the phones before. In fact, they'd seemed to work pretty well, taking the Reagan and Bush administrations through twelve years of successfully handled world crises, including the downfall of the Soviet Union and the victorious war in the Persian Gulf. To many, the White House phone system was more than adequate, it was one of the wonders of the Western world—capable of finding anyone, anywhere, at any time.

But President Clinton thought the phone system was "impossible" because he couldn't make personal calls without the assistance of White House switchboard operators.

For most of us, the problem wasn't the White House phones, it was the people who were answering them. Time after time I would call an office within the White House, only to hear a Clinton staffer respond, "Hello? I mean, Public Liaison. Hello. Um, just a minute. Ummm, ah, who's this?" Then I had to convince them I wasn't kidding. "I really *am* an FBI agent. Really! Now please put your supervisor on the line."

Being put on terminal hold was something I came to expect. I got used to being disconnected, too. When the Clinton staffers weren't intentionally hanging up on me, they were doing it by accident. During the Bush administration, I could usually reach the desired party in less than a minute. In the Clinton White House, it sometimes took half an hour.

The ex-take-out pizza guys and gals in the Clinton administration—of whom there were quite a few—did fairly well with the phones. Everyone else seemed to be struggling. We learned later that the real problem was that most Clintonites just didn't *want* to answer the phone.

Early in the administration, a senior Clinton staffer tried to call the vice president at his residence. The call was placed after 9:00 P.M., and the veep's schedule indicated that he and Tipper Gore were at home. Even if they'd gone out, staff would be there to answer any call.

The phone rang and rang. Nobody answered. Immediate panic set in, as White House staff wondered what had happened. The staff called the White House switchboard; the switchboard called the White House Communications Agency, and phone technicians were rushed to the veep's residence. They went through the gate, walked to the front door, and were met by one of the vice president's staff. The technicians explained why they were there, and Mrs. Gore was summoned.

Tipper appeared, and the mystery was solved. Couldn't they see that it was after 9:00 P.M.? The staff had been instructed to shut off the ringers on the vice president's phones. The Gores did not want to be disturbed after nine.

Another of Clinton's complaints about the phones was that the system was overloaded now that so many more people wanted to call the White House. So the new phone system was set up to *shred* calls.

How do you shred a call? Simple. Instead of using human operators, use voice mail that shunts public calls to a call "dump." This innovation was instituted at the direction of Patsy Thomasson and David Watkins at the Office of Administration, two of Bill and Hillary Clinton's closest friends.

More than $27 million was spent on this new and improved phone system that offered each staffer a "secret," unpublished phone number, a number that even the FBI was not allowed to know. Each "personal" phone number also had voice mail, but that was secret, too. Offices also had a main number where messages could be left in a generic voice mail "pool," essentially a mini call dump. So, if a staffer wanted to avoid a call from a pesky FBI agent, it was easy. These were public servants, but they weren't very interested in being publicly accountable.

The White House also had an e-mail system, and we had computers, but David Watkins and Patsy Thomasson saw to it that the FBI Office could not hook up to the e-mail system, in spite of our repeated requests.

One day, deeply frustrated by my inability to get appointments and meet deadlines, I tried to call Patsy Thomasson directly to request a list of the "secret" phone extensions. The phone was answered by a machine, and the message went something like this:

"Hello. You have reached the Office of Administration, Main Office. Nobody is here to take your call right now. Please leave a message. If you are calling to request a tour of the West Wing, press one, now. If your call is about. . . ."

Nobody is here right now? It was the middle of the day.

Later, I met a good friend in the hallway, a permanent employee who saw Patsy Thomasson frequently.

"Gary, there is no secret phone list." Her eyes swiveled to check if we had been overheard.

"Sylvia, it's sure as hell secret if *I*, an FBI agent, can't get it!"

"Well, all right, Gary. But *please* don't call it secret—it makes people around here nervous."

The next day a very muted and intimidated Sylvia called me. "Gary, I passed your request on to Patsy, and you don't want to hear what she said."

"Aw, go ahead. Nothing would surprise me anymore."

"When I told Patsy you wanted the list, she said, 'Screw the FBI! To hell with the FBI! They're not getting this list!'"

In addition to making it tougher to reach people, the new phone system was a security nightmare. The old system was self-contained, manned twenty-four hours every day. The new system was computerized and, therefore, *not* self-contained.

In preparation for this book, I interviewed a White House telephone company official who requested confidentiality.

"Gary, as you know, the Secret Service has always had a say in the past on changes to the phone system. This time they were effectively told to 'sit down and shut up.' The system was installed without any of the usual input or approval from the Secret Service."

"Aw, come on, you're kidding. What bonehead cut the Secret Service out of the loop?"

"No, I'm not kidding. It was Patsy Thomasson and David Watkins who were the boneheads, Gary."

I heard many complaints from Democratic congressmen that they could not get through on the new Clinton phone system, and if they did, by chance, their names were often not recognized, and they often weren't called back.

Another problem with the new phone system was how to pay for it. On 11 October 1994, it was revealed that more than half a million dollars worth of charges were rolled up on the new White House phone system. But since each of the several White House agencies was funded separately by Congress, and no one had arranged for them to be *billed* separately, there was no legal way to pay the bill with the appropriate funds.

While David Watkins and Patsy Thomasson tried to figure out what they had done, a White House spokesperson explained it this way, "It's not that we are delinquent. It's just that we cannot legally pay the bill."

With the phones now squared away, the Clintons decided to "upgrade" the White House computers. The Bush computers were IBMs and IBM clones. The Clinton administration preferred Apples and didn't want to waste time receiving training on how to use IBMs. So new Macs were installed, and the staff who were on hand to train them on the IBMs were fired.

The Clintons also fired roughly two dozen people from the Office of Presidential Correspondence.

The result was chaos. Huge canvas bins loaded with mail were parked end to end all around the halls like some enormous wagon train. Vast numbers of tables were set up and overflowed with mail.

Reportedly more than one million pieces were unread, unanswered. Most of it was protest mail.

The fired employees would have been an enormous help to deal with it. They were professionals, most of whom had worked for presidents of both parties. And when President Clinton was elected, several came out of the closet as vocal Democrats.

Ellen Strickhartz, the correspondence analyst, was one of these. She made no effort to hide her joy at Clinton's victory. She was also one of the first to be fired by the Clintons. The day that happened, she walked around the OEOB, literally in tears, stopping everyone she knew, including me, and cursing the Clintons.

"I *voted* for them. I can't believe they've done this to me. I'm a registered Democrat! I have a family to feed. A mortgage to pay. There are no jobs. What am I going to do?"

No amount of pleading would dissuade Marsha Scott, the Clintons' director of correspondence, from firing these "little old ladies."

And what was Marsha Scott's connection to the Clintons? She told a California newspaper that she was a former girlfriend of the president and they had remained good friends. Her friendship entitled her to a salary close to $100K and the right to fire loyal public servants.

Scott also reported that in the 1970s she'd been a wanderer, driving her old Volkswagen bus from town to town. When the bus ran out of gas, she decided that was the place she would live.

Scott's office in Presidential Correspondence, like every other office in the OEOB, had gone from being immaculate to being a pigsty. At first, Marsha Scott reminded me of David Watkins, because she greeted me with such insincere, excessive friendliness that I felt uncomfortable. Then I wondered whether or not she was violating the Clinton "dress code." She was wearing a very short skirt and—like Sharon Stone in the movie *Basic Instinct*—kept ostentatiously crossing and uncrossing her legs. But Marsha Scott is no Sharon Stone.

After I returned to my office, I told Dennis about the Scott interview and asked him if he'd met her. He had, and she had tried to "ruin his concentration," too.

In the meantime, the mail stacked up. And then it was gone. Just like that.

I wondered what had happened to it. One day as I was taking a bag of FBI memos and duplicate copies of investigative forms to the grinding room in the basement of the OEOB, I found out what happened to at least some of that mail. Stacked in the hallways near the huge shredding machine were boxes and boxes of postcards, telegrams, and letters—most of it apparently protest mail. "So *this* is how they're catching up," I thought, as the people's voice was turned into the people's garbage.

Perhaps shredding the mail was the only way they could keep up, as heads kept rolling from the Correspondence Office. I remember seeing the supervisor of the Mail Analysis Office, a distinguished, older woman named Lillie Bell, coming out of Marsha Scott's office. Her eyes were red, and she had a Kleenex in her hand.

"Lillie, what's wrong? Can I help you?" I asked.

"No Gary," she said sternly, her voice shaking. "Just don't pray for something you think you want, unless you are very sure you want it! As a black Democrat, I prayed to God that I could end my career working for someone like Bill Clinton. And I got what I prayed for. And now, I've just turned in my retirement papers. I am leaving early, Gary. These people are doing things that are *so wrong!*

"Our office used to work so well, and now they've destroyed it. I told them I would stay on to get things working again, but I can't. I'm leaving. I just cannot be a part of what they are doing. It's just *wrong*."

It turned out that Lillie had been luckier than Betty Dunn, a long-serving employee of the Correspondence Office. Dunn was absolutely destroyed by the news she was going to be fired. She called her elderly husband. It was a worse shock for him; he suffered a fatal heart attack.

Dunn called her supervisor, "This cannot be happening. I'm losing my job and my husband on the *same day!*" Her supervisor begged Marsha Scott to reverse Dunn's termination. The answer? "Nope. Can't help ya." After all, they needed that slot.

Did Presidential Correspondence improve under its new management? The short answer is, *no.*

To give a parochial example, when the Bush administration sent out a letter of congratulations to a retiring FBI agent, they worked from a general format, but always personalized each letter to make it special, taking account of each agent's individual achievements.

The Clinton administration quickly did away with such nonsense. They had one form letter and used it over and over again, simply changing the name of the retiring agent.

It was for this and other such time-saving innovations that Marsha Scott got paid the big bucks.

Dennis and I soon discovered that appointees could make big bucks in the Clinton White House without any sort of expertise, relevant experience, or even basic knowledge.

One day, Dennis entered the office shaking his head and chuckling. "Gary, I just had the most amazing interview with that congressman's wife who got hired as deputy assistant to the president and deputy director of public liaison under Alexis Herman."

I nodded. I'd heard about her.

"Well, we finish the interview. So I get up to leave, and she says, 'Do you know what I'm supposed to do here?' I thought she had a question about security or about her pass, but she says, 'No, no, no. I'm talking about this job, this job here at the White House. What are my duties? Do you know what I'm supposed to do?' "

"Gary, I just stood there and stared at her. I couldn't believe it! This woman is getting $85K a year, and she hasn't a clue of what her duties are! How do they choose these people?!"

It was a good question—one we asked ourselves again and again when confronted by the petty antics of the new Clinton staffers.

One day I was getting my lunch in the canteen. The picture was the usual scene out of *Animal House*, with staffers going first to the drink machine, then ordering a sandwich or burger, all the while sipping their drinks, and then returning to the drink machine to "top them off," before they sat at a table—of which there were too few. And they stayed there, even after they were finished, while dozens of other staffers, including some elderly volunteers, stood waiting.

Now, I knew the canteen manager, a good fellow named Tom. He had told me that his margin of profit was very close, so as to keep prices down. Tom's success at managing the canteen depended on customers who didn't, for instance, double-dip at the drink machines. He clearly was not going to do well with this Clinton crowd. That day I saw a new scam—a "twofer." It combined the elements of thrift *and* good health!

The frozen yogurt machine was about fifteen steps from the cash register. Near the register was a scale where you weighed the yogurt or whatever else you bought that was chargeable by the ounce, like salads, self-made sandwiches, or self-serve pasta. A man dressed in a business suit, an *expensive* business suit, and about thirty-five years old, approached the yogurt machine, selecting the largest cup. I noticed that he had a spoon in his hand. He must have picked it up on his way in. He pulled the handle on the yogurt machine and filled the cup, and then while he stood in line for the cash register, in full view of anyone who wished to see, he wolfed down as much yogurt as he could.

Bernice, the canteen cashier, saw him too and groaned. There wasn't much to weigh once he got to the scale. I studied his badge to see if I could identify him so I could let his supervisor know about his rude, cheapskate, and dishonest behavior. But his supervisor was Hillary Clinton. He was working for Hillary's Health Care Task Force.

The only way to keep these Clinton staffers honest, I thought, would be to weigh them entering and exiting the canteen and charge them accordingly.

But they didn't cheat only on yogurt. The Secret Service has a small gift shop in the basement of the OEOB. It sells gifts to benefit the families of Secret Service agents injured or killed in the line of duty or in need of funds because of illness or other personal calamity. Craig Livingstone actually had to issue warnings to the Clinton staffers and interns that passing bad checks to the handicapped man who ran the Secret Service gift shop would not be tolerated.

For me, that kind of dishonesty—cheating the families of injured or murdered Secret Service agents—would eventually come to characterize the Clinton administration. I wasn't at all surprised when a source close to the White House Credit Union told me that Clinton staffers' accounts were full of irregularities and that one senior staff member in the Clinton administration was using his federal credit union account for check kiting, while he waited for his FBI background investigation to be completed. I guess he figured that in this White House, check kiting was no bar to getting ahead.

Chapter Four

ROSE LAW-NORTH

Rules for Radicals: "The fourth rule of the ethics of means and ends is that judgment must be made in the context of the times in which the action occurred and not from any other chronological vantage point. Ethical standards must be elastic to stretch with the times. In politics, the ethics of means and ends can be understood by the rules suggested here."

George Washington's Rules of Civility and Decent Behaviour: "Superfluous compliments and all affectations of ceremony are to be avoided, yet where due, they are not to be neglected."

There was nothing gradual or subtle about the changes at the White House. By the second week in February, Dennis and I and our Secret Service chums knew we were in for what writer John Podhoretz said of the Bush administration—"a hell of a ride." Each week, every month, the incidents piled up. The permanent staff was bewildered, and they would often come to our office to unburden themselves of the latest outrages they'd seen or heard. Some of these became public, like the scandal of the Clinton staffers stealing U.S. Navy towels during the president's trip to Normandy. Some were not so public, like the story of a staffer on that same trip who intentionally kicked over a small American flag on a soldier's grave so that when the president and the news cameras arrived, our commander-in-chief could be photographed lovingly replacing the flag.

Some of these tales were funny, but most were not. In the best tradition of the White House, these permanent staff members would couch their remarks in the most generous terms, so as not to insult

52

the president or his senior staff, but they would get their message across. The message was, "What the hell is going on here?"

What we were seeing went beyond politics. It was a matter of basic standards of civility, of deportment—even legality. Clinton staffers would show up at checkpoints without any identification, or with friends who didn't have any ID, or even, on more than one occasion, with friends who were wanted by the law and would become outraged when the Secret Service denied them access.

In one instance, a Clinton staffer came in on a weekend with a group of friends to show off his office and give them a tour of the West Wing. He possessed a temporary access pass, also known as a "T" pass, and the rules prohibited staff members who had not successfully completed an FBI background investigation from bringing in visitors. It was a basic security procedure, and for most people, no big deal. But this staffer reportedly "lost it" when he was turned away. Moreover, he attempted to get the officer at the gate disciplined for enforcing the security policy. Within hours, the rule forbidding uncleared staffers from bringing in visitors was waived. Apparently, one staffer's ego was thought to be more important than the security of the president of the United States.

It was also very annoying, apparently, for the "T" pass staffers to have briefcases and bags searched as they went through the security checkpoints. All permanent staffers could walk right through the magnetometers, because they had been cleared. The "T" pass holders saw this search, and the wait, as an insult. They considered the bag searches "discrimination." Before long, that rule was also rescinded, even though one Clinton "volunteer" from Texas was caught trying to bring in a pistol. He wasn't intent on harming anyone; he just wanted to protect himself in Washington, D.C.

Every day in the Clinton White House we were surrounded by people who had not been properly screened or properly searched. To be responsible for security in these circumstances was unnerving, to say the least.

In February I got a chance to bring my concerns to the White House Counsel's Office, because I needed to interview Bernard Nussbaum.

The counsel's number-one job is to keep the president and the White House out of trouble. Dennis and I saw the White House heading for *major* trouble down the line, if something wasn't done to make Clinton staffers cooperate with our background investigations and unless White House security policy was enforced.

The lead players at the Counsel's Office were Nussbaum, the White House counsel; his deputy, Vince Foster; and the associate counsel, William "Bill" Kennedy. Foster and Kennedy had worked in Little Rock with Hillary Clinton at the Rose Law Firm. So had Webster Hubbell, now at the Department of Justice. But most people knew very little about these lawyers or about the Rose Law Firm.

When Nussbaum was announced as the president's White House counsel, I remember that he was referred to as a "brilliant New York attorney." All New York attorneys, in my experience, believe they are "brilliant." But Nussbaum was already having trouble.

It was the day after Janet Reno was nominated to be attorney general. The FBI had not yet conducted an investigation, because, once again, President Clinton had announced his choice before the FBI had a chance to look into Reno's background. Three failed AG nominations in a row? It was a serious possibility.

Dennis and I knew we were getting close to Nussbaum's office in the West Wing of the White House when we smelled the cigar smoke. Hillary had proclaimed that the White House would be smoke-free, but apparently Nussbaum smoked cigars in his office anyway.

Nussbaum had chairs set up around a coffee table, and he motioned us to sit there. He introduced himself. We spent an awkward moment on small talk, then Nussbaum got down to business.

He obviously anticipated our complaints, because he tried to bury us with effusive praise for the FBI, how important he thought our work was, and other bombast that sounded extremely insincere. Nussbaum's heavy New York accent was an interesting contrast to the soft-spoken, gentlemanly manner of Foster, whom I'd meet the following day. Foster was tall, the polite southern gentleman. Nussbaum was short, pushy, and imperious.

As Nussbaum rattled on, he must have noticed by the look on my face that I was not impressed. He said, "Look, we made some mistakes with the Baird and Wood nominations. We have taken steps to avoid making the same mistakes again."

"Like what?" I thought to myself. But the AG wasn't as much my concern as the White House staff was.

I asked Nussbaum why staff members weren't cooperating, why in some cases they were openly hostile, and why nothing was being done about this problem.

He didn't seem surprised by this revelation. Nussbaum assured us that the staff would cooperate. He said he'd advised Vince Foster to let him know if anyone was not fully cooperative. His dismissive tone offended me, so I called him on the Janet Reno appointment.

"Mr. Nussbaum," I began, "I have seen no evidence that Janet Reno has submitted any documents to the FBI to enable us to conduct a proper background investigation, but her nomination was announced yesterday." Nussbaum didn't say anything.

I turned to Dennis and asked, "Dennis, do you have any paperwork on the Reno investigation?" Dennis, of course, answered no. Nussbaum's face was turning beet red. He stared at me for a long time. I stared right back. I had the distinct impression that he was considering whether he should squash me like a bug. All he had to do was pick up the telephone and have me thrown out of the White House. One call to FBI Director William Sessions, and I would be on my way.

I had made a big mistake, if I had my heart set on staying at the White House, and I knew it, but the security of the president of the United States *was* my mission, and I could not stand idly by while President Clinton, or any other president, had his life put in danger because of the dissembling of a cocky New York lawyer. Nussbaum stood up, signaling that the meeting was over. Grim-faced, he walked us to the door. I knew that I'd made an enemy, a big one.

The next morning I was to meet with Vince Foster. Privacy Act provisions prevent me from telling you about the background investigation of Vince Foster, but I can tell you that he had one, just like everyone else in the White House, and I was the FBI agent who conducted the investigation, at least the part that was conducted inside the White House.

I sipped my coffee and reviewed the standard forms that Foster had filled out about his life and background. As part of his responsibilities, Foster would need to see many of the nation's most secret secrets. But as yet, he had no basis for a security clearance. Foster had never been investigated by any agency responsible for national security.

Foster was the third most powerful White House appointee after Chief of Staff Mack McLarty and Bernard Nussbaum, but except for the fact that his references were the president and the first lady, we knew very little about him.

What was public about Foster was that he was a graduate of the University of Arkansas School of Law, Class of 1971. He was a partner at the Rose Law Firm in Little Rock, Arkansas, and reported to William Kennedy, who was his senior and managing partner at the firm. He was married to Lisa, and they had two sons, Vincent and John, and a daughter named Laura. Foster's father was deceased, but his mother was living in Hope, Arkansas, where Foster was born and reared.

His two older sisters, Sheila and Sharon, lived in Washington, D.C., and Little Rock, respectively. Sheila was an attorney who joined the U.S. Department of Justice shortly after Clinton's election. When Foster moved to Washington, he lived with her.

Foster's SPIN investigation would serve to determine Foster's good character, allow him access to classified information, and give him unlimited access to the White House complex. It would also allow him unlimited access to intelligence agencies throughout the Executive Branch, including the FBI, the CIA, the National Security Agency (NSA), and the entire Department of Defense.

Of particular interest to me that morning was the fact that Foster had been at the White House for almost a month, but we were just now getting the paperwork necessary to conduct his investigation. Given his high position, we should have been asked to complete his investigation months ago, so he could have his permanent access pass and security clearance before the inauguration. Foster would need at least a top secret clearance, and should have had a basic understanding of how the system worked. In addition to being briefed by President Bush's counsel and deputy counsel, he received a full briefing from *me* about the system on 12 February, after I had finished his interview. But understanding security and agreeing with the need for it are two different things.

Foster quizzed *me* very thoroughly. He was interested in the function of the FBI at the White House, as well as the clearance process. Using composites of troubling cases that I was aware of or had personally handled in the past, I pointed out why it was important to national security and to President Clinton that the staff be "cleared" prior to granting permanent passes.

I reviewed the issues of suitability, physical security, and national security, and I also reviewed how the previous administration had dealt with problems associated with negative background investigations.

I left my meeting with Foster thinking that here, at last, was someone who seemed to understand the need for security.

When I saw Foster again, a few days later, he asked how things were going. I told him that key individuals, even low-level staffers, were stiff-arming us. He promised to do something about it and asked me to let him know if the problem continued.

As a response to my complaint, Foster wrote a memorandum directed to "All White House Staff," ordering everyone to turn in their FBI forms and make time for Dennis and me when we called. The memo, dated 17 February 1993, was unprecedented. For one thing, it was puzzling to see William Kennedy's name on the memo along with Foster's. For another, that the deputy and associate counsel would have to scold White House employees for failure to cooperate with the FBI and Secret Service was truly amazing.

I recall that the memo read something like this: "There are a large number of staff members yet to be interviewed and only a few weeks left to complete the interview process before your temporary clearance expires. Avoid the last-week crunch and the risk of expiration of your temporary clearance."

I wasn't entirely happy with the memo. The decision to delegate this troublesome security mess down to the associate counsel level—to William Kennedy—was a big mistake. The responsibility was Nussbaum's, and the staff would have taken the memo more seriously if his name had been on it. Security was still getting low priority in the Clinton administration.

George Saunders, the veteran White House security consultant, complained to me that his day had been reduced to waiting for phone calls that never came. George had also been moved from the fourth floor of the OEOB to a former supply room in the Office of Administration. Apparently, David Watkins, in charge of space in the OEOB, didn't think very much of George—or his job.

I met William Held Kennedy III on or about 22 February. He was dark haired, mustached, and bulkier than his white long-sleeved shirt wanted him to be; his tie was loose, and his collar was unbuttoned.

Kennedy always had a hangdog, forlorn expression on his face, as if he had been set upon, mistreated, or in pain. In hindsight, if anyone appeared to me to be depressed, it was Kennedy, not Foster. (I recently saw Kennedy testifying in front of the Senate Whitewater panel. He still had that "you are ruining my life" expression.)

I introduced myself and briefed him on the role of the FBI in the White House. I specifically recall telling Kennedy that I had twenty years of experience with white-collar criminal investigations and that my education and investigative experience was in accounting. He seemed *very* interested in this information, asking me about what kinds and types of financial investigations I had handled. I told him that I had specialized in investigating embezzlement and political corruption and had jailed bureaucrats, politicians, and lawyers. (I always enjoyed telling lawyers about those experiences. For some reason, it always seemed to get their attention.)

Kennedy reached down into his center desk drawer and pulled out the Foster–Kennedy memorandum of 17 February 1993. He handed it to me and asked me if I had anything to do with it. I admitted that I had spoken to both Nussbaum and Foster about the problems we were having and I reiterated them.

Kennedy was clearly unhappy. "I wouldn't have written this. I'm not happy with this. Vince should have checked with me before he sent this out."

I wasn't sure what part he objected to, but I didn't much care. After all, as long as FBI agents had been ordered by an Executive Order signed by the president himself to clear the president's staff, I felt justified in supporting embarrassing memos written by a deputy counsel, if that's what it took to get the staff's attention.

I began, "Look, Mr. Kennedy . . ."

He interrupted. "Call me Bill."

Where had I heard that before? "Look, Bill, I understand that everyone is busy, and everyone is reluctant to go through this in the first place, but I've got a job to do here, and it's been very difficult so far. If we can get the new staff off to a good start, we can avoid problems down the road with 'emergency' deadlines, and so forth. Rushed investigations are never a good idea. Your staff is acting as if this is personal or that *I* want to know about their backgrounds. I don't. All I'm trying to do is get this information back to the president so he can do his job and we can ensure his security. That's all. I wouldn't have complained if I didn't believe we were having serious problems."

Kennedy was paying half attention. He always seemed to be distracted by something. "Well, okay, Gary. Tell you what. Let me know if you have trouble interviewing anybody, and I'll call them and ream them out."

"Bill, I can't do that."

"Why not?"

"Well, I have to work here just like everyone else. My success is dependent on making the least number of enemies as possible. How long do you think I would last if I called you up each time a senior staff member tried to dodge my interview? They'd find a way to sink me, sooner or later. I wouldn't be here very long if everyone thought I was a *snitch*. Besides, why shouldn't your staffers cooperate with sworn federal officers?"

"Gary, look, these people, are, well, just a little different from the crowd you're used to working around. They don't like telling strangers about their personal business. They think it's too intrusive."

"I couldn't care less how anybody *feels* about this process. It's just too bad if they don't like it. This is the only way we know to protect the president, the White House, and national security. We've been in the White House since Johnson, and this process has been accepted by presidents and staffs since Eisenhower. It's also the law. It's the FBI's job to see to it that these people are investigated, and I'm less concerned about hurting feelings. The White House has standards of suitability. If these folks have that much to hide, they shouldn't be here."

Kennedy was surprised by my candor. So was I. But I didn't unload completely on Kennedy, because I couldn't without alienating him. David Watkins was one of Kennedy's good friends, and Watkins was one of my problems.

All of the senior staff were closely tied together in a web of personal and professional relationships. Still, I didn't suspect that Kennedy would be anything other than a help, a cooperative party to enforce the security system. At that time, I could not imagine that Kennedy would actually be in charge of *dismantling* the security program. The thought that the Clintons would try to "get around" the FBI and Secret Service was so alien that I just could not have absorbed it.

We finished our conversation, but not before Kennedy had let me know that he was not pleased with leaving Little Rock, working at the White House, or getting stuck with this nettlesome security assignment.

Soon after that, I saw Kennedy again. I had other background investigations that required his being interviewed. Kennedy greeted me with his usual sad face and Southern friendliness. Then he asked, "How's Gary feeling today?" I thought, "Poor man, he can't keep Dennis and me straight."

I must have looked puzzled. He tried again, "How's *Gary feeling*?" Then it dawned on me. He was asking how *I* was *feeling*. Was I about to be hugged here? When they weren't shouting at each other, which they did frequently, the Clinton staffers often talked about their "feelings." Kennedy was inviting me to *share*.

"Bill, if you mean how is my day going, I would say fairly well." He didn't look happy with my answer; but if I wanted to complain to somebody about my feelings, I would call my wife, not confess to the associate counsel to the president.

Clearly, we were not bonding. I asked him about the cases I was working on, and we took care of business. He cooperated with my questions, and there was no problem completing the interviews. He seemed to be in a hurry, but he indicated he wanted to talk to me some more. He told me he was late for a flight taking off from National Airport and needed to catch a cab. I offered to drive him.

On the way to National, he told me he was flying to meet his wife to pick up an adopted baby. It was his second adoption, as I recall. He told me his wife was still living in Arkansas, and he did not indicate when, or if, she would be joining him in Washington.

Our conversation drifted back to security issues at the White House, and I remember it ended with Kennedy saying dismissively, "Let's not stand on ceremony." I dropped Kennedy off at the airport terminal, and he trudged off to catch his flight, still frowning.

From the time I met him, until the Travel Office firings, now known as Travelgate, Kennedy certainly worked hard to avoid "standing on ceremony"—or standing on Executive Orders, or policy, or procedure, or the law. Kennedy was a close personal friend of Hillary and Bill Clinton, Vince Foster, David Watkins, Bruce Lindsey, Patsy Thomasson, and all the other high-level Clinton insiders at the White House. He was also a very close friend of Webster Hubbell, who was already being referred to as the "real" attorney general. So he was confident in his power and position. He wasn't likely to be shoved aside. But that didn't mean he cracked the whip on the Clinton staffers to fall in line and cooperate with us. I had the distinct feeling that we were just excess work he didn't want to deal with.

Dennis and I were called to a meeting in Bill Kennedy's office to offer suggestions about how the White House, the FBI, and the Secret Service could work better as a team. Dennis had requested the meeting, and I agreed it was a good idea.

I told Kennedy that one problem was that the White House Counsel's Office, the SPIN unit at FBI headquarters, and the field office did not have a collegial, harmonious working arrangement in spite of the fact we were all on the same mission.

I suggested one solution might be for the White House Counsel's Office to host a simple "Coke and peanuts" get-together, maybe in the Indian Treaty Room. Counsel's Office could provide a speaker to tell the FBI personnel how much their work was appreciated and so forth. Having everyone in the same room for a friendly gathering might help iron out some of the friction that existed between the parties.

Kennedy said he thought it was a good idea and asked me to prepare a proposal, including a list of guests who would attend from the FBI.

Dennis was more direct, as he usually was. "Bill, things are really screwed up at FBI headquarters. There are about a dozen things HQ does on a regular basis that, if corrected, could mean a smoother, better, more comprehensive SPIN for the White House."

Kennedy was clearly not interested, but he told Dennis to put the suggestions on paper and he in turn would suggest them to headquarters, if he agreed.

Dennis balked at giving him anything in writing. "Bill, you can't be serious—if FBI headquarters or anyone else saw a list written by me, telling them that they could do things better, that would be curtains for me. No agent knows more than the bureaucrats at FBI headquarters! Everyone knows that. It's the law!"

Kennedy seemed amused. "Dennis, do you think that I would *ever* do that? Just give me the list, and I'll do the rest."

For days after, whenever Kennedy saw Dennis or me, he would ask for our respective lists. Something in the back of my mind kept telling me, "Watch out." Kennedy's persistence bothered me; this couldn't be high on his list of things to do. I decided to run the idea by Tom Renagahan, my field office supervisor. Of course, I anticipated that Tom would do nothing—he rarely did anything other than carp about deadlines—but, having told Tom about it, I knew I could then tell Kennedy that I had kicked the idea upstairs for action, and I'd be off the hook. I was already having second thoughts about it. Kennedy's interest seemed phoney, but I didn't know what his game was.

Dennis gave in to Kennedy's persistence. He typed the list of "sins" on plain bond, as a personal note to Kennedy, and gave it to him. Weeks went by, and nothing happened.

But on the evening of 19 May 1993, Tom Renagahan came down to the White House to review our White House operations and suggest ways for Dennis and me to meet the background investigation deadlines in a more consistent manner. "The deadlines thing again," I thought. Tom was very adept at ignoring the real problem.

We had our meeting and then took Tom to meet Kennedy. Tom said he'd never spoken to Kennedy, but I wondered. I also wondered how Kennedy had time to see us for what was essentially a social call. But Kennedy saw us right in. There was the usual small talk, as "Tom and Bill" got to know each other.

Then a curious thing happened. Dennis joked that one of the best things about his White House assignment was the fact that his supervisor, Tom, could never just drop in on us because of the access pass requirement (Tom didn't have one). Ha, ha.

Kennedy and Tom didn't smile. Kennedy turned to Tom and said, "That's easy. We can sure fix that in a hurry. We'll order you up a pass today!" Dennis looked as if he had just watched somebody run over his puppy.

It was not fair of Kennedy to cut Dennis off at the knees like that. It was a clear warning. But Kennedy wasn't finished. A few minutes later, he administered the coup de grâce when he reached in his desk and pulled out Dennis's list of FBI headquarter's sins. I thought, "We're dead!"

Kennedy handed it to Tom and said, "What do you think about these ideas that Dennis and Gary have given me?" My name was not on the note, but I had agreed with Dennis in our initial meeting with Kennedy that certain simple administrative changes would make things go better, and some of the changes had referred to FBI headquarters. Oops.

Tom read the list in silence, while Dennis and I tried to make our-selves as small as we could. I would not have blamed Dennis if he had just got up and walked out. But Dennis believed in his sugges-tions, and he intended to defend them to the death, or at least to the transfer.

Tom stammered, as only Tom could, "Ah, ah, um. Well, some of these might, ah, um. Some of these things could, ah, um." He was trying to support his agents, but he could not. I guess he could only wonder at what the FBI headquarters management would do to *him* if they found out his agents had gone off the reservation.

Kennedy let Tom keep the note, and the meeting was over. He had managed to embarrass us and possibly neutralize Dennis and me in one masterstroke.

Smart, but snakelike. On the way out, Kennedy caught up with Dennis and me. I, for one, felt only disgust and anger toward him for setting us up. I vowed henceforth never to believe anything Kennedy had to say. In fact, from that moment on, I avoided him like the plague that he was.

He tried to make up. "Look, guys, sorry. By the way, tomorrow you guys are going to hear about something you aren't going to like, but you're going to thank me for keeping you out of it."

I turned to Kennedy, "What are you talking about?"

"I can't tell you now. Just read the papers. You're going to thank me for keeping you out of this thing. Just read the papers."

At the same time Kennedy was meeting with us, Dee Dee Myers, about one hundred yards away, announced that the FBI would be conducting a criminal investigation of the White House Travel Office.

Dennis and I had done just about as much as we could to alert the FBI and the Counsel's Office to the problems we and the Secret Ser-vice were facing with staffers who were uncooperative, deceptive, and potentially dangerous to the president, but we weren't getting any-where.

One problem for us was that the FBI was distracted by its own internal difficulties. FBI Director William Sessions was fighting charges of ethics violations, and the president and the AG were non-committal about whether they intended to support him. (He was eventually fired in July.) Director Sessions did not want to leave the

FBI, and everyone knew that. So for six months, Clinton had the FBI effectively compromised with a lame duck director. Sessions and the FBI were effectively wounded, if not neutralized.

Was it possible that Kennedy, understanding that Sessions was compromised, figured he had the FBI "handled" and, as a result, didn't have to take two of its agents very seriously? This scenario would explain why we never got anywhere.

In spite of our best efforts and the real risks that Dennis and I had taken (when we complained, we were on thin ice), persons continued to be named for posts *and then* we were asked to investigate them. This virtually guaranteed that our reports would be irrelevant, because having announced someone for a post, the administration would be reluctant to pay the obvious political and public relations costs involved in retracting his or her name, even if we found something.

The president was entitled to have the people he wanted. But this prerogative rested on the assumption that the president would require basic standards of suitability. If a person didn't meet these standards, he was out. But the Clinton administration had very different standards. So in order to maintain an appearance of propriety—while hiring staff that previous administrations would have regarded as a security risk—they needed to keep the security personnel in place while they dismantled the security system.

In order to do that, Kennedy disconnected the security consultant, George Saunders, from the security procedures but kept him on as an employee. To the outside observer, the fact that Saunders was still working at the White House would be evidence that everything was the same as before.

Next, and more important, Kennedy had to get the Secret Service out of the business of reviewing the background investigations. The Secret Service insisted it must review background investigations, so that if anything went wrong it would have an idea of possible suspects.

If a staff member had shown behavior in the past that indicated that he or she did not conform to normal rules, regulations, and laws, then that nonconformity, which most security officers would consider a character issue, would be known to the Secret Service.

If that nonconformity was severe enough, the Secret Service could raise it with the Counsel's Office, expressing its concern. If a staff member displayed behavior that was illegal or aggressive or bizarre, then the Secret Service could make a case for denying that individual access, at least access to the West Wing where the president could usually be found.

In the past, the Secret Service had a right to determine the potential "dangerousness" of an individual and advise the Counsel's Office accordingly. In the past, there had been no question that the experts—the Secret Service, not the associate counsel—was the agency responsible for security, and its recommendations carried great weight and were rarely, if ever, overruled. To shut the Secret Service out from receiving the SPIN results would change the Secret Service into a reactive body. Without access to the background investigations, the Secret Service could not *prevent* security problems; it could only react once they had occurred. In other words, denying the Secret Service access to background investigations would mortally wound its capacity to protect the president and everyone else who worked in the White House.

Kennedy's problem was that he needed to hire the Clintons' appointees, regardless of character issues that were considered irrelevant by the group as a whole. The yardstick by which persons were selected to work in the Clinton administration was different from any yardstick used by the FBI or the Secret Service. The Clintonites adjusted the White House security system accordingly.

During the early months of the Clinton administration, the Counsel's Office and the Chief of Staff's Office behaved as if they had no idea how to run the security program. They wanted everyone to believe that they were just a bunch of dumb clucks from Greasepot, Arkansas. Dumb like a fox.

Foster actually told his wife that the Bush administration had "walked off the job" and had taken all the memos that could have been used by the new administration to help them run the White House. This was pure claptrap.

When Dennis and I met with Nussbaum, Foster, and Kennedy, they behaved as if they had never heard of the concepts of "security" and "suitability." They failed to acknowledge at least three meetings that took place before and after the inauguration, when they were personally provided with more information than they would ever need to staff the White House properly. The fact that the Clintons did everything sloppily and at the last minute was not the fault of the Bush administration or the Executive Branch permanent employees.

During the transition, Bush Administration Associate Counsel Greg Walden and Assistant Counsel Robert Swanson met with Clinton lawyers Steve Neuwirth and Cheryl Mills and provided them with a general explanation of how security, ethics, and the hiring process worked. Walden had long been ready for the meeting and wondered what had taken the Clinton people so long to meet with him.

Walden and Swanson spent more than two hours with the Clinton lawyers and provided them with packages of documents that covered the laws and procedures for selecting White House appointees, their terms of employment, and much about the ethical considerations that any new administration faces. These same documents could also be used to "vet" an appointee so that the president could be protected from persons who might either embarrass the administration or even possibly endanger national security.

Walden recalls that before the day ended, Bernie Nussbaum and Vince Foster appeared in his doorway and introduced themselves. They explained that they had just finished a meeting in the West Wing with Deputy Counsel John Schmitz and Counsel to the President Boyden Gray. Nussbaum and Foster said that Counsel Gray had suggested that Walden was the person they should talk to in order to find out more about the mechanics of the ethics reviews which relied upon FBI background investigations and other components.

Walden explained to Nussbaum and Foster that, though he'd be happy to meet with them, he had just finished a lengthy meeting with Steve Neuwirth and Cheryl Mills on the same subjects and had given them the extensive documentation, so they might want to touch base with their own lawyers first. Nussbaum and Foster thanked Walden and said that they would get together with Neuwirth and Mills.

On February 16, Walden honored a request to lunch with Bill Kennedy and Beth Nolan, and he went over some of the same material again. Walden told me that although he was no longer a White House employee on the day he met with the Clinton White House representatives, he was enthusiastic to help the "keep the White House out of trouble." Walden, just like the rest of the departing administration, had been ordered by President Bush to "make this the best transition in the history of the White House." Not everyone was happy to help the Clintons, but nobody wanted to disappoint President Bush.

Walden told me he stressed to Kennedy and Nolan that the security system at the White House worked "fine" and as far as he could tell, "the people in the White House security office were competent, professional, efficient, and trustworthy." Walden was surprised that so much time was spent on the security and clearance process, and "so little of our luncheon meeting concerned the ethics and issues such as financial disclosure, travel, gifts, and ethics briefings," the essence of Walden's expertise.

Staffing and presidential appointments weren't the only security risks at the Clinton White House. A related risk came from the new administration's total disregard for the security of classified information. Just as they ignored the need for FBI SPIN investigations, so too did they deride the idea of needing security clearances to handle or read classified documents.

Emma Horton, an employee in the Office of Presidential Personnel headed by Bruce Lindsey, a close, personal friend of the Clintons, was talking to me one day about classified material. She was a new Clinton staffer, not yet cleared by the FBI. I was curious. I asked her if classified material came across her desk. She would not answer directly. Instead, she asked, "What if I open it inadvertently?"

Horton worked directly for Jan Piercy, an old associate and former classmate of Hillary Clinton's at Wellesley, and one of the hardest persons to interview that I ever encountered in the Clinton administration. Piercy simply would not return my calls. I finally complained to Lindsey about her, but nothing improved. Piercy's job at the White House was pre-vetting White House and Executive Branch candidates.

Lindsey's and Piercy's office often received secret and top secret material from the FBI and other agencies about some of the candidates under consideration. Presidential Personnel needed to process the paperwork, but could not "see" the paperwork—except, of course, *inadvertently.*

It took the Bush administration *hundreds* of employees with security clearances to handle the same volume of paperwork. But according to a GAO report made public in October 1995, from 20 January 1993 to March 1994 there were only twenty-four employees in the entire Clinton administration who had been cleared to handle the thousands and thousands of classified documents. There was no way they could have handled the workload. I believe that classified material passed through the hands of Clinton employees without security clearances. After all, little or no regard was given to any other security-related policy or procedure. Why would they treat classified documents any differently?

Handling classified material without a clearance—or *allowing* classified material to pass through uncleared personnel—is a violation of federal law. But think of what it means for national security when just about anyone can handle classified material. It wouldn't take a KGB genius to infiltrate the Clinton administration. Apparently, most White House documents are freely available to whomever might look at them, however "inadvertently."

Early in 1993, while we struggled to understand the Clintons' hostility to normal security procedures, an incident occurred that shook up the Democratic National Committee (DNC) headquarters. An individual who was not a DNC employee, and who was suspected of being with the media, was caught inside the building, wandering around without an escort.

Worse yet, this individual was observed trying to read a memo on someone's desk. David Wilhelm was reported to be very upset with this "serious security breach." He immediately instructed all personnel of the DNC *to apply for and get a pass, and wear it at all times!* DNC employees were reminded of the seriousness of the security breach and the potential "damage" that could occur if such a person had been able to read an important memo, one that might reveal some DNC political strategy, for example.

So, down at the DNC they understood the concept of security perfectly well. There was no confusion, no ambivalence, no hesitation to clamp down on security scofflaws.

This incident drove the point home that the Clintons, their staff, and associates like David Wilhelm knew perfectly well what security was and why an organization should have it.

The White House's security program was not a complex and mysterious operation beyond the grasp of the newly arrived administration, whose lawyers had been extensively briefed by Bush administration counsels.

The Clinton administration knew how the system worked. And as I would come to understand, they knew *exactly* what they were doing.

Chapter Five

THE UNRAVELING OF VINCE FOSTER

Rules for Radicals: "A sense of humor enables him to maintain his perspective and see himself for what he really is: a bit of dust that burns for a fleeting second. A sense of humor is incompatible with the complete acceptance of any dogma, any religious, political, or economic prescription for salvation."

George Washington's Rules of Civility and Decent Behaviour: "Do not express joy before one sick or in pain, for that contrary passion will aggravate his misery."

I was looking forward to another meeting with Vince Foster. I had seen Foster from time to time after our meeting in February, but because the security program had been delegated down to Bill Kennedy and Craig Livingstone, I didn't see Foster as much as I would have liked.

There were indeed *plenty* of security issues on which I needed the Counsel Office's assistance, but I had no intention of speaking to Kennedy about them. I had concluded that Kennedy was dishonest. In fact, after Travelgate—in which he'd gone around Dennis and me and abused the FBI, using us as political cover for the Clintons' pointless hounding of the Travel Office—I had no use for Kennedy at all.

When I passed Foster in the hallways or saw him under informal circumstances, he was invariably pleasant and friendly. We would stop and chat about generalities, but I did not make any effort to speak to him in such informal settings about my security concerns. I never noticed any evidence of depression, and if Foster was suffering, he hid it well. I believe I would have seen it, if it was there.

It was July 1993, and all the Clinton staffers were still walking around the White House with temporary passes, including Foster. In the Bush administration, a temporary pass was very easy to see, because of the very large "T" on it in big bold black print. Clinton's Counsel's Office and the Office of Administration changed that in a hurry. Instead of a big "T" that could easily be seen by the Secret Service, they modified the pass's design to a tiny "t". This was how Nussbaum, Foster, Kennedy, and Watkins were able to get around the pass "standoff" with the Secret Service, who insisted it would not issue permanent passes to Clinton staffers until it was able to review the FBI background investigations in order to know which staffers might be a danger.

But with the tiny "t" pass, staffers wandered the White House unrestricted, unless sharp-eyed Secret Service agents caught them where they weren't supposed to be. And given that so many Clinton staffers chose to wear no badges at all, Secret Service agents had their work cut out for them.

I knew all this going into my meeting with Foster, and it weighed heavily on my mind. I had reached the conclusion that working at the Clinton White House could be *dangerous.*

What could Foster do at this late date? I intended to address the issue of White House security with him, but at the same time I wondered if it might be only a "fool's errand" that would come to nothing and cause me a lot of trouble. How much power did Foster really have?

Even though he exhibited an interest and some understanding of the need for security screening, I had to assume that Foster was bogged down with his work as Hillary's attorney, managing her blind trust and other legal affairs. I also suspected by this time that Bernie Nussbaum or someone above him had, for some reason, thrown sand into the works.

What I could not understand was the enormous risks the Counsel's Office was willing to take by keeping the FBI reports out of the hands of the Secret Service. To be into the middle of summer of the administration's first year and have hundreds of staff members without permanent passes, and many without FBI background investigations, was, in my opinion, foolhardy.

How could I know that Foster did not want the Secret Service to have access to *his* own FBI background check?

Foster was one of the few who kept his appointments with the FBI. As I entered Foster's office, he rose to greet me, extending his hand with his usual warm, friendly smile. Again, I saw no sign of depression. He seemed upbeat, positive, happy. We quickly took care of the formal interview I had to conduct. Unlike most in the administration, Foster was known for his candor and openness. It made the process simple and painless.

Then Foster turned to the question of security, as I had anticipated and hoped that he would. "How is security around here?"

"Not good at all, Mr. Foster."

"What's the problem?"

"If the FBI knew I were offering you my own opinions on the faults of White House security, it could cost me my assignment or even my job."

"It's all right, Gary, this is just between you and me. You've got my word on that. Now tell me what the problems are."

I told him the security process was still stalled and that I was seriously worried about how the Secret Service had been blocked from seeing our reports.

"Blocked? Who blocked them?"

"Well, Mr. Foster, it was the Counsel's Office."

He seemed surprised to hear this.

He asked about the magnitude of the character issues we discovered during our investigations. I told him they were numerous and serious. I also told him that I was not comfortable giving him information about any specific staff member; after all, many of these persons were his friends and there were questions of protocol and discretion. Any negative comments from me about any specific individual could be misinterpreted or even misused. Foster should simply order copies of the FBI summaries, read the results, and judge for himself.

There was a long-standing FBI policy that held that agents made no recommendations, offered no opinions. We were investigators, seekers of facts. We asked questions and made our reports—that's it. This was a new administration, and while I liked Foster, I did not trust him completely. Besides, it would have been improper of me to offer an opinion about any particular staffer, although several immediately came to mind.

There was also an element of self-preservation in my reticence. If I had identified any one individual as being a security risk, as I understood the concept, and if that person turned out to be a good friend of the president, I would be a goner. At that time I did not fully appreciate how many "Friends of Hillary" staff members there were. Vince Foster was one of them.

"At what level of staff are you finding character problems?"

"At the highest levels."

He thought for a moment, appearing very troubled. "Are they using George?" he asked, referring to George Saunders.

I suggested that he should speak directly to Saunders about that, not wanting to speak for George, but I indicated that he would get a negative response from him.

"How about Kennedy? How's he doing with the program?"

"Not so good," I replied.

Foster now began to take notes. "What are the problems, the issues here, in your opinion? What do you think I should do?"

"Well, Mr. Foster, I suppose that some of the senior staff are afraid that they will not be able to remain in the White House or get the necessary security clearances, if the investigative results become known to the Secret Service. But this is a very dangerous and shortsighted approach."

I became impassioned. I spoke of former presidents and how they had suffered from scandal and how such scandals could have been easily avoided by a simple background check. I told him of many instances where the background checks were ignored, with disastrous consequences.

I reminded Foster that it was one thing for an individual to lie to FBI agents. It was quite another situation for staff members to confess serious character problems and have the administration cover them up. I told him I thought that this was dangerous and stupid, because ultimately it was the president who would be held responsible for the failings of his staff, no matter how little he himself knew about them.

I reminded Foster that presidents since Eisenhower had issued executive orders requiring background investigations and they had also set forth minimum standards for employee suitability. It was simply unthinkable—incomprehensible!—to abandon the security umbrella around the president, and yet the unthinkable had become reality.

I told Foster that I could not stand by in silence and watch as the president or national security was placed in danger. It was my job, my mission, to see to it that the president was kept safe. I ended my "speech" by reiterating that Foster should call for the FBI investigations and review them himself. He indicated that he would. I thought that when he did, *if* he did, he would probably be in for quite a shock, thinking back to one case that I had called my "litmus test." Months had gone by, time enough for someone to read the FBI summary, but that senior staffer was still working in the West Wing.

But, ever the optimist, I still felt that the security program had been broken by ignorance, not willfully destroyed by someone with a sinister purpose. I thought they still had time to get things back on track. How wrong and naive I was.

Foster continued his inquiry. "Are all of the staff members in the West Wing required to have FBI security background investigations?"

What? Hadn't he been paying any attention to what I was telling him? With that question, Foster told me more than he could ever know. When he asked me if his own staff needed to be cleared with an FBI investigation, I realized just how deep the problem was. Foster did not have a clue, and no matter how much I lectured him, he still wouldn't have a clue.

I answered that, yes, everyone needed to be investigated; they all needed clearances. I told him that during the previous administration nobody was allowed to work in the West Wing until the FBI investigations were completed *and* reviewed *and* were found to be free of character problems.

But this was crazy! Here was the deputy counsel to the president of the United States, and he didn't have the remotest idea of security procedures of the White House. If the Counsel's Office didn't know the whys and wherefores of security, who in this administration would?

Foster changed the subject. He asked me about the status of the FBI, inquiring about morale and attitude. He wanted to know if I thought Bill Sessions, our FBI director, was being treated unfairly, having been left hanging for so long.

Sessions was being investigated for allegedly misusing FBI assets and personnel, including using an FBI jet to carry firewood to Washington. A "review" of the allegations by Attorney General Reno was still under way, but months and months had gone by. The report wasn't that long and the issues not that difficult to assess.

Having a director in limbo was not good for the FBI. I told Foster that and said if the director had misused FBI resources, I could not understand how he could stay in that position and remain an effective leader. On the other hand, I had no way of knowing whether the allegations were true. That was Attorney General Reno's job—and it was long past time for her to make a decision.

I would be happy to know, Foster said, that the "Sessions problem" would soon be "taken care of." I was amazed. Was Foster telling me that a decision to keep or fire the director of the FBI, my director, was imminent? Foster asked, "What do you think about appointing a younger man as director? How do you think the agents will react to that?"

With that question, I was certain he was telling me that Sessions was a goner. I couldn't believe Foster would cross that line. Any doubts about what I thought he was trying to tell me were erased when he asked me about the most recent name floated by the administration to take Sessions's place, Judge Louis Freeh.

I told Foster that my wife was a former FBI agent and had worked with Freeh and had a high opinion of him. He seemed pleased. Foster asked, "Do you think Freeh's youth will be acceptable to the older agents?"

I told him the fact that Freeh was a graduate of the FBI Academy and had experience as an FBI agent would outweigh any age factor. In fact, a younger director might be just what the FBI needed. Foster thanked me for my time. He told me he was going to look into the security problems immediately and told me to call him if my concerns continued.

As I left the Counsel's Office, I felt pretty good about our meeting, which had taken about an hour. But on another level, I was really concerned that Foster didn't seem to know anything about the concept of security.

Also, the fact that Foster would brief me on what the White House intended to do about Sessions, and basically tell me that Judge Louis Freeh was probably going to be the new director, proved he obviously did not understand Washington at all.

After all, Sessions and the FBI higher-ups would very much have liked to have the information I had just been given. With one phone call, which I did not make, the entire bureau would know Sessions's fate before he did. They would also know who the new director would probably be.

Why couldn't these Clinton people learn the elementary principle of discretion? If I made that one call, it wouldn't be too long before such sensational news would be leaked to the media, and the White House would have yet another mess on its hands, as if there weren't enough messes. Was it possible that Foster wanted me to call FBI headquarters?

I continued to wonder why Foster told me about Sessions. Did he really want my opinion, or was he just trying to keep me on the reservation by throwing me a prime tidbit? I drove home and had a quiet dinner with my wife and told her about Foster and his comments about Louis Freeh. I put the fear of retribution out of my mind, believing that I had dumped the problem on Foster, right where it belonged.

I arrived home by about 6:30 P.M. At about that same time, Vince Foster was joining his wife Lisa and other family members for dinner at a local restaurant. It was supposed to be a celebration. But Foster announced his intention to resign his position as deputy counsel to the president. His family members, however, talked him out of doing it, suggesting that things would get better. His wife, in fact, encouraged him to write down what was troubling him about his job—a list of grievances that was later found in Foster's briefcase, torn into twenty-seven pieces.

July 19, 1993, was a sad day for the FBI. Judge William Sessions became the first FBI director to be fired. It took two calls from President Clinton to convince Sessions that he should turn in his FBI property and leave the FBI headquarters building.

Sessions left the FBI a disgraced and broken man, having failed to understand the group he was trying to direct and having failed to size up the nature of the persons who now ran the Executive Branch. All of his posturing to ingratiate himself with Janet Reno had done nothing to save him.

On 20 July Louis Freeh was announced as President Clinton's choice for FBI director. That night, however, another of the Clintons' most important appointments met a different fate.

I was watching President Clinton on the Larry King show. Clinton had been on for an hour, and King asked him to continue for another half hour. He agreed, and they broke for commercial. During the break, somebody told Clinton that Vince Foster was dead. Clinton did not come back for the last half hour.

Vince Foster's body was found in Fort Marcy Park, dead from a gunshot wound to the head, the victim of an apparent suicide.

At 10:00 A.M. the next morning I met a Secret Service buddy in the hallway of the OEOB. We were both in deep shock, not only because we knew Vince Foster, but because we understood the possible ramifications of his death. What if Foster had shot himself in his office? What if he'd first turned the gun on others? The fact was the Secret Service had never examined Foster's FBI summary and had no idea what risks he might pose to himself or other staffers.

I thought the security mess would hit the fan now, and we might be called in front of a congressional committee in a major battle between Congress, which had oversight responsibility, and the White House over the unconscionable and inexcusable risks that were being taken with the president's security. And I knew who would get the blame—the FBI and the Secret Service, not higher ups and not the Bernard Nussbaums, who knew how to cover their tails.

I also felt pangs of guilt. If Foster had indeed committed suicide, might I have unwittingly added to his woes with complaints about security, unsuitable staff members, and the potential for future embarrassments?

At the time, I didn't fully appreciate that Foster was perhaps one of the biggest security problems that the White House had, being a depressive with a gun, worried about his own ability to obtain and keep a security clearance and a permanent White House pass, and knowing that his deep involvement with the Clintons was about to be probed in painful detail by aggressive investigative reporters.

Did he carry his gun into the complex or into the West Wing that morning? He could have. Was it in his briefcase? Had a suicidal man brought a gun into the White House, *with the intent to use it?*

It is precisely to prevent dangers like this that we have the FBI to conduct background investigations, a Secret Service, security fences, alarms, magnetometers, and *access passes*. All of these things are supposed to prevent the very kind of thing that Foster did. Who would have thought it possible for a high-level staff member and a close friend of the president and first lady to commit such an act? Who needed to be in a position to predict and prevent it? The FBI and Secret Service, that's who.

We will never really know why Foster did what he did or where he did it. If we are to believe that he was deeply disturbed, deeply depressed, could he also have been angry at someone in the White House? Could Foster have been a danger to the president or the first lady?

The Secret Service agent asked me if I was aware that Foster's office had not yet been sealed. It was 10 A.M. the morning after the suicide. My astonished reply was, "What? You've got to be kidding me!" The office should have been sealed immediately after the White House learned of Foster's death, to prevent any accidental or intentional tampering of evidence.

It was a day of surprises. Later, I learned from media reports that the Park Service was going to be conducting the investigation of Foster's "suicide." I was astounded.

The FBI had never before taken a pass on such an investigation. Had the acting director, Floyd Clark, refused the case? And if so, why? The FBI had always been the agency of choice in previous administrations when there was a need for investigations of this kind.

We were good enough to investigate the Travel Office staff on trumped-up charges of an allegedly missing $50,000, so why wasn't the FBI asked to investigate the death of the president's third highest White House staff member? The Park Service is a fine organization, but it works under the supervision of the secretary of the interior, not the Justice Department. The Park Service has neither the depth nor the experience to investigate a case of this magnitude, unless, of course, the White House meant to limit the scope of the investigation. And I believe they did.

The White House was like a morgue for about a week. Getting interviews with the Clinton staff had always been hard. Now it was impossible. We didn't even have Vince Foster to help us any more. I got busy with administrative work and took care of my other FBI duties that were not related to the White House.

A few days after Foster's suicide, my partner Dennis was crossing West Executive Drive on his way to the West Wing to conduct some interviews, when he ran into Bill Kennedy. They stopped to talk, it being the first time they'd seen each other since Foster's death. Dennis described Kennedy as solemn, but then Kennedy always appeared to be in pain of some kind.

Dennis offered his condolences, and they discussed the circumstances of Foster's death. Kennedy denied that Foster's White House tour or his new life in Washington had anything to do with his alleged suicide.

Kennedy would know better than most about that. The Travel Office fiasco—where innocent permanent employees were persecuted because Hillary wanted an excuse to fire them and replace them with her friends—had been engineered by Kennedy and Watkins, with Foster's acquiescence.

As Rose Law Firm partners, Kennedy and Foster were also both deeply involved in the Whitewater mess, where it looked ever more likely the Clintons might be pinned as accomplices to what was essentially a bank robbery with a pen rather than a gun. If these matters had anything to do with Foster's death, Kennedy would know. He told Dennis they didn't: "Vince brought his problems from Arkansas to the White House. It wasn't anything that happened here," Kennedy said.

Then, on 11 August, Director of Security Craig Livingstone called me and asked me to meet him in the White House Counsel's Security Office. He sounded very mysterious, and he wouldn't tell me why he wanted to see me.

As I walked down to the first floor of the OEOB, I wondered if I was going to be told anything about Foster and the suicide. Livingstone didn't indicate that I should bring notes of any particular case with me, so I knew our meeting was probably not about a routine background investigation matter.

I thought I might be in for some interesting information, since Livingstone was extremely close to the Clintons. He would have known Foster and his family well. I hadn't talked to him since the funeral, but I knew he was deeply involved with monitoring the Foster investigation.

Livingstone was my usual point of contact in the Counsel's Office, and we had become friends to the extent that it was possible under the circumstances. I thought then, and I think now, that Livingstone was really trying to do his best to protect the president. But he was an amateur, and he was getting no support from Kennedy. I also knew that Livingstone trusted me and took me for a serious, professional security man just trying to do his job.

Livingstone motioned for me to follow him into the walk-in safe that was located within the security office. He told the staff to leave. Then he closed the thick steel door behind us so that we couldn't be heard. The walls and the door of this safe, which was also where the FBI reports are kept, are made out of solid metal and are about a foot thick. What he told me about Foster in that hour that we met inside that closed vault made the hair stand up on the back of my neck. I kept thinking all the time he was talking, "Why me, Lord?"

Livingstone was clearly shaken by Foster's suicide and admitted it. He said, "Gary, I had to go to identify Foster's body with Bill Kennedy. It was terrible. Then we drove to Foster's town house in Georgetown to be with Mrs. Foster."

"Craig, I feel terrible about this. I know how close you were to Vince. The entire White House seems to be in shock; the whole place seems to have shut down. But look, I have a confession of my own. I think I added to Foster's depression by telling him too much about my troubles on the job, and I feel awful about it."

Craig seemed keenly interested in what I had just said. "What do you mean? How could you make Foster more depressed?"

"No offense, Craig, but you know how I've been complaining about security. Well, I had a chance to talk to Vince on the twelfth of February, and I took the opportunity to let him know how dangerous things are around here. He didn't have a clue. He was clearly shocked.

"I saw him again on July ninth, just eleven days before he killed himself, and I *really* let him have it. I told him the security here was a real mess, a significant problem. I figured you'd hear about that."

"What did you tell him?" Livingstone asked.

"Well, all the same things that you and I have discussed. He didn't know, for example, that there were hundreds of people walking around the White House, many through the West Wing, who had not had their security clearances completed. Foster didn't even know whether or not his own staff, right outside his office, should have a background investigation!

"He didn't know much of anything about the process. In fact, he knew so little I didn't see how he could do his job. And then he asked me if there were any staff on board who shouldn't be allowed in the White House. I told him, yes, there were many—too many. He asked me at what level, and I told him at the highest levels. I'm afraid I added to his woes by dumping all this on his lap."

"Gary, I assure you, none of that stuff had anything to do with his death. He had bigger problems on his mind. He was worried that rumors about his affair with Hillary were resurfacing. We had that problem during the campaign, you know, after the business with Gennifer came up. You remember, when Bill and Gennifer were doing their thing? Vince and Hillary were doing *their* thing. Vince thought if it surfaced it would ruin his life, his reputation, and his marriage, and he thought it would impact *big time* on Hillary and the presidency. He was worried sick about it."

"What? An affair with Hillary?"

Livingstone looked genuinely surprised. "You don't know? You're kidding me, right?"

I couldn't believe what he was saying. I remember that my hands were sweating. Why the hell was he telling me this? I had no business being in on this revelation.

Craig went on, "There are some people down in Little Rock who are talking. About this and other stuff. We thought it was all put to bed, but it's resurfacing."

"So what? If it's not true, big deal. Those kinds of co-worker rumors happen all the time. Why would Foster kill himself over some rumor?"

Craig didn't answer. He just stared straight ahead, and in his non-answer, I believe he was telling me that he knew that the "rumors" were true. We sat there in silence while I thought of what to say next. I was very uncomfortable, and I tried to change the subject.

"All right, Craig, I don't know about all that, but the fact remains that the security system is broken, and now the only guy who seemed to give a damn about it—the only guy who could do anything about it—is dead. What do we do now?"

"You think you're telling me something I don't know? I know it's a mess. It's all screwed up. The whole system's falling apart." He pointed to a stack of files immediately to his right. It was a high stack.

He said, "See that stack of files over there? Each one is about a staffer who needs to be fired, right now! And I can't get Kennedy to do anything with it."

I knew that nobody was being fired or otherwise affected by the FBI SPINs. Now Livingstone was admitting it.

"You mean to tell me you've discussed these staffers with Kennedy? Does he know what the problems are? Does he understand?"

"Oh, yeah. He knows. Not only that, he won't give me the budget or the manpower even to run this office."

I knew that already. Craig had many more responsibilities than his predecessor, Jane Dannenhauer, and yet he was being paid about one half of what her salary had been. Jane ran a good shop, but she limited herself to flagging issues and sending the SPINs on to Deputy Counsel John Schmitz.

"Kennedy! Kennedy's not the right man for the job, Craig. For one thing, he takes nothing seriously. And for another, he's a snake."

"What do you mean, a snake?"

"He's tried to set Dennis and me up, get us into trouble with our supervisor and the SPIN Unit so we'd be neutralized or transferred out. He's always trying to compromise us. Going to him with our problems is like the CIA going to the KGB. And then this Travel Office mess. That was abuse, Craig. He should never have forced the FBI to be involved in that sordid political game."

At the mention of the Travel Office, Livingstone really got going. "That f---ing Watkins. I told them that Watkins was going to screw everything up. Gary, I sat in a meeting when it was decided that the Travel Office guys were going to get fired and that they would be reported to the FBI. I told them they were nuts. Look, we'd heard rumors that the press was taken care of by the Travel Office guys, bottles of wine in their rooms, easy customs exams, and stuff like that, but it was stupid of Watkins to suggest that the FBI be brought into it.

"There was no wrongdoing, no illegal acts that we could prove. The only good rumor we had was some reporter bringing in a carpet illegally through customs. That was it. I argued very strongly against bringing in the FBI. It was wrong. We unnecessarily ruined their reputations. It was Watkins and Kennedy, Gary. This was their big idea of how to get rid of them. I told them it was a stupid idea that would never work."

"What do you mean, 'you told them,' Craig? This wasn't your department, was it?"

"Look, Gary, I'm the security guy around here. Whatever happens regarding security, I'm *in* it, even if I don't decide, and even if I'm just told what to do. I'm still in the meetings. They know that I deal with the FBI all the time, so they would naturally want me to know what's going on. I've been in most of the meetings about security and the FBI. Your director calls me all the time. He knows me by my first name."

I was dumbstruck. "Craig, just what *do* you *do,* related to security?"

"Well, for one thing, I do a lot of the security advance for the president. Recently, I went with him to the Law Enforcement Memorial. Your director was there. I started to walk up to Louis Freeh, and your agents got all huffy about it." Craig was clearly annoyed that the FBI agents didn't know who he was. "I said, 'Hey, I'm Craig, and I'm a friend of your director. Back off.' " According to Craig, Freeh came over, said, "Hi, Craig, howya doing?" and signaled for the agents to back off.

Craig went on, "I don't think I'll have this job very long anyway, but Bill [Kennedy] is f---ing up my chances to get anything good around here. He won't give me staff, he won't give me resources, he won't back me up on who we should fire. He's no help at all."

I said, "Well, I'm not happy about what's going on here myself. I came here in 1990, found a good security program that works, and now I watch while the Clinton administration basically trashes it, disregards it. Why, Craig? Why don't you all just use the same system that's worked for thirty years?"

"Gary, look, you just don't understand how things are here. It's me against Kennedy, and who are they going to believe?"

"Maybe they won't believe you, but what if I backed you up? What if it was you and a senior, experienced FBI agent saying it, too? Don't you think 'they' would listen?"

"Yes, maybe so. Would you be willing to do that?"

I admit I was caught up in the moment, sitting there in the vault with Livingstone, him confiding in me and giving me hope that I might have a serious ally to improve the security situation. I figured, "What the hell? What have I got to lose? What are they going to do to a guy who is just saying, 'Let's do a better job of protecting the president of the United States'?"

"Okay, sure, Craig. I'll do it. When do we talk to Nussbaum?" I didn't like the little guy, but maybe the two of us could get his attention.

Craig looked at me like I didn't have a brain. "Nussbaum? It's not Nussbaum we gotta talk to. We'll be talking to Hillary."

"What? You're kidding? No? Look, Craig, I said I'd help you, but an FBI agent meeting with the first lady. . . . Uh, that's beyond me. Are you sure? I mean, this is my career. I have a family to take care of, a wife, three kids. What if she thinks I'm out of line? I mean, one word from her and I could be in serious trouble!"

"Hillary is the one to talk to, trust me. And I'll be talking to her tonight. I've got to join them on a trip on Air Force One. She'll understand the risk you're taking. You don't have to worry about her hurting your career. I know her well enough. She'll be interested to hear what you have to say. And she's the *only* one who can change things."

I reluctantly agreed, thinking all the time that the great personal risk I was taking might be worth it.

In hindsight, I was an idiot. It was naive of me to believe that Hillary Clinton gave a damn about me, or about calling me in to give my report, or about White House security at all. Of course, where does that leave Livingstone? To this day, I think he still *believes* she *does* give a damn.

As I drove home that night, leaving a very emotional Livingstone and the White House in my rearview mirror, I felt like I was living a real-life spy novel, and I didn't care for it one bit. I was worried that Livingstone might have second thoughts about confiding in me. I was involved in a dangerous situation.

If Livingstone ever confessed his extremely disloyal act of confiding in me to the Clintons, he would be fired. But *my* name would be mud, my FBI career would probably be over, and I might even be in danger, if the stories coming from Little Rock were true—about how so many enemies of the Clintons ended up having fatal "accidents."

On Monday morning, and for several mornings after that, I waited for a call from Livingstone, ready to face my fate. The call never came, and Livingstone never mentioned the possible meeting to me again. I was just as glad he didn't.

And there was something else to consider. I assumed this whole extraordinary interview took place because Livingstone needed to let off some steam, some pent-up emotions, from the whole Vince Foster tragedy. But there was another possibility. The administration had Foster's notes, and it could have known of my conversation with him. Perhaps the interview was a way of finding out how much I knew. I doubted that possibility, but the fact that I even thought about it showed how worried I was.

In February 1995 I was talking to a computer expert from the White House Information Resources Management Division about how I could clear deleted documents off my hard drive so that some computer thief wouldn't get access to classified material.

"Well, Gary, there are several ways a hard drive can be made unreadable. First, we can take the hard drive out and take it apart, actually break it into pieces. That's one very obvious way. Or, I could take out the hard drive and just give it to you. You could then take it back to the FBI or do whatever with it, but you'd have to give me a new one to replace it, and a new one costs about $500."

"The FBI isn't about to give me $500 to solve this problem. I'm not sure that they'd know what to do with my old hard drive, except throw it away."

"Well, Gary, there is also a government-approved 'scrub' program we can use to erase the hard drive completely. When you're ready, call me, and I'll send a technician over. He'll put in the program, and in about four hours the disk will be clean."

We digressed a bit, talking about the Clintons, their staff, and what we had both witnessed over the past two years. Then he said, "Speaking of computers, have you heard about the Foster computer?"

"What about it?"

"You aren't going to believe what happened to it. Months after the suicide, someone finally got around to thinking about Foster's computer and ordered us to track it down. I can't believe that Fiske and your FBI boys didn't seize it right away, but they didn't. We tracked the computer by its serial number. We then ran a review of all repair and installation documents related to it, and guess what we found out? Foster's computer had been taken out of his office after his death because it wasn't being used, and someone else needed it.

"But when it was turned on, when someone tried to use it, it wouldn't 'boot up'—the hard drive wouldn't function. A call was placed to the shop that repairs computers, and the guys came over to take a look at it. Sure enough, the hard drive wasn't operating. They took the machine apart, and found the hard drive was so badly damaged it couldn't be repaired.

"The computer repairman didn't know the history of the computer, that it had been Foster's computer, so he simply took the old broken hard drive out and installed a brand new one. He programmed the new drive and took the old hard drive back to the shop and tossed it into the scrap barrel. A couple of months later someone came along and emptied the scrap barrel."

"This is unbelievable. How could this happen? You *do* know that the FBI is investigating obstruction of justice charges in this case? Does anyone else know about this?"

"Yeah, one of the guys testified about it to Kenneth Starr's group or was interviewed about it; I don't know which. Staff knows about it, but I don't think anyone knows who 'did' the hard drive."

" 'Did' the hard drive? Wait a minute. Are you saying that the hard drive was destroyed by someone? How do you destroy a hard drive?"

"Gary, there's only one way I know of to destroy a hard drive. You turn on the computer and order it to perform a function of some kind, and while the hard drive is working to finish the function, you pick up the case and you drop it sharply on the floor, or on some other hard surface. The disk will usually self-destruct on impact, and then it can't be used and can't be read easily, if at all. Of course, even if we could read it, it's long gone now because all those investigators didn't think to ask about it."

"This is crazy. Why didn't they seize the computer as evidence? They should have done that first thing."

"Gary, I've known you for years, and you know I like the FBI, and I think you're an excellent FBI agent, so please don't be offended by what I'm about to say about your FBI. Everyone around here is asking the same thing. How could the FBI agents assigned to this case be so *stupid* as to miss something this basic?"

"Don't blame the FBI. We get blamed for everything, but when we work for a special prosecutor, there isn't much we're able to do on our own. There isn't any real independence. Look, when there's a case like this, the prosecutors go into micromanagement overdrive. They're absolutely terrified that the FBI agents working for them will make a mistake if they're not micromanaged, or that the FBI will think of something that they haven't thought of first—something that'll take away from their moment in the spotlight. It's not like you think at all. We don't run these investigations, we take orders. FBI agents working for an independent counsel have virtually no say in what is done or not done. It hurts our ego to admit it, but it's true. The good old days of the independent FBI are over. The FBI gets the blame, and the prosecutors get the credit. That's how it works these days."

"Well, then the prosecutors really blew it. If *we* all know they should have seized the computer, why *didn't* they?"

Chapter Six

"GOOD MORNING, MRS. PRESIDENT!"

Rules for Radicals: "The eleventh rule of the ethics of means and ends is that goals must be phrased in general terms like, 'Liberty, Equality, Fraternity,' 'Of the Common Welfare,' 'Pursuit of Happiness,' or 'Bread and Peace.' "

George Washington's Rules of Civility and Decent Behaviour: "In your apparel be modest and endeavor to accommodate nature; rather than to procure admiration, keep to the fashion of your equals, such as are civil and orderly with respect to times and places."

On 2 February 1996 the president of the United States attended an annual rite—the National Prayer Breakfast at the Washington Hilton. The media reported attendance of about one thousand of the most powerful persons in government and business.

In what had to be one of the most unlikely stand-ins in modern times, U.S. Senator Carol Moseley-Braun, a person who has been accused of numerous financial wrongdoings, including stealing from her own mother, spoke in place of the Reverend Billy Graham, who was too ill to attend.

Senator Braun began her remarks by acknowledging the presence of the president and "Mrs. President"! If ever there was a slip that could be called Freudian, that was it. Maybe God spoke through Braun that morning to make sure the rest of the country knew what was going on in Washington, that we had traded in our Constitution for a new, bizarre experiment in the Executive Branch, a co-presidency.

Early in the Clinton administration, the media was full of stories about FOBs—"Friends of Bill." But many of the appointees I investigated were really FOHs—Friends of Hillary. Nowhere were her thumbprints more pronounced than on the Health Care Task Force—the most important domestic project of President Clinton's first term.

The health care debate looked very different inside the White House than it did to the public. While the public was inundated by hard-luck stories of suffering poor people who had lost their insurance, the Clintons themselves were behaving like the most cutthroat corporate downsizers.

In an effort to make good on candidate Clinton's promise to cut the White House staff by 25 percent—a target the administration never reached—many longtime federal employees were fired. To staff the White House, the administration brought in a flood of interns and volunteers who worked not only without insurance, but also without pay (and frequently without professional standards of behavior).

Kept very quiet by the Clintons was the fact that many White House employees were hired as officially "part-time" staff to be paid at only thirty-nine hours a week or less, even though there was plenty of work for them to do and they wanted to work full time. But denying them that extra hour of work a week allowed the White House to deny them a variety of benefits, the chief of which was *health insurance!*

During "the health care crisis," a friend of mine named Karen, who had worked in Bush's Visitor's Office, called to see how I was doing in the new administration.

"Oh, pretty good, Karen. You know, the usual grief that comes with presidential transitions. But we'll work through it. How about you?"

Karen told me she had joined a U.S. Senate campaign and if her candidate won, she might take a job in his Washington office.

"Congratulations. Good luck. I hope he wins."

"Thanks, Gary. But I'm calling for another reason. I want to know what the heck is going on with Hillary Clinton."

I wasn't sure what she meant.

"I have a friend up here who just returned from a conference at the White House, and if what she tells me is true, Hillary must be really wacky!"

"Like what?"

"Well, three health insurance company executives hired my lobbyist friend to go with them to the White House to present their solution for the health care crisis. They wanted personally to present their case to the task force, hopefully directly to Hillary. They got their chance. They were able to get an appointment with the first lady. They went down there in a group, were brought into the West Wing, and were told to wait in the Roosevelt Room. They had sent advance copies of their plan, and they were looking forward to speaking to Hillary about it."

"How did your friend get caught up in this?"

"Well, she's the sister of a classmate of Hillary, and it was thought that if a call was made. . . . You know the rest, right?"

"Yeah. So tell me, what happened?"

"They were kept waiting an hour. Then Hillary walked in, slammed their proposal on the table, and said, 'Gentlemen, I have looked at your proposal, and it's pure bulls--t! Now, you've had your meeting! Get out!' So my friend, who was really humiliated and very angry, got up from her chair, looked Hillary square in the eye and said, 'Mrs. Clinton, my sister warned me about you when she set up this meeting for me. She told me that I would be sorry that I ever asked her to set this up, because she said you are a real bitch. She was wrong! You're a *f--king* bitch!' So, with that, they all got up and walked right out of the White House. Gary, could this really be true? Is Hillary that screwed up?"

Screwed up? That's a matter of opinion. Tightly wound? Ready to pounce on enemies, real and imagined? Abusive of White House staff? *That* I had on good authority.

One White House staffer, who must obviously remain anonymous, told me a story that was typical Hillary. At midnight, hours before a long-planned overseas trip, Hillary Clinton called the Usher's Office and "ordered" three tubes of Blistex.

The assistant usher tried, gently, to tell the first lady that the White House pantry and supply room did not maintain a drug store. He didn't get very far.

Suffice it to say, ears still ringing, the assistant usher drove around Washington in his own car looking for an all-night drug store, bought the Blistex with his own money, and was neither thanked nor reimbursed by the first lady.

"Mrs. President" doesn't seem to know how to moderate her behavior even when she's among friends. A senior permanent employee, who I knew to be a strong supporter of the Clintons, had looked forward to meeting her. He held a position that ensured that some day he would. One day he saw Hillary Clinton walking in his direction down a corridor in the OEOB. She looked in no particular hurry, so he thought it might be a good time to say hello. She approached with her Secret Service agents walking several paces behind her.

Working up his best smile, he said, "Good morning, Mrs. Clinton." She stared right through him. He told me it was as if she had "pierced his skull with laser beams."

My friend still works at the White House, and I cannot use his true name for very obvious reasons. He has a family to feed. But he told me he recovered and walked on down the hall, dumbstruck. He knew Barbara Bush; that day he learned that Hillary Clinton is no Barbara Bush.

Another staffer, also permanent, witnessed the event from her cracked office door and approached my friend.

"John, I guess you didn't get the word?"

"What word?"

"When 'Queen Hillary' walks down the hall, you're not supposed to look at her. You're actually supposed to go into an office if there is one nearby. She doesn't want staff 'seeing' her. And I know she sure as hell doesn't want to meet you or any other staffer!"

"You have to be kidding me!"

"No, we got the word in a staff meeting. It's true. Look around. Do you see anyone else in the hall?"

John looked around, and sure enough people were starting to emerge, like prairie dogs peeking out of their burrows after a hawk has flown past.

My partner Dennis had a similar experience. In February 1993 he was walking to the Residence to interview Head Usher Gary Walters about a new employee. He saw Hillary Clinton coming from the opposite direction. She was carrying a box that appeared to be heavy, and she was about to come to a double door that would have been hard to open, even if she had not been carrying a heavy box. He noticed the Secret Service agents making no effort to assist her. He stepped forward to help, but a Residence staffer close enough to Dennis to whisper without being heard by "Queen Hillary" said, "Don't!"

When Hillary was safely away, the staffer told Dennis that Hillary insisted that no man should assist her in any way.

Another close source, this one in the Secret Service, told me that Hillary had ordered her Secret Service protective detail to "stay the f--k away from me!" and to keep at least ten yards of distance between her and them at all times.

The Secret Service agent told me that it was much harder to protect her from a distance of ten yards, and she was told this, but she didn't seem to care what the Secret Service said. He also told me that it was obvious that she had a clear dislike for the agents, bordering on hatred, in his opinion.

Along those same lines, another source reports that two Secret Service agents heard Hillary's daughter Chelsea refer to them as "personal, trained pigs" to some of her friends. When the friends had gone, the senior agent on the detail tried to scold Chelsea for such disrespect. He told her that he was willing to put his life on the line to save hers, and he believed that her father, the president, would be shocked if he heard what she had just said to her friends. Chelsea's response?

"I don't think so. That's what my parents call you."

In a way, that Chelsea story didn't surprise me, because Hillary Clinton's roots were deep in the 1960s counterculture, where equating law enforcement officers with "pigs" was commonplace. I knew that as a college student, Hillary had made the cover of *Life* magazine as an example of student radicalism. She had also attended the Democratic National Convention in Chicago in 1968, where the radical Students for a Democratic Society (SDS) and others had orchestrated the "Days of Rage" riots, chanting "Death to the Pigs" while throwing bags of human excrement at the police.

After graduating from Yale, Hillary Rodham was invited to the House Judiciary Committee, where she worked with Bernard Nussbaum in the effort to impeach President Nixon. That effort was led by Congressman Thomas P. "Tip" O'Neill, who went on to become Speaker of the House.

To make his case for impeaching Nixon, O'Neill built a 718-page report, researched and written by the legal staff on the House Judiciary Committee. This document provided the rationale for allowing the committee to continue its work, to subpoena and subpoena until eventually they acquired the Nixon tapes, which became the basis for three articles of impeachment. Without the 718-page report it is quite possible, as O'Neill related in his memoirs, *Man of the House,* that his impeachment efforts would have been stalled.

Much of the research and writing of this book was done by none other than Hillary Rodham and her mentor, supervisor, and close personal friend, Bernard Nussbaum.

In *First in His Class,* David Maraniss describes the relationship between Hillary and Bernie as close. He points out that both Nussbaum and Rodham worked night and day, seven days a week, on the effort to impeach Nixon. Rodham was known to refer to Nixon as "evil," especially with reference to his politics. Strictly speaking, comments like that would have violated her oath of office as a Judiciary Committee lawyer who is supposed to be objective. But how objective could Hillary be? Before graduating from Yale Law School, she and her live-in boyfriend, Bill Clinton, had worked on the McGovern presidential campaign.

Moreover, she and Nussbaum reportedly made no pretense that their purpose working on the committee was to get Nixon. According to Maraniss's sources, "the impeachment staff experience was much like that of a political campaign," or, in other words, an extra-electoral means of ousting the man who had defeated Bill and Hillary's candidate for president.

Now Hillary was herself in the White House. Her Watergate mentor was White House counsel. And they showed they'd learned some important lessons from their past experiences. In his book, Tip O'Neill observes, "Those tapes are what undid Nixon. If he had destroyed them, he could have remained in office until the end of his second term," and, "not to destroy them was irrational."

In 1973 Rodham and Nussbaum worked overtime to get those tapes. In 1993, twenty years later, Nussbaum, while defending his decision to forbid FBI agents from searching the dead Vince Foster's office, said, "A smart New York lawyer would have made the documents disappear *before* the subpoenas arrived." Maybe that's why President Clinton let his wife choose his lawyers for him. He certainly seemed to have no qualms about having her choose much of his staff and run much of the government for him as well.

One day, while Dennis was waiting to interview Mack McLarty, he overheard McLarty's executive assistant talking to another assistant, "Do you think she'll get away with it?"

"Well, if she doesn't, it'll be the *first* time she's lost a battle around here."

"I don't know what she's trying to do. If we route all of McLarty's incoming and outgoing mail through her office, it's just going to create another step and delay things even worse!"

"Yeah, but Hillary wants to see who's coming in to see Mack and what he's reading and writing and working on. She wants to control this office. That's the long and the short of it; Hillary is trying to be the chief of staff!"

"I guess we should just get ready for it, since nobody around here seems to know how to say 'no' to Hillary."

Traditionally, the first lady's role is dominated by running the "domestic" side of the White House. But, by becoming de facto chief of staff or, more accurately, co-president, Hillary not only ran the domestic side of the White House, she ran domestic policy as well.

Some of this was done by high-level staff appointments, such as putting her law firm partners Vince Foster and Bill Kennedy in the Counsel's Office and making her good friend Carol Rasco director of the Office of Domestic Policy.

But Mrs. Clinton was also the de facto White House counsel and director of presidential personnel, selecting and clearing staff.

There were *some* staff members with obvious links to the president—like Catherine Cornelius and another West Wing employee, both young attractive blonds—but the president generally kept a low profile in the staffing and management of the White House. I saw no evidence of a power *struggle* between the president and the first lady. The power was all hers. The president's role seemed limited to taking the blame.

Most of the staff was linked to Hillary, and in many cases she approved of new hires only after interviewing them personally. Indeed, in Elizabeth Drew's book *On the Edge* it was reported that Hillary attended personnel selection and placement meetings about 80 percent of the time. Evidently, Mrs. Clinton was also responsible for the personnel decisions made by the transition team.

There *was* a clearance process for White House employees—they had to be approved by Hillary. And Hillary, if my thousands of interviews were representative, had an affirmative action program that favored tough, minority, and lesbian women, as well as weak, minority, and gay men. It was also apparent that when Hillary wanted a candidate, character issues were brushed aside. That might sound broad brush. It is. But it is justifiable. I know. I was there. If you compared the staffers of the Bush administration with those of the Clinton administration, the difference was shocking. It was Norman Rockwell on the one hand and Berkeley, California, with an Appalachian twist on the other.

In the Bush administration, Deputy Counsel John Schmitz reviewed the FBI SPIN investigations. Schmitz made his recommendations to the president's counsel, Boyden Gray. Gray would weigh Schmitz's recommendation and sign off on the final paperwork that would allow a White House staff member a security clearance and a permanent pass. If, during the course of the SPIN investigation—or perhaps earlier, in the pre-FBI scrubbing that could give early warnings of unsuitability—serious issues were developed and proven, then the president's counsel would tell the president that "Joe Blow" wouldn't be joining the White House staff. If the president asked why, he would be told that there was a problem in the FBI investigation. President Bush would never have asked, "Can we ignore it, or get around it?" That would have been ridiculous. How did I know that? Because I personally handled investigations of persons President Bush wanted for particular slots, and when these persons couldn't get through the FBI investigation, they were immediately dropped from further consideration.

In the Clinton administration things were very different. The function of approving and issuing security clearances and permanent passes was done in a loose and dangerous way. To start with, the authority to grant passes was delegated down from Bernard Nussbaum, the counsel; to Vince Foster, his deputy; to Bill Kennedy, the associate counsel; and in many cases, from Kennedy down to Craig Livingstone, who was the director of the Security Office, but who was not an attorney and had no security experience. I learned that all of these individuals were handpicked for their respective roles by Hillary Clinton.

Other major changes were made, the most significant being the deletion of "character" as a component to determine suitability. No attempt was ever made to dismiss a staffer after he or she had been selected by Hillary or Bill Clinton, no matter what character problems one might find. During a conversation with Elizabeth Drew in February 1993, Communications Director George Stephanopoulos explained it this way: "We've learned about the power of the president's voice. When he says something, it pretty much drives everything else away."

This was Stephanopoulos's explanation for the Zoe Baird and Kimba Wood fiascos. What he didn't admit was what we all eventually knew—that choosing the attorney general was Hillary's prerogative. Hillary had been told that Baird and Wood had problems, but she didn't care. She wanted them, and that was that.

If the Clinton White House had had a real counsel with real authority, these two nominations would have been vetted by attorneys knowledgeable about background investigations and suitability. When Baird and Wood caused such trauma to the Clinton administration, Nussbaum and Foster didn't get the blame, because they hadn't made the decision. Hillary had.

The Clintons and their staff did *not* have a reputation for being good listeners, but they *did* have a reputation for losing their tempers. The president and Mrs. Clinton, especially, were frequently observed flying into rages at each other or at staffers. They evidently thought this was a healthy and constructive way to air differences, but it had the inevitable effect of creating chaos and cowardice in the White House—not to mention lots of shouting—which ensured that bad personnel choices initiated from the top were never questioned.

This made me wonder what the working atmosphere at the Rose Law Firm of Hillary Clinton, Vince Foster, William Kennedy, and Webster Hubbell must have been like. In any event, the Rose Law Firm certainly has left its mark on Washington with a suicide, several scandals (Hubbell, for one, is today peeling potatoes in a federal penitentiary), and Hillary's seizure of power, which might extend even to the humble halls of the FBI.

Evidence has surfaced to suggest that Judge Session's replacement, Louis Freeh, like every other important Clinton presidential appointment, was made by Hillary in collaboration with Bernard Nussbaum, Susan Thomases, and Vince Foster. But the picture is murkier than that. Among those recommending Louis Freeh for FBI director was Robert Fiske. Freeh was appointed in July 1993. On 20 January 1994 Fiske was appointed special counsel to investigate the Clintons' involvement with Whitewater.

Fiske's investigators are on loan from the FBI. Obviously, the potential for conflict-of-interest is rife in this web of mutual friends. Although there is no evidence of misconduct on the part of these agents, they should never have been put in this situation in the first place.

There is a word for what is missing here—and it's "ethics." Ethics were something the Bush administration took great pains to enforce. Advising the Bush administration on day-to-day ethics questions was, in fact, the prime responsibility of Associate Counsel Greg Walden. This emphasis on ethics by President Bush was evidently not shared by the new administration, whose co-presidents, interestingly enough, were both lawyers.

There was still the matter of the social side—the domestic side—of the White House. In past presidencies, this large function took the full-time effort of the first lady and about twenty fine staff members, as well as a number of volunteers and a long list of "helpers" who could be available to come down to the White House and help out as needed.

The Residence itself was a major operation. It was well-managed by Chief Usher Gary Walters, but certain major decisions had to be made by the first lady. Hiring, firing, promotions of Residence staffers, and the style of food served in the Residence were prerogatives of the first lady.

In the world of Hillary it might take a village to raise a child, but it takes only one hard-driven Rose Law Firm partner to run the entire government. It quickly became evident, however, that the first lady's traditional functions were beyond Mrs. Clinton. The first warning signs came shortly after the inauguration.

Janet Green was a Clinton administration employee who, like many others, didn't know where she would be assigned to work. She ended up as an assistant to David Watkins. When I met her I recall her demeanor as polite, but not overly serious. Green had "the Clinton administration smirk" that many staffers had when they met an FBI agent. I could not imagine Green being put in charge of evaluating serious functions at the White House. But she was. Ms. Green's job was to interview personnel in each of the offices she was assigned to examine, and after she had "sized up" whatever White House operation she was studying, she was to report back to Hillary and tell her what she had found. Based on her report, staffing needs would be addressed.

It was late December, and although a new president was about to take office and one would expect general chaos to reign in the White House, much of the White House continued to hum along as always, because many of its functions were not political.

The Visitor's Office was one such apolitical function, although not long after they took office, the Clintons politicized the Visitor's Office, too, by withholding tours requested by members of Congress, thus punishing them if they had not voted for the president's agenda.

The Visitor's Office is located in the East Wing, on the first floor just under the first lady's suite of offices. During the Bush administration the office was headed by Director Janet Johnson. I knew most of the staff in the office—they were younger women, typically of impeccable backgrounds, the "girl next door" types that I had learned to expect in the Bush White House.

They handled hundreds of phone, fax, and mail requests for White House tours every day. The phones were constantly ringing. Though the Visitor's Office was one of the busiest places in the complex, the staff were poised and simply delightful; they were supposed to be.

They had been carefully selected for their personalities. They dealt with thousands of citizens every week, many in high places. The staffing of this office had been high on the list of matters overseen by First Lady Barbara Bush.

Among its other responsibilities, the Visitor's Office organized the many special and social events that occurred each year. The Christmas parties and tours, the staff's Fourth of July celebration on the South Lawn, the annual Easter Egg Roll, and the president's helicopter arrivals and departures. Whenever an event took place in the Residence, or on the Residence Lawn, the Visitor's Office was responsible for making it work. They prepared the guest list, ordered the little American flags that everyone waved, and made sure everyone was cleared through the Secret Service. The Visitor's Office performed an important White House function, but it was only after the inauguration that Ms. Green contacted the office. Janet Johnson was happy to hear from *anybody* from the Clinton administration at that point, as the social business of the White House needed to continue. For example, contracts needed to be negotiated and signed for many coming events—including the Easter Egg Roll, which was looming on the horizon.

The Easter Egg Roll is a tradition on the South Lawn of the White House. Children are invited to enjoy clowns, balloons, flags, surprises being given out at booths, a visit from the Easter Bunny, and the "roll" of the Easter eggs—a contest to get an egg from one point to another without breaking it. The Easter Egg Roll is one of the rare times average citizens get to enjoy the grounds of the White House. But entry is conditional—you must bring a child. Children love the Easter Egg Roll. To commemorate the event each child is given a wooden egg with a picture of the White House on it. I took my own children to two of these celebrations.

When Green presented herself at the Visitor's Office, she seemed impatient and in a hurry. She wanted a quick and easy summation of the office's work so that she could report back to Hillary for staffing decisions.

Johnson tried to walk her through the various responsibilities and tried to impress on her the volume and importance of the work of the Visitor's Office. Green didn't seem interested or impressed.

Johnson tried to bring Green up to speed, using the Easter Egg Roll as her best example of why the staffing of the office should be addressed soon.

"Well, I don't think Hillary or Bill will care very much about this. Maybe we can cancel it. I just don't think they will want to do this 'egg' thing."

Johnson was astonished. "Hillary and Bill? First of all, Miss Green, we refer to the Clintons as Mr. President, and the first lady, or Mrs. Clinton, *not* Hillary and Bill."

"Well, I call them Hillary and Bill."

"And, in the second place, Miss Green," Johnson continued, "the Easter Egg Roll at the White House is an important tradition, one that is very famous. It has taken place here for many years. Most people have heard about it. Apparently, you have not. Maybe before you dismiss its importance you should talk to the president or Mrs. Clinton about it. Because if you don't, in my opinion, you are making a serious mistake!"

According to Johnson, Green continued to dismiss the event—*and* the Visitor's Office overall—as inconsequential. Johnson could not fathom how such an immature person could have been placed in charge of evaluating the Visitor's Office—or any other White House function. Johnson's worst fears were, in fact, realized, as the Clintons, following Green's advice, botched the staffing of the Visitor's Office. When Janet Johnson told me this, I felt sorry for her and her staff. I knew they'd put their hearts into helping people see the White House and maintaining the high White House standards people expected. Now it looked like their work was being thrown away.

I drove to Washington midmorning on the day of the Easter Egg Roll. I saw unhappy parents and toddlers all over the place, many lined up past the entrance I usually used at the OEOB. The line stretched for hundreds of yards from the entrance gate.

In years past, the event was over by noon. "Why are they still here?" I wondered. I soon found out. As I approached the gate, I overheard a young mother complaining to another mom, as both of their four-year-olds screamed their lungs out, "Can you believe this? We've been waiting four hours now, and the line isn't moving. My kids are hungry, and there's no food. They're squirming, and they have no place to go to the bathroom. Can you believe these people? Don't they have kids? Don't they know kids get hungry, need to use bathrooms?"

The other mom replied, "Man, I would have never come if I knew that it would be like this. It's supposed to be fun. This is a nightmare." And with that, she turned her stroller around and stomped off in the direction of the nearby McDonald's, where she could at least be assured of a snack for her child and a bathroom.

What had happened? What went wrong? I asked my Secret Service buddy, whose officers had to pull extra duty during such events. "Damn Clintons. They can't do anything without screwing it up! We've got a mess from one end of the complex to the other, and hundreds of angry mothers! What the hell were they thinking?

"They simply won't listen. I *told* the new director of the Visitor's Office that they were setting it up all wrong! They invited too many people, left the gates open too long. Now they've closed the gates because the place is overrun, and they haven't even told the people in line yet! Wait until those tired and hungry moms and their children hear they've waited in line for nothing! I don't wanna be here for that! *And,* they've run out of eggs! Can you believe these people?"

Although the event turned out to be a catastrophe, the news media made little mention of it.

Janet Green didn't last very long at the White House, but not because of the Easter Egg fiasco. Green worked for David Watkins, which was her bad luck. Rumors were rampant throughout the White House that Watkins discriminated against women.

Watkins had already taken out Cerda and Cornelius, his two deputies. They couldn't stand to be around him and moved to different posts. They had nothing kind to say about their former boss.

Dennis told me that when he began to ask Watkins questions about Green for his background investigation of her, Watkins gave Dennis the "time-out" signal.

"Why are you wasting your time on this case? I'm just going to fire Green anyway."

"Why?"

"Look, Dennis, you look like a bright guy, and a man old enough to understand what I am about to say, but if you ever repeat what I'm going to tell you, I'll just deny it. Dennis, I'm going to fire Green for one reason, and one reason only, and do you know what it is? I can't *stand* to work around women!"

Shortly afterward, Green was out the door.

The Easter Egg Roll wasn't the only Clinton Visitor's Office disaster. Next came the Fourth of July. I had planned to bring my kids down for the event, but at the last minute my boy came down with the flu, which turned out to be fortuitous. Things on the South Lawn got pretty ugly, according to some FBI agents who told me about it later.

Apparently, someone took exception to the rule that only staff and their immediate family could attend. Since it would have been judgmental and controversial to define "a family" in this administration, each staff member was allowed to bring four guests.

The Secret Service must have taken one look at the line winding around the White House that Fourth of July night and collectively thought, "Oh, s--t!" The "diversity" of Clinton families and guests meant a bigger crowd than the Secret Service could have expected or the grounds could accommodate. Before long the South Lawn filled up, and there were people everywhere, even climbing the trees. The Secret Service didn't know what else to do besides close the gate early to stop the overcrowding.

But then all hell broke loose. The Clinton staffers and their friends shut outside simply climbed the fence! They broke into the White House! How *dare* the Secret Service ruin their evening? The Secret Service caught them, or at least most of them, and the invaders were promptly thrown to the ground and arrested, and rightly so.

And then later, they were unarrested. To my knowledge, not a single staffer was ever punished for this juvenile, outrageous, dangerous, and illegal act, nor was a single "guest" prosecuted for breaking into the White House. Thus another Clinton White House Visitor's Office fiasco passed quietly into the history books, unreported by the media.

Has the performance of the Visitor's Office staff improved since these catastrophes? I'm told that although they work very hard to make the White House available to the public, it is not unusual for Bill, Hillary, or someone on their staff to decide at the last minute that it's time to "party down." When that happens, hundreds of people who traveled hundreds or thousands of miles and who stand in line for hours to see the White House are greeted with a "Sorry-We're-Closed-Come-Back-Another-Time" sign.

At the beginning of the Christmas season, usually December 5, the staff at the White House Residence implements its holiday decorating theme. In order to create a first-class presentation, thousands of hours of work goes into the plan—at least six months worth—and thousands of volunteers throughout the country participate in the making of tree ornaments for the many trees displayed in the White House and the Residence.

Many people in the arts–crafts–decorating industry participate to send in ornaments they hope will be good enough to hang on a White House tree. If the ornament is especially well-made, there is a good chance it will be selected for the tree in the Blue Room, the first lady's tree.

The first lady's tree is the "Mother of All Trees" and the one that's supposed to capture the "message" of the first lady herself. I was astonished when I was invited by the White House Residence staff in 1992 under the Bush administration to help decorate the White House Christmas trees. I just couldn't believe it. I came home and told my wife, "Nina, there are only forty people in the entire nation who are invited to do this, and I am one of the forty!"

Actually, I found out later that they didn't want me for my decorating talents, which was good, since I didn't have any. They wanted me because I had a strong back and the magic blue pass that allowed me to go anywhere in the White House.

Decorating Saturday rolled around, and I arrived at dawn with everyone else. We sat in the Residence near the formal dining room. The Residence staff split us into teams and assigned us rooms, wreaths to hang, and trees to decorate. Most of my fellow decorators were professional florists.

The decorating work, which was to last until 10:30 P.M., was organized with military precision. It was going to be the best-decorated home in the world, or we would all collapse trying. That was the mood. This occasion was as close as I had ever worked with the Residence staff, and my impression of them as hardworking, amazingly decent people was reinforced.

This year's theme for the first lady's Christmas tree was needlepoint, which was one of Barbara Bush's hobbies, and the place was filled with boxes of needlepoint ornaments. When we were done, late that night, we stood in silence and smiled, deeply satisfied. It was terrific. It was just breathtaking how beautiful the White House, and especially the first lady's tree, had become—capturing the joy, the spirit of goodwill, even the religious meaning of the holiday season. It was one of the highlights of my time in the White House.

Sure enough, in 1993, I was invited back to assist in hanging the Christmas decorations, but I declined. I was fed up with the attitude of the Clinton administration and its endless scandals.

Just before Decorating Saturday, I ran into some of my old team members from the previous Christmas. They were next to the Oval Office working on wreaths. None of them was cleared to be in this part of the complex (you needed a permanent pass), but then again, no one seemed to need clearance for anything anymore.

"Gary, how you doing? I hear you can't help us this year. Why not?"

I made a flimsy excuse and avoided eye contact.

"Well, don't feel too bad about it, pal. You aren't missing anything. You wouldn't believe what they're calling 'Christmas decorations' this year. It's unbelievable. In fact, it's downright disgraceful. There's this one ornament, a clear lucite block, and inside are some old computer parts, and that's a Christmas ornament, see?"

My other former team member chimed in, "Yeah, it's true, and there's all of this carved dark wood, not resembling much of anything—just sticks and twigs tied together. They look like fertility gods or something. We can't tell."

"Yeah, and there are pots, and carvings, some that look kind of obscene, and boxes, but nowhere can we find anything that resembles *Christmas*. Nowhere."

"And have you seen Bertha?"

Yes, I had seen Bertha—big, ebony Bertha. Bertha was a statue that Hillary had selected to be placed along the public tour line. About eleven other examples of modern art were in the Jackie Kennedy Garden (the companion garden to the Rose Garden). Bertha was twice life-size and was very naked. In addition, Bertha had enormous buttocks, far out of proportion to the rest of her body.

That is why the permanent White House staff named her Bertha, which was short for "Bertha's Big Butt." This is what the first lady considered appropriate for the eyes of the thousands and thousands of visitors who daily toured the White House—Bertha's Big Butt.

I could just hear my child asking, "Daddy, why doesn't that woman have any clothes on? Daddy, why is her bottom so big?"

Later that same day, I drove to the Cannon House Office Building for some interviews. As I waited for a stop light, I looked over at the national Christmas tree. What a sight it was. Gone were the multi-colored Christmas balls and other ornaments that traditionally symbolized the holidays. Gone was the star from the top of the tree, symbolizing the night when Christ was born.

Instead, on top of the tree was a large stainless-steel ball pierced by colored shafts. It looked like the ball that sat atop the Daily Planet building in the Superman comic books I read as a child. This ball and the square and triangle tinfoil ornaments made the tree look like a robot. I couldn't wait to see what the Clintons and their friends would do the following year.

When I returned to the White House the next day, I ran into Tom Hufford, one of the holdovers from the Bush administration, now working in the Office of Administration. Tom had worked very hard to convince the Clinton crowd that he was indeed apolitical, and I knew that he was.

"Hi, Tom. What's up?"

"Hi, Gary, how are you? Still here, I see."

"Well, sort of Tom. I don't spend much time here anymore. Most of my time is spent on the Hill, talking to congressmen."

"Did you want that?"

"Yes, I did. I needed a change, a fresh perspective. I've been here long enough."

"I think I know what you're getting at, Gary. I'm about ready to go myself."

"Is your office still the place to pick up the Christmas cards?"

"Yeah, if we ever get the cards made. We're about two weeks out, and they're still fighting over what kind of card, who's going to be on it, and so on and so forth."

"Who's fighting about it?"

"Gary, who do you think? The president and the first lady, who else?"

Right. Fighting over Christmas cards. How seasonal.

The most noticeable thing about the Christmas cards when they arrived was that the first family had lost Chelsea. She wasn't on the card. Maybe she was hiding in shame, because that Christmas *The Los Angeles Times* and *The American Spectator* ran their stories on Troopergate and the Clintons' extramarital escapades as governor and first lady of Arkansas. It wasn't the sort of news that those of us intent on preserving the reputation of the presidency wanted to hear.

Fast forward to one year later. Again I was asked to help decorate the White House. I didn't get it. There wasn't much to do. The Clintons didn't like tinsel—not one tree had any tinsel—nor was there any fake snow, nor did there seem to be much for decorators to do. Christmas 1993 had been pretty stark, but then, it's always hard to hang wooden fertility symbols and lucite blocks with old computer parts; the branches keep bending and breaking.

But I agreed to help. It might be a last chance to help the permanent staff with the decorations. I could see retirement up ahead, just six months out, and though I had loved working at the White House, the Clintons had made the idea of retirement particularly sweet for me.

I arrived early. Everyone was in a good mood, but I was surprised to hear the first family was at home. They had not gone to Camp

David, as was traditional—that way, the decorating could go on undisturbed and they could be surprised when they returned for the great unveiling. Perhaps Hillary didn't trust us. She had, in fact, "hired" some volunteers of her own. While in New York, Hillary had seen an office she thought was well-decorated. She ordered the staff to find the decorators and bring them down.

The permanent White House staff wasn't wild about this idea, but, after all, it *was* the first lady's show, and everyone understood that it would be done the way Hillary Clinton wanted it done.

"Gary, you and your team will work on the Blue Room tree."

What? I had been "fired" two years before from the Blue Room tree, the first lady's tree, for complete decorative incompetence. "They must have forgotten," I thought.

I went out to unload a truckful of ornament boxes. They had been received at another location and then X-rayed and examined to make sure nobody sent the White House a ticking bomb. We brought the boxes into the hallway just north of the Green, Red, and Blue Rooms, between the State Dining Room and the East Room.

The GSA, the Park Service, and the Residence maintenance staff had erected all the trees. Some staff were on high ladders, hanging evergreen garlands. We gathered around folding tables to unpack the ornament boxes.

It took about ten seconds to get the first reaction. "What in the world?"

Then another. "What the hell?"

Then another. "Look at this thing! What *is* it?"

"Hillary's ornaments is what!"

From one end of the hall to the other, about forty people were picking up these "things," staring at them, turning them around, trying to figure them out or stifle their embarrassed laughter. I turned to one of my team members. "What *are* these things?"

"I heard the theme is The Twelve Days of Christmas, as interpreted by art students from around the country. Hillary sent a letter out just two months ago, really late actually, asking budding artists to send in an interpretation of The Twelve Days of Christmas, and this is what they came up with."

I couldn't believe what I was looking at. "This stuff is just childish garbage! We can't hang this stuff on any White House Christmas tree! This is a bad joke."

"Gary, the orders from the First Lady's Office are to hang these. It's what she wants, so we have to hang them. Anyway, many of them are from 'blue ribbon' art schools, as designated by the Secretary of Education. The whole administration has a stake in this."

"Well, if this is blue ribbon, then we're in serious trouble, educationally." I pulled out one ornament that was five real onion rings (five *golden* rings) glued to a white styrofoam tray, with a hook attached to the back so it could be hung. But where? Maybe in Bill Clinton's bedroom so he could rip off a midnight snack?

I was disgusted, but some of it was actually pretty funny.

"Gary, come here, look at this!" It was a mobile of twelve lords a-leaping. They were leaping all right. The ornament consisted of tiny clay male figurines. Each was naked and had a large erection. My friend said, "Whoops!" and he dropped it on the floor. Then, "Oh, no," as he stomped on it. He joked, "Man, I hope I don't get in trouble with Hillary for that!"

Some of the ornaments were silly and some were dangerous, like the crack pipes hung on a string. We couldn't figure out what crack pipes had to do with Christmas no matter how hard we tried, so we threw them back in the box. Some ornaments were constructed out of various drug paraphernalia, like syringes, heroin spoons, or roach clips, which are colorful devices sometimes adorned with bird feathers and used to hold marijuana joints.

Two turtle doves became two figurines that had the shells of turtles but the heads of birds; there were many of these. Four calling birds were—you guessed it—birds with a telephone, and there were at least two miniature phone booths with four birds inside using the telephone. There was a partridge in a pear, without the tree—a clay pear with a partridge head sticking out of it. Three French hens were French-kissing in a ménage à trois. So many of the ornaments didn't celebrate Christmas as much at they celebrated sex, drugs, and rock and roll. Several of the birds had dark glasses and were blowing saxophones.

"Hey, Gary. Come over here." I walked over. It was another leaping lords ornament. Each "lord" had a wooden body with a photograph of Rush Limbaugh for a head. A dozen ditto-heads, suitable for hanging, but nobody had the guts to hang Rush Limbaugh on Hillary's tree, so back in the box it went.

First, though, I held the Limbaugh ornament up, while someone took a picture of me. It was like holding twelve sticks of dynamite in my hand, because with my bad luck, I expected one of the Clinton folks or maybe the Clintons themselves to walk around the corner just as the camera flash went off. But I was lucky this time.

I went over to one of the tables I hadn't looked at yet. What's this? Of course. Two turtle doves, but they didn't have shells this time—they were joined together in an act of bird fornication.

I picked up another ornament that was supposed to illustrate five golden rings. One of the male florist volunteers grabbed my arm and laughed and laughed.

"What's so funny? What are you laughing at?"

"Don't you know what you're holding?"

No, I didn't, but he was happy to explain it to me: the golden rings I was holding were sex toys known as "cock rings"—and they had nothing to do with chickens.

Another mystery ornament was the gingerbread man. How did he fit into The Twelve Days of Christmas? Then I got it. There were five small, gold rings I hadn't seen at first: one in his ear, one in his nose, one through his nipple, one through his belly button, and, of course, the ever-popular cock ring.

I couldn't believe the disrespect that these ornaments represented. Many of the artists invited to make and send something to hang on the tree must have had nothing but disgust, hatred, and disrespect for the White House and the citizens of this country, a disgust obviously encouraged by the first lady in the name of artistic freedom.

I thought of all the children, grandmothers, and grandfathers walking past the White House's Blue Room, looking at the first lady's Christmas tree and wondering what in hell had possessed the White House.

Here was another five golden rings ornament—five gold-wrapped condoms. I threw it in the trash. There were other condom ornaments, some still in the wrapper, some not. Two sets had been "blown" into balloons and tied to small trees. I wasn't sure what the connection was to The Twelve Days of Christmas. Condoms in a pear tree?

When we were through, the first lady's tree had all the beauty and majesty of a landfill.

Hillary's social secretary, Ann Stock, came down, carefully looked at the tree and its decorations and pronounced it "perfect" and "delightful." My shoulders sagged. Stock had been our last, best hope to clean up this "mistake." But instead, she thought it was "*neat*." At least we had turned the gingerbread man around so that his golden rings didn't face the tour line. I came back later and took some pictures of the tree and "Mr. Gingerbread Man" with rings side *out*. I knew nobody would believe this without photographic proof.

While I was working on the tree, Craig Livingstone happened to stop by. He was surprised to see me placing ornaments on Hillary's tree, but I told him I was an old hand at this decorating business. Livingstone was leading Oliver Stone and Michael Douglas in a tour around the White House. Stone was making *Nixon,* and Douglas was making *An American President.* Stone *looked* stoned to me, as he gazed around, obviously thinking of this "shot" or that. I wasn't impressed. Still, this must have been a great moment for Livingstone, our White House security director, whose goal in life was to become a Hollywood producer.

But the cameras, surprisingly enough, soon fell not on Michael Douglas or on the dazed Oliver Stone or the photogenically challenged Craig Livingstone; they fell on me. I was interviewed by Martha Stewart, who was doing a Christmas special to be aired later on a major network morning show. She promised she would not blow my cover when she learned I was an FBI agent.

As she looked around the tree she made "hmmmm" sounds. If she didn't like the tree, she was very diplomatic about it. I wondered what she really thought. It seemed to me most people could have only one thought: "Throw a tarp over it!"

Aside from displaying sex toys and self-mutilation devices on the nation's Christmas tree, there was another "change" in the way the White House celebrated Christmas. Hillary decided to delete spouses from the invitation-only staff Christmas party. This caused a bit of a stir, not only because it broke with tradition, but because it raised a question I had heard several permanent staffers ask: "Why is Hillary so hostile to families?"

I think it's because they represent a sphere of loyalty outside her control. And Hillary likes to be in charge.

Chapter Seven

DRUGS

Rules for Radicals: "Men don't like to step abruptly out of the security of familiar experience; they need a bridge to cross from their own experience to a new way. A revolutionary organizer must shake up the prevailing patterns of their lives, agitate, create disenchantment and discontent with the current values, to produce, if not a passion for change, at least a passive, affirmative, non-challenging climate."

George Washington's Rules of Civility and Decent Behaviour: "Let your recreations be manful not sinful."

It was Sunday morning, 4 December 1994. I was sitting at my kitchen table, drinking a cup of coffee and watching Newt Gingrich being interviewed for *Meet the Press*. It was assumed that Congressman Gingrich would be the next Speaker of the House, when the new Republican-controlled 104th Congress convened in January.

I nodded in agreement when Gingrich said the Clintons and their staff were throwbacks to the 1960s counterculture. Then, to drive his point home he said, "I had a senior law enforcement official tell me" that many Clinton White House staffers had used illegal drugs within the past five years.

I choked and spit my coffee across the table. There couldn't be more than two dozen "senior law enforcement officials" who could have told Newt Gingrich about White House drug use, and some people would think that I was one of them. My first thought was, "There goes my job." I was not an "official," but I was "law enforcement" and I was "senior." I was also assigned to both the White House and the House of Representatives.

108

Craig Livingstone knew about my bifurcated assignment at the White House and the U.S. House of Representatives. Livingstone had quizzed me before about who might be talking to Congress about Clinton White House shenanigans. And the Clintons controlled the Department of Justice, under Janet Reno, and the FBI. I would be at the top of the Clintons' short list of suspected whistle-blowers. Even though I hadn't leaked anything, I was likely finished; they had a perfect excuse to fire me.

Gingrich hadn't completed his interview before I received my first "Did you hear what Gingrich just said?" phone call. I received calls all day Sunday and Monday from fellow agents, friends, and family who were worried for me. I assured them all that I was not Gingrich's buddy. But if my own friends thought Gingrich was referring to me, how much more would the Clinton administration see this as their opportunity to put me out to pasture?

Of course I knew that there were probably multiple leaks, and it would not have surprised me to learn that many law enforcement officials in the FBI, the Secret Service, and elsewhere were complaining to Congress or anyone else who would listen about the Clinton White House staff and Executive Branch political appointments.

Monday passed, and nothing happened. On Tuesday morning, however, Livingstone asked me to come down to see him as soon as I could. Livingstone said, "Gary, I just hung up with your director. I told Freeh that I didn't believe you were the leak." He was watching me closely for a reaction, but I gave him none.

"Gary, do *you* know who is telling Congress all this, this sh-t about drugs and stuff?"

"Craig, look, I don't know. Nobody, anybody, everybody. You should know by now that you can't hide anything in this town, especially in this White House. I've told you that before. There are dozens of people who might be in a position to comment on drug use on the part of your staff. Drug use has not been my main concern, and you know that."

"Well, okay. Listen, on another topic, I've been wondering what you're going to do after you retire? Made any plans yet? You said you were going to retire soon. I'm just curious."

"Uh, no, Craig, I really haven't made any plans. I might go into the private investigations business; I don't know. I guess I have to start thinking about that." Our conversation had suddenly taken a very puzzling turn.

"Well, would you consider taking over George's place? You know, be the White House security consultant?"

I was shocked. From suspected leak to employee-of-the-month, all in one conversation.

"Craig, I can't say yes or no, but I'll consider it. Have you checked with, uh, you know, the 'higher ups' around here to see if that would be okay with them?" I believe Craig knew that I was referring to Hillary Clinton, since Craig had already told me that she called the shots on security.

"Yes, yes, don't worry about that. You're trusted. It's a done deal. Just think about that, okay?"

"Okay, I will. But where is George going? Has he announced his retirement?" George hadn't indicated to me that he had any interest in leaving, and in fact he seemed to be content with his new, if very limited, role. "No, ah, he doesn't know anything about this. Ah, he's, you know, getting old, and, well, I think it's time for George to retire."

I was dumbstruck. As I pondered what Livingstone had just said, I began to wonder. I thought, "Nah, he can't be offering me a promise of a job to silence me because he thinks I'm the leak . . . a job to shut me up? No way, that's too obvious."

Yet, I remembered that the Clinton administration had offered jobs to some of the state troopers in Little Rock after they started talking to the press about the personal and professional problems the Clintons had had while Bill was governor. In one case a trooper was contacted directly by the president of the United States, and he had indeed become a federal employee, earning a salary of almost $100,000 a year. Another trooper had been contacted by an intermediary and had turned down a job offer, saying he couldn't uproot his family, even though the offer was tempting.

The offer of the security consultant position was something that got my attention, because I had actually thought about seeking the job if George Saunders ever retired. But George seemed to go on and on, like the Energizer Bunny. During the Bush administration, the job meant something, and it looked like an attractive post. But now to take Craig's offer would mean immediate compromise. The administration had already neutered the position and now—maybe—they were using it to bribe me. Of course, I also knew that by turning down the offer I would become a marked man by the Clintons. Maybe they thought they could buy an FBI agent, like they had bought a state trooper in Arkansas. I was six months from retirement and I was looking for a new job. Now I'd received my first offer—from the Clinton administration. But I had resolved I wouldn't remain in the Clinton White House one day past my retirement date. I'd come to the White House to get away from crooks and drug dealers, and now I was surrounded by a *White House* staff full of people who had been major drug *buyers*—or maybe worse.

One only had to look at Clinton associates like Little Rock businessman Dan Lasater, who was convicted of cocaine distribution (and later pardoned by then-Governor Clinton) and whose former business partner is current Clinton director of White House Management and Administration Patsy Thomasson (responsible for drug testing at the White House), or at the cocaine distribution convictions of Clinton's half brother or of Surgeon General Joycelyn Elders's son to get a hint of possible murky depths.

If I had to guess, about 10 percent of the persons coming to the Bush White House had tried an illegal drug—which was about a third of the national average—and it was almost always marijuana, and only once. Prior use of cocaine was very rare; use of more serious drugs was unheard of. The illegal drug use was invariably confined to an individual's college days.

Though the age breakdown in the Bush and Clinton administrations was probably about the same, illegal drug use in the Clinton administration was much higher and *not* confined to minor drugs like marijuana. Generally, if marijuana was used, it was not confined to the college years, either. In fact, a striking number of cases began to emerge in which the use of marijuana, once started in high school or college, continued into one's twenties, thirties, and sometimes even forties. We were talking about *decades* of *illegal* drug use.

There was another important difference between the Bush and Clinton staffs. In the Bush administration, more of the younger, post–baby boom staffers had managed to get through college with no drug use at all. They were a reflection of the national downward trend in drug use inspired by Nancy Reagan's much-mocked, but effective "Just Say No" campaign. But in the Clinton administration it was harder to find young staffers who hadn't experimented with marijuana, cocaine, and heavier drugs. Apparently, they couldn't "Just Say No."

The minority of Bush applicants who "experimented" and admitted inhaling didn't try to defend their use of illegal drugs. They were invariably apologetic: "Yes, I did smoke marijuana once or twice. I was in college and everyone was doing it, so I tried it. I stopped using marijuana after I left college, but I'm ashamed that I ever did it, because it was stupid. I'm sorry agents like you were risking your lives fighting drug traffickers while I didn't have the guts to stand up to peer pressure."

By contrast the Clinton staffers, older or younger, made no apology for their illegal drug use, which was more extensive, and included many "heavy" drugs like cocaine, crack, LSD, and methamphetamine. Many were actually "in your face" about it, using the FBI interview to try to debate me on the merits of making drugs legal. Of course, when I asked them how they obtained their drugs, the lies began.

It was a rare Clinton staffer who ever purchased any drugs. Almost all of the Clinton staffers were given drugs "by friends," or "could not recall" who gave them the drugs, or "used the drugs at a party" where "they didn't really know anybody there."

In the Bush administration the Secret Service rarely, if ever, approved a permanent blue pass for applicants with confessed drug use beyond college. In fact, the Secret Service didn't want drug users anywhere within the complex, let alone near the president.

But this was the Clinton administration, and things were going to be a lot different. Of all the character issues I investigated, I ranked casual drug use as no more important than simple dishonesty. Nevertheless, I had no criticism or argument for law enforcement officers taking a harder line, because many character problems were often driven by substance abuse. It was, in itself, a serious character flaw.

In an effort to illustrate a typical Clinton–Gore illegal drug user, I will need to craft a composite person. I will call this young man, Finew Linew, as in "first name unknown, last name unknown." Last time I checked, lots of Mr., Mrs., and Ms. Linews were still working in the Clinton–Gore administration.

Mr. Linew presented himself at the appointed time and sat in the "hot seat," the chair where most of my interviewees were asked to sit. We went through the normal introductions, and I explained what we were going to do and the possible ramifications. Mr. Linew was told that it was a formal interview, "an interview that would be reduced to a formal report, and sent to the president's counsel."

I learned that, like so many other Clinton administration staff members, Mr. Linew had a personal and professional relationship to the Clintons. So many of the staffers had worked for the Clintons in Little Rock, had then worked on the campaign, and then had been invited to the White House. Many of the younger staff's parents had also worked for the Clintons, and so the loyalty to the Clintons was personal, professional, *and* familial.

After graduating from college, Mr. Linew had been a waiter or pizza delivery boy. He then worked for the state of Arkansas before coming to the White House.

We finally got to the section regarding the use of illegal substances. Mr. Linew had typed, "some experimentation—most during college." He had not provided any further information. I needed to define his use so the reader of my report could judge Mr. Linew's exposure to illegal drugs and illegal activity, since the use of illegal drugs *is* an illegal activity.

"Mr. Linew, tell me more about your use of illegal drugs."

"What do you mean?"

"Well, what you have indicated on the form doesn't tell us very much. For example, when did you start using illegal drugs?"

"Look, I don't know what this has to do with anything. I haven't used drugs recently. I'm not using drugs now. Why should I tell the FBI about this anyway? It's none of your business. I'm a friend of Bill and Hillary's."

"Look, Mr. Linew, I couldn't care less about your drug use. Let me tell you something. You say you're a good friend of the president and first lady? I am going to give you the extension for the president's phone. If you wish, you can call him now, and tell him that you don't want to talk to me about this drug use. But I think you should know that this investigation process is authorized by, and for the benefit of, the president of the United States. He had a choice whether to continue this process, and guess what? President Clinton signed the Executive Order that instructs me to ask you about your drug use. So, what about your drug use? When did you first start using drugs?"

"I used some marijuana in high school and then in college."

"Mr. Linew, from when to when did you use any illegal substance? Just give me the dates."

"Well, from 1986 to about sometime in 1992. It was grass, mostly."

"Mr. Linew, can you tell me how many times you used grass from 1986 to 1992?"

"How am I supposed to know that?"

"How often did you use it regularly? If you smoked grass once a week, then we can guess that you used grass about fifty-two times a year, and we can multiply that by your years of use. It's simple, Mr. Linew. Now how many times did you use grass?" (I should point out that fifty-two times would be an extreme case. I never had such a case in the Bush administration. But this was the Clinton administration.)

Mr. Linew began to count the times in his mind. I was getting tired of Mr. Linew, real tired. He, like so many others, had simply disregarded the law in favor of satisfying a personal desire. This is called hedonism, I believe. I was a professional FBI agent, and I had seen so many things in my career that I didn't like, but I guess I had thought I wouldn't have to be around such people *in the White House.* Lord knows it was accepted that a law enforcement officer would have to be around dirtbags; that was part of the job. But in *the White House?*

When Mr. Linew had an answer, I got ready to copy it down in my notes. "Okay. I think I would say that I used marijuana about four hundred times. Yeah, maybe four hundred. Maybe more." I paused, staring at my notes, at my pencil. I looked up to see if my partner Dennis had heard the answer. He had. Dennis was grinning like a polecat and shaking his head. He was trying to control the same response I was having, but he could smile because Mr. Linew had his back to him.

This was it. I had spent many an hour with many of the Clintons' "best and brightest," and I had heard so many things. They came to see me in t-shirts. They came to see me in jeans and earth shoes. They came to see me in short skirts without stockings or modesty. They came from Pizza Hut and Domino's and Joe's Bar and Grill, and off campaign airplanes where they had been flight attendants. I couldn't stand it. I wanted to shout, "THIS IS THE WHITE HOUSE, DAMN IT!" I collected my thoughts and tried to regain my composure, but I just could not let this moment pass.

"Mr. Linew, what did you conclude?"

Mr. Linew looked puzzled.

"Mr. Linew, what did you find out?"

"I don't get it. What do you mean?"

"Well, Mr. Linew, *you* described your drug use as 'experimental.' Obviously, you conducted many 'experiments,' maybe more than four hundred experiments. Surely by now you have reached a 'scientific conclusion.' Can you tell me what that might be? Have you concluded that you are *addicted,* Mr. Linew? Or, have you concluded that you love marijuana? What is your scientific conclusion about drugs based on your experiments?"

With that, Dennis broke up laughing, and so did I. Clearly, Mr. Linew was not amused, and while I had my laugh, I also figured *this* might be my last day at the White House. But by now I had already decided that the Clinton White House was not my kind of White House. I had worked many years on the side of law and order, and I thought that my last years in the FBI should be spent someplace where my work meant something. Maybe someplace where my co-workers and associates shared my values. That place was certainly not the Clinton White House. Marijuana one hundred times a year, for four years? Hell, Mr. Linew was defined as "a hard-core drug user" by Clinton's own drug czar!

Mr. Linew stood up. "This is *not* fair. This is *not* professional. I resent this!" He moved toward the door.

"Mr. Linew, look, I'm sorry. Why don't you sit back down, and we'll move on and finish this thing so you don't have to come here again." He sat down, and we went through the last of it. We finally got to the loyalty question. Sure enough, when I asked him about his loyalty he immediately concluded I was talking about "Bill and Hillary," as almost all Clinton staffers did. Bush staffers understood this question to be about loyalty to the United States and the Constitution. *They* had it right.

"No, Mr. Linew, this isn't about your loyalty to the president and the first lady. That's taken for granted, or they wouldn't have hired you in the first place. I'm asking you about your loyalty to your country, the flag, the Constitution. . . ."

"Oh yeah. The country. Sure."

Mr. Linew was shown the door. Whenever Dennis and I saw Mr. Linew—we called him "the scientist"—in the hallway, he would glare at us, despite the supposed mellowing effects of his experimentation.

A second example, whom I'll call Balls O'Leary, another composite, will serve to illustrate another well-represented type of Clinton staffer.

Balls was a middle-aged guy who had graduated from college in the early 1970s, and then basically "hung out," as he put it, for about a decade. Then he took a job on the Hill in one of the more liberal House or Senate committees, or maybe he worked for a public interest group, an environmental law firm, or a women's rights group.

Balls came up to my office. In the course of the interview, I asked him about an arrest in the 1970s for possession of an illegal substance. He said, "You know, man, that 'longhairs' like me got rousted all the time."

"Oh, you had long hair? That's it?"

"Yeah. That's it. You know, man, you cops didn't like people with long hair in those days."

"Well," I thought, "I guess he's got me there." It's true; as a young FBI agent, I really *didn't* like guys with long hair because they were usually the violent felons I was trying to track down. And a lot of them smelled bad.

"But what about your *arrest?* Tell me about it."

He explained that he was pulled over by a redneck cop (in a Northern state—how was that possible?), and the cop pulled him over only because he had long hair. And then the cop made an illegal search of his car and found (of course!) *somebody else's* marijuana. He was arrested, and the cop did not advise him of his rights! Can you imagine that?

So there it was. I wrote it all down and sent it in to my headquarters. At about the same time, an agent was interviewing O'Leary's ex-wife about this "victim of police brutality." She had quite a different story. According to her, Balls was really a "head," a serious user of any and all kinds of drugs. On top of that, he was an alcoholic. *On top of that,* he used to beat the snot out of her on a regular basis. Others we interviewed echoed his ex-wife's claims.

I received these additional reports and, I admit, I wasn't surprised by what I read. After more than twenty years in the FBI, I was pretty good at sizing people up, and I *knew* that Balls had more strikes against him than just long hair. I called him up and told him to come to my office immediately. He meekly complied.

He came in and sat down. "What's up? What's wrong?"

Nothing much, just lying to an FBI agent, which is a federal felony, for openers. I began, "Look, ah, we have some real problems with what you told me last time, Balls. We've talked to quite a number of your former associates. They claim you had a real history of substance abuse and that you were an alcoholic. Did you use marijuana on a regular basis? Did you use cocaine, LSD, mushrooms, speed, whatever you could get your hands on, as these former friends of yours have claimed?"

Balls was red-faced. "I cannot believe this. This is so, so, so kafkaesque!"

Nevertheless, I was able to extract the required confession out of Balls without electrodes or rubber hoses, but by that point, I was pretty sure that he would be at the White House on the day that I retired anyway. You know what? He was.

Another composite, I'll call him Willie, was a middle-aged fellow and a mid- to high-level staffer who also had a long history of illegal drug use. Nothing on the scale of Mr. Linew or Balls O'Leary, but his use was just a little more recent. "Like, you know, during the campaign." He was high enough on the food chain to have his own office. I interviewed him there.

I found the same perpetual smirk that told me that he was "in the know" about the fix being in on the FBI investigations. No matter what we found, *he* was one of the chosen and would be rubber-stamped by the Counsel's Office for even the most sensitive post with access to classified material. I came to the section about drugs and noted that he had listed use in late summer of 1992.

"Well, Willie, I see we have some recent marijuana use here. What about it?"

"Yeah, sure. We were on the campaign, you know, and like, some friends of mine had tickets to a rock concert, you know? They invited me along, and, you know, they told me that they, like, knew the band well. We had front-row seats. At a break in the concert, the band leader leaned down and invited us up to his hotel room, you know, like after the concert and everything? We went up there, and there was the band, and some others sitting around a bong pipe. What was I supposed to do, man?"

It was not my place to lecture a man in his thirties working for the then-governor of Arkansas about all the reasons why he might have excused himself from that room. If he didn't understand the reasons, and he clearly didn't, then what could I possibly tell him? I took notes of what he said. I finished the rest of the interview, and he saw me to the door. Then he said something I will never forget.

"The things we'll be able to tell our grandchildren!" I thought he was talking about working in the White House for the president of the United States.

He said, "Just think, I'll be able to tell my grandchildren that I smoked pot with the Great Whatever Band!"

The White House staff *did* meet some standards. They met the standards that the Clintons set. If those standards were low, if they reflected the morality of the counterculture, then the Clintons are the only ones who can be blamed.

This was proven to me, beyond a reasonable doubt, by the individuals Hillary chose to run the background adjudication process of the Counsel's Office—Bill Kennedy, Craig Livingstone, and their respective staffs.

Associate Counsel Bill Kennedy was responsible for keeping persons of questionable character away from the White House. But as a gatekeeper, he wasn't terribly strict. For one thing, he didn't seem to regard serious drug abuse as a security risk. In one case Kennedy summoned George Saunders to his office. He told Saunders that during a background investigation a staffer had admitted to serious illegal drug use over an extended period, including recently.

Kennedy asked George how he would approach the case. If he had to decide whether to keep or reject the staffer, what would he do? George said he would get him out of the complex, *immediately.*

Kennedy was surprised. Why should the staffer be denied access to the White House or a security clearance? Saunders pointed out that the staffer was not some "kid" who had been experimenting in college. He was a middle-aged man who should have known better. The drugs in question were hard drugs, not just marijuana.

Kennedy thanked Saunders and said he wouldn't deny the staffer access or clearance. "I can hardly fire somebody for being honest to the FBI now, can I?" This was probably a "test," and if it was, George obviously failed it. After that, George's participation in the security program was greatly curtailed. The staffer, by the way, is still on board.

Need another example? On 27 September 1993 Craig Livingstone called me to discuss the new student interns. One intern working in the security office had expressed an interest in becoming an FBI agent. She had attended the briefing I'd given and was interested in learning more about the job.

Craig wanted me to know that he had been very "firm" with her about not wasting the FBI's time. "Gary, I told her that she needed to understand that the FBI and the Drug Enforcement Administration (DEA) and other such agencies are very 'straight' and would require full disclosure about her background, including a polygraph.

I told her that she could not hide her past. *I mean, it isn't like the White House, where you can use drugs before, and skate past other indiscretions, and still work here."*

I hung up the phone and stared out the window. There it was. The MHT.

Incidents like these convinced me that word had trickled down to the Clinton staff that the system was rigged, and it didn't matter if we found their paperwork to be incomplete, illegible, or downright fraudulent. They knew the FBI and Secret Service agents were just paper tigers. I didn't know it in the beginning, but they knew it, and they laughed at us.

Yes, a few token staffers were fired—mostly for financial problems we discovered in their backgrounds. But these were the little people, the secretaries and clerks. The big fish remained in place, and *they* were the ones who were the most worrisome. *They* were the ones who most often posed a clear and present danger to the security of the White House—and, from our perspective—to *national* security.

In November 1993 I met with Congressman Charles Rangel of Harlem, New York. One of his staffers who had worked on the Select Committee on Drugs was moving over to the Office of National Drug Control Policy. Congressman Rangel had known and supervised this staffer for years and was a key interview in my FBI SPIN.

Congressman Rangel arrived just a few minutes late but was apologetic and made an effort to make me feel at ease. He was friendly, warm, and seemed sincere. While I was waiting for the congressman I had some conversations with his polite and friendly staff, and I thought to myself how much more welcoming they were than the Clinton staff.

Congressman Rangel had a reputation for being very liberal, and the very "liberal" liberals I had met and interviewed usually treated FBI agents with suspicion, if not hostility. But Congressman Rangel was different.

"Well, what brings the FBI down here today? Good to see you," Congressman Rangel said, extending a big hand for a firm handshake. He had a twinkle in his eye and no sign of any clintonesque hostility.

I explained my mission, and we got down to business. I asked my questions, and he gave me good, honest answers. I thought as I sat there, "Man, did I make the right decision to spend more time on Capitol Hill and away from the Clinton White House." Congressman Rangel was helpful and professional. This was the way my job was supposed to work—and *had* worked in the Bush administration.

"Gary—do you mind if I call you Gary?—how do you like your new FBI director?"

"I'm very hopeful, Congressman. He seems like a decent and intelligent man. Best of all, he's a former agent, and I think that experience will serve him and us well, sir."

"Louis Freeh wasted no time getting up here to pay a courtesy visit. And I told him that I wanted to see the FBI maintain its very strong presence in the drug war, what's left of the drug war since Bill Clinton got hold of it. Clinton called me to let me know he was bringing 'Out of Town Brown' from New York to serve as his drug czar. That's before he gutted the drug czar's Office, of course. I said, 'Bill, what in the world are you doing to me? I got kids getting shot by kids, and you're spending all of your time on NAFTA, gays in the military, and now you're doing this, hiring a lightweight for a heavy-duty job!' And he says to me, 'Charlie, you're talking about apples and oranges,' and I said, 'No, Mr. President, I'm talking about oranges and oranges! All of these yuppie college kids and Wall Street types are having their nose candy, keeping the cocaine flowing right into the inner city where it's turned into cheap crack. The damn rich get to have their recreational drugs while my people die in the streets, and in the meantime, you want to raise the quality of life in Mexico and stick me with 'Out of Town Brown'?' "

The congressman and I had a long talk about drugs and crime, and it was clear to me that he was very concerned, knowledgeable, and astute. He didn't believe in playing games with drug smugglers, sending them to treatment programs or halfway houses. He thought they belonged in the slammer, period.

Our talk continued. "Gary, did you know that Janet Reno was supposed to be the drug czar, but when the president and Hillary botched up the AG appointments, they had to switch Reno over to Justice? She's all for the drug court concept, you know: 'rehabilitation,' without punishment or a criminal record. It's nonsense!"

"Congressman Rangel, sir, can you tell me how you know that—about Janet Reno being drug czar?" That was quite a promotion, I thought, from drug czar to AG. It might explain why she took the unprecedented step of firing all U.S. attorneys shortly after her appointment. She wouldn't want to be shown up by U.S. attorneys more aggressive than she was—not to mention that it would slow down investigations into Democratic Congressman Dan Rostenkowski, point man for Hillary's health care plan, and into Whitewater and other Little Rock mysteries.

"Sure I can. The president told me that. And when he moved Janet Reno to AG and brought in Lee Brown as drug czar, I said, 'Mr. President, I think you are making a big mistake. Lee Brown didn't do anything when he was up in New York, and he ain't gonna do anything down here.' "

I learned Congressman Rangel had a background in law enforcement, and that gave us more to talk about. By this time, the staff was bobbing heads in and out of his office, signaling Congressman Rangel that his schedule was stacking up. He walked me to the door.

"Gary, I've enjoyed talking to you, and you know what? From what you've told me about your job here and at the White House, I think you have the best job in the FBI. In fact, Aldrich, you got the best job I ever heard of, next to mine, of course!"

I thanked him, and as I walked away I thought, "Congressman Rangel, I used to think so too."

On 9 December 1993 I met Lee Brown, the new director of the Office of National Drug Control Policy (ONDCP). By the time I met him, ONDCP had been slashed by David Watkins to one-quarter of its former size.

The Clintons had changed the direction of the drug war from prevention and prosecution to treating drug abuse as a mental disorder. By the time I met Lee Brown, article after article had appeared in magazines and newspapers suggesting the Clintons were sufficiently "soft" on drugs that they might consider legalizing them. But when Surgeon General Joycelyn Elders broached the idea, coincident with her son's arrest on serious drug charges in Arkansas, the administration was stung by the national backlash.

Elders drew back, and the idea of legalizing drugs was effectively retired—at least until a second term. I was curious about what Director Brown would say about Elders and her theory.

I asked him questions about the investigation that had brought me there, and then he opened the door by asking me what I thought of Louis Freeh, the new director of the FBI, and about changes at the

FBI, and soon the conversation drifted into the issues related to drugs, as I knew it would. I asked, "What do you think of the surgeon general's comments on legalizing drugs?"

"I'm very unhappy with what she said. She should stick to her business and leave the matter of drugs to me. I think she did a lot of damage, and she should keep her personal ideas to herself. If she doesn't learn soon, she'll be looking for a job. By the way, I just met with Freeh, and I think he'll do a good job on drug control."

I was curious to know what Director Brown thought about Congressman Rangel. I asked, "Did you see the debate between Congressman Rangel and William F. Buckley on *MacNeil-Lehrer* the other night?"

"No, I didn't catch it. What did they say?"

"Congressman Rangel criticized the administration, saying it was inactive in the war on drugs and making things worse."

"Ah, Charlie Rangel. He thinks he's still running a drug committee over on the Hill. He hasn't figured out that that's in the past. He's made it his life's work, his agenda," Brown said with undisguised derision.

Under Brown's leadership the ONDCP's mission shifted from stopping the flow of drugs and locking up the smugglers to putting people who frequently didn't want to kick drugs into drug treatment programs—with predictable, unsatisfactory results. Drug abuse by young people jumped dramatically during the first years of the Clinton administration, no doubt, in part, because the "users," the "heads," were now running the bully pulpit. They were in domestic policy positions in the Clinton administration. There was even one charter member of the National Organization for the Reform of Marijuana Laws, or NORML, working in the White House, and this staffer (no volunteer, but a federal employee) claimed to be a close, personal friend of Hillary Rodham Clinton.

Nobody ever asked Hillary if she had smoked dope or if she had ever "inhaled," but Hillary was running the entire domestic policy machine at the White House. So, under the circumstances, why was it so important to know if *Bill* inhaled?

While for me, the war on drugs and fighting crime were matters of law enforcement, for the Clinton administration, it seemed a matter of politics.

One day I received a call from Jack Quinn, Vice President Gore's new chief of staff. Quinn is now counsel to the president, having moved steadily up as vacancies have occurred.

Quinn and I had talked several times of my interest in stemming the tide of violent crime. He knew I was interested in doing anything I could to assist in this effort, including sharing my thoughts with the Domestic Policy people in the Clinton administration who would be in a position to influence the administration's stance on crime, and what to do about it.

Of course, I had explained to Quinn, "I am just one FBI special agent, and I don't speak for the agency, but if there is anything I can tell you about my experiences with the Criminal Justice System, I'd be happy to." After all, twenty years of chasing crooks and doing a pretty good job of it was worth something, wasn't it?

Quinn told me that he had sent a memo over to Carol Rasco, assistant to the president for Domestic Policy, and she had agreed that I should talk to the administration's crime expert, Jose Cerda, a senior policy analyst.

Now I knew that Jose Cerda was the brother of Clarissa (I'm not a secretary) Cerda, the Watkins deputy who had barked at me that first day after the inauguration, but I couldn't hold that against him.

So I skipped lunch and met the Clintons' twenty-seven-year-old *senior* crime policy analyst. Oh, he was well educated—at Harvard Law School—but how did he get to be the administration's crime czar? It turned out that his only experience with law enforcement was as the Clinton campaign's political liaison with law enforcement groups, and as a campaign adviser on crime policy. Oh yeah, and he had "a cousin in Chicago who's a cop."

We talked for a while, and then he gave me the Clinton smirk. "Between you and me, during the campaign we realized that Clinton's media reputation for being 'tough on crime' was an absolute gift. And, man, we didn't look a gift horse in the mouth! Only, we were scared. We kept waiting for the Bush campaign to drop the 'Crime Bomb' on Clinton, because we felt vulnerable. If they opened the record, they could have blown us away on crime. But it never happened."

He was right. I went back and counted President Bush's campaign speeches. Of the hundreds he made, his advisors had given him a grand total of *two* on the subject of crime, and neither one of them went after Clinton's record—and you didn't have to look hard to find holes in it.

For example, Governor Clinton had given a pardon to his good friend Dan Lasater, a convicted drug smuggler and the person who supplied the president's half brother Roger with cocaine. President Clinton had brought Patsy Thomasson, Lasater's business partner, to the White House to be his director of Management and Administration, and a special advisor to the president. These were very strong signals about where this president stood on the issue of illegal drugs.

"Look, Jose. I've been in this business a long time. I am telling you that people are absolutely fed up with crime, especially violent crime. And from my experience, I know there is only one way to get control of the situation—and that's to lock them up and throw away the key."

"Well, Gary, you gotta understand one thing about the Clinton administration. We're a house divided about what to do about crime. Some say, lock 'em up. Some say, give them more help when they're young. The 'root causes' people are winning the argument here."

We finished up our talk, and made plans to talk again, after the selection of a new FBI director. Sessions was just about finished, but he was the only one who didn't seem to know it.

Before I left, Cerda gave me a prediction: "The Republicans have always owned this 'tough on crime' issue, Gary. But we're going after it, and we're going to take it away from them. Watch and see."

I didn't care who "owned" the issue. As a professional in law enforcement, I just wanted something done on the issue I cared about most. But after Vince Foster's death, I stopped participating in crime discussions at the Clinton White House. Instead, I avoided any issue not directly related to background investigations. I could see big trouble ahead, and I didn't want to have any part of it. Many of my permanent staff buddies were taking identical positions. We climbed into our foxholes, hunkered down, tightened the straps on our helmets, and waited for the "incoming."

One day in early March 1993, I walked into the Office of Presidential Scheduling to talk to Mike Lafrano about a background investigation. He had been given the deputy slot. His office had the new Clinton staff look. The office walls were bare, partially unpacked cardboard boxes were spread haphazardly on the floor. On the filing cabinet sat a motorcycle helmet. Half-empty coffee cups were strewn about. The place looked like a college dorm room.

Mike Lafrano was looking right at me and was talking to me, but his words made no sense at all. He waved at me while he talked, and I wondered if he had gone crazy. I knew scheduling the president could be stressful, but . . .

Of course, he wasn't talking to me at all. He was wearing a miniature headset, like a telephone operator might wear, and he was speaking to someone somewhere about an upcoming presidential visit. I gestured an offer to leave, inasmuch as he clearly was not ready to talk to me. I was annoyed that I'd been sent into his office without being told he was on the phone. But Lafrano indicated I should stay.

My meeting with Mike Lafrano was short and to the point. He was a Clinton loyalist, of course, but even Mike Lafrano reached his limit. On 29 September 1993 he called me and asked if I remembered him. Sure I did.

"Gary, do you mind if I ask you a question? How do you FBI guys do your jobs here in the White House?"

"Well, Mike, ah, you know, we just call folks and line up interviews, and. . . ."

Mike interrupted, "No, no. I'm asking you how you can clear people through the security system when there *are* no standards."

"What are you trying to say, Mike?"

"Gary, I'm telling you, I know a lot of these people, and I cannot believe that they are here, in the White House. Don't you people have any standards at all?"

When I felt like Mike Lafrano, that the Clinton administration had thrown every standard to the wind, I did what I could to get away from the White House, to fulfill one of my other FBI responsibilities. One of these was brushing up on my marksmanship.

FBI agents were required to train in the use of firearms several times a year, and I always looked forward to a day at our training facility at the Marine Base in Quantico, Virginia. It was a chance to get outside, get some fresh air, and visit with agents I hadn't seen for a while.

We were well into the new Clinton administration, and we knew we had a problem on our hands. The agents who conducted the SPIN investigations were the first to see the disturbing trends and patterns of the new administration.

Next to see the problems were the analysts at FBI headquarters who received the reports and saw the character flaws we were unearthing: drugs, bizarre sexual behavior, failure to pay taxes, failure to honor financial obligations, severe credit problems, bankruptcy, civil suits, liens, loan defaults, failure to repay federally funded student loans. There was a long list of character issues.

Of course, drug use stood out, mostly because it was blatant, and there was a pattern of serious long-term and recent use.

"Lifestyle" was also an issue that we had to address, because homosexuals were now present in the White House in large numbers. This created special problems for our background investigations, because we were still required to ask if a person was homosexual and investigate those who lied about it. Did the Clintons care if there was a potential for blackmail? It was hard to think they did, especially after having made "gays in the military" their first big policy fight. And there were certainly plenty of homosexuals in the White House who flaunted, rather than tried to hide, their sexual persuasion. I remember walking out my door one day to see two men with identical ponytails, earrings, turtlenecks, tight-fitting jeans, and jean jackets, holding hands. And it wasn't that unusual a sight.

In the Bush administration, candidate-staffers were so well scrubbed, we were virtually reduced to asking questions like, "Did you actually *see* him take the pen?" Now we were being asked to look the other way when we found serious character issues that would previously have meant immediate dismissal.

During a break in target shooting, some of the SPIN agents confronted me. "What the hell is going on at the White House, Gary?"

"Look, Joe, don't ask me. I've never seen anything like it."

"Are you *sure* you haven't seen these people before? Think about it," said an agent who had worked for years in foreign counterintelligence. " 'Kill the pigs.' 'Ho, Ho, Ho Chi Minh, the Viet Cong are gonna win.' That's who they are, Gary. They're the people we used to arrest."

I remember it was a chilly day. The army fatigue jacket had been borrowed from the rack at the Quantico training facility where we had received our briefing the night before. We were not yet full-fledged FBI agents, but it was an "all hands on deck" situation.

Black armband, red headband, army jacket—I looked just like a Vietnam vet against the war. I fit right in, and it was "right-on!" We had fanned out; none of us had a partner. We were to walk around and observe. If we overheard any plans to storm the White House or the Department of Justice, we were to get on a pay phone and report it immediately. I also had a camera, but I didn't stand out because lots of the protesters had brought cameras.

I collected a few tracts related to various radical splinter groups and listened as SDS leaders from around the country called for over-throwing the government, by violence if necessary. The Washington Mall was packed with half a million disaffected young people.

At one point I saw Park Police on horseback being assaulted by rocks and bottles. One rider was thrown to the ground. The young crowd cheered and shouted, "Off the pig! Off the pig!" They surged forward as a mob. The Park Police, a hundred-strong, surged right back.

That riot having been stemmed, I moved on down the Mall. There were Vietcong flags everywhere, and many protestors were carrying Chairman Mao's little red book, very popular reading on campuses in those days. The red headbands were not about war wounds. The headbands were the communists' way of identifying each other. Every so often I would stop and listen to the ranting.

Some of the rhetoric was about getting the U.S. out of Vietnam. Most was about "killing the pigs," "f--king Nixon," burning down the White House, storming the Pentagon, taking over the Depart-ment of Justice, and taking revenge on the hated FBI and CIA.

They shouted about the necessity of "offing" undercover FBI agents and informants. I raised my arm in a power salute with the others and chanted, "Right on, death to the scum FBI pigs!"

I came to a police barricade. There were D.C. police on one side of the line and a riotous crowd on the other. They were nearly toe to toe. The police looked scared but determined. Many were as young as I.

The rioters were in their faces, screaming obscenities, warning that their days were numbered. They would be drawn and quartered, hung from lamp posts, hunted down and shot in the head.

Rocks and bottles started flying from somewhere back in the crowd. The police retreated a step or two and donned gas masks. They pulled pins from tear gas canisters and tossed them high in the air. Other police loaded tear gas guns, ready for total assault.

Everyone started screaming, and the protesters bolted in all directions, howling with rage. The hatred I saw in the protesters' eyes was incredible. They wanted anarchy; they wanted violence; they wanted Washington in ruin, the Constitution in flames, simply because they believed the government was repressive, corrupt, and beyond repair.

Earlier that same day, in another time zone, five hundred protesters from Oxford led by William Jefferson Blythe Clinton marched on the American Embassy. Many carried little red books and Vietcong flags, shouting "Down with the United States" and "Ho, Ho, Ho Chi Minh!"

It was a coordinated effort, set up by the Vietnam Moratorium Committee, or VMC, an organization run by Sam Brown, a good friend of Bill Clinton. On this side of the Atlantic, I stood at a police barricade and hoped the officers would be able to return safely to their wives and children that night.

On the other side of the Atlantic, the future president of the United States was leading a march against his own country's embassy.

Chapter Eight

TRAVEL OFFICE TRAGEDY

Rules for Radicals: "An organizer working in and for an open society is in an ideological dilemma. To begin with, he does not have a fixed truth—truth to him is relative and changing. Everything to him is relative and changing. He is a political relativist."

George Washington's Rules of Civility and Decent Behaviour: "Be not hasty to believe flying reports to the disparagement of any."

When I was being trained as a new agent at the FBI Academy at Quantico, Virginia, the instructors warned us about abusing our power. We had the power to arrest, the authority to shoot to kill, and the devastating power to investigate a person's past and current activities. The mere *existence* of an FBI investigation can lead to an individual's personal, professional, and financial destruction. An actual indictment is like dropping a house on someone.

FBI agents, at least senior ones, are well aware of this, and they use their power wisely. We have seen how businesses can go under, banks fail, marriages dissolve, and prosecutors become famous and defense attorneys become wealthy as a result of a single visit from an FBI agent.

Imagine, if you will, that the president of the United States and his spokesperson have announced that *you* are suspected of a criminal act and that he has ordered the FBI to solve the obvious crime that has been committed within the walls of the White House. Can you imag-

129

ine the impact that the president's allegation might have on your life? If the FBI has enormous power, what kind of turbo-boost to that power results when the president gives the orders and the encouragement?

That power was turned on seven good and innocent men in the White House Telegraph and Travel Office because the Clintons believed in the spoils system—stripping loyal employees of their jobs and giving those jobs to friends.

Billy Dale's window of vulnerability was that he paid foreign customs officials the "fees" they required to ensure that on presidential trips, the media's boxes and bags sped through customs without delay.

The nightmare scenario he was trying to avoid was having a president ready to sign a historic agreement in some foreign country, pen poised, waiting for the photo dogs stuck at the airport. Why the media didn't deal with this problem themselves is not known to me, but Billy took the fall for it.

Maybe that's why so many media giants, like Sam Donaldson, showed up to testify in Billy's defense. They knew what had really happened, and they felt sorry for Billy. So did I.

When Dennis heard that the Travel Office was under the microscope at the instigation of David Watkins and his assistant Catherine Cornelius, he went to Kennedy and told him about the Travel Office/media/customs delay problem. He told Kennedy that this less-than-savory arrangement was *not* a scheme to line the pockets of Travel Office personnel; it was a mixture of realpolitik and courtesy (to the media). But Kennedy and Cornelius had their orders to create some vacancies.

Hillary Clinton was pressuring her Counsel's Office and Watkins, who ran the Travel Office, to take action. "We need the slots," is how one memo recalls her words. The trick was how to open those "slots" without inviting the same sort of criticism that greeted the "meat cleavering" of the grandmothers in the Correspondence Office.

The Travel Office guys were good at what they did. They had been in the White House for decades. But, most of all, these guys were *loved* by the media. Why? Well, not only did they pay the "fees" demanded by the foreign customs officers, but they also got the media hotel rooms when officially there weren't any to be had and made sure that the media weren't left stranded by canceled flights or bungled hotel reservations or any other travel disasters normal people put up with. In short, the media were treated presidentially by Billy Dale's crew.

In my meeting with a very emotional Craig Livingstone on 11 August, he described a meeting attended by Watkins, Foster, Kennedy, and himself wherein he argued against involving the FBI to investigate rumors of suspicious activities in the Travel Office. There was no mention of missing monies or "gross mismanagement," which was eventually claimed by the White House as the reason for firing the seven.

Livingstone blamed David Watkins for the "stupid idea" of bringing in the FBI, but some of the others must have agreed with him. According to Livingstone, they knew of no evidence that would prove any illegal acts. The point was to force the FBI into an investigation that *might* discover wrongdoing *that took place during the Reagan and Bush administrations.* Then the Clintons could get rid of the seven, create the "slots" Hillary wanted, and leave the press without much room for protest. After all, who would defend seven assumed criminals investigated by the FBI? Bill and Hillary's good buddies, Mr. and Mrs. Harry Thomason, would then get the travel contracts, worth millions of dollars, and Catherine Cornelius, who was already complaining about Watkins's abusive behavior, could get a much better job in the administration, away from Watkins.

How had White Houses of the past handled internal problems, including fraud, corruption, and the like? Simple. With a very efficient and quiet Secret Service investigation. The Secret Service was good at these kinds of investigations, and more important, it was their jurisdiction, not the FBI's.

Why didn't they use the Secret Service then? Because Secret Service agents had been traveling with Billy Dale and his crew for years and had never seen even the slightest evidence of theft or fraud.

What else could the White House do? They could have called the SPIN Unit at FBI headquarters and ordered a review of the background investigations of the Travel Office, focusing on "lifestyle" issues related to credit and living within one's means.

In the Bush administration, I had handled a number of such cases, which were accelerations of routine updates. The Counsel's Office would advise me of "additional information" or new allegations that I would then investigate. This was an appropriate, legal use of the FBI and an effective means of clearing up personnel problems.

The FBI SPIN would be submitted to the White House counsel, who would then decide a course of action. But all of this implied allegations that truly deserved investigation—something the Clinton administration didn't have.

Clinton's White House Counsel's Office certainly knew about accelerating routine background checks of staffers because they'd used it before—and, as in the Travel Office investigations, with ulterior motives.

I know, because early in the Clinton administration I began receiving requests for investigative updates on Residence staffers, years before such updates would normally occur.

I asked Craig Livingstone why, especially given that the administration showed so little interest in having anyone else—especially new political appointees—investigated in the normal fashion. "Have they done something wrong? Are they accused of anything?"

"No. We've just lost their files. So we need to update them."

"I know an easier way," I said. "Getting copies of the files isn't a problem. Just give me a list of the cases, and I'll have the FBI SPIN Unit send you a new copy." I'd done plenty of investigations of Residence staff, and I didn't remember any serious issues coming up. More than that, I had enough work to do without taking on entirely unnecessary new investigations.

Craig looked pained. "Uh, I'll think about it."

Later, I got a call from my supervisor telling me that the clock was running on requested update investigations of Residence staff and I had better meet my deadlines. So that was that.

The real reason for the updates, I later discovered, was not because the files had been lost, but because the Clintons considered the Residence staff "disloyal." The investigations were a punishment, and if we turned anything up, no matter how minor, long-serving staff would be history.

Bill Kennedy didn't ask me to update Billy Dale's file because he knew the odds were high I wouldn't find anything. After all, I'd already investigated Billy Dale in 1991.

Did the White House Counsel's Office make that investigation and other records related to Billy Dale available to his defense? The answer is "no." Steven Tabackman, Billy Dale's defense attorney, learned about the 1991 SPIN summary by accident, just before the trial.

That's why in the fall of 1995, when two special Department of Justice prosecutors brought Billy Dale to trial after a thirty-month investigation by numerous FBI agents, I, a now-*retired* FBI agent, was subpoenaed to testify as a character witness. As it turned out, there were so many character witnesses—including my buddy Dennis—that I was never called to the stand.

The single charge against Billy Dale was that he had mixed some press money with his own in a personal bank account. His explanation? It was easier to cash the checks that way.

I was standing in the hallway of the federal court building in downtown Washington, D.C., while Billy Dale's trial dragged on. I was talking to Dale's brother-in-law. He told me why he couldn't believe the government's charge that Billy stole more than $50,000.

"Mr. Aldrich, I remember one time that Billy brought his kids over to the house for a Friday night get-together. We were going to order some pizzas. I said, 'Billy, what kind of pizza do you want me to order for your kids?' Billy told me plain cheese, because he said his kids didn't like sausage or pepperoni.

"Well, when the pizzas arrived, some plain with just cheese and some with the sausage and pepperoni, Billy's kids tore into the pizzas with the meat and didn't even look at the plain ones. I said, 'Billy, I thought you said they didn't like anything but plain pizza.' Billy said, 'Well, the toppings cost two dollars extra. We get plain pizza at my house.' "

Would a guy like Billy steal $50,000? The jury didn't think so either. They returned an innocent verdict in less than two hours.

Sometime after the trial, I had a chance to get together with Dennis. Not only had Dennis testified against White House witnesses, he had testified against the evidence presented by his own agency. And he was now being subjected to minor harassment—such as anonymous letters sent to FBI headquarters lodging false accusations against him.

I asked Dennis if he thought his testimony had been important to Dale's acquittal. He didn't know; but he was under oath and told the truth. He testified that he'd seen Clinton staffers, volunteers, and persons wearing visitor's passes going through desks and file cabinets in the Travel Office, tossing documents into the trash that was headed for the shredder.

Dennis told me that late one night after the trial he walked into the Security Office and found Craig Livingstone alone at his desk, staring out the window.

"Oh, it's you! I'm surprised you'd show your face in here. I don't appreciate what you did for Billy Dale, Dennis. It wasn't helpful."

"Craig, I just came down here to clear the air. I was subpoenaed, I was under oath; I had to tell—hell, I *wanted* to tell—the truth. What did you expect me to do?"

"The truth, Dennis? Don't you know that truth is relative? Your testimony was *your* version of the truth. Truth is whatever you want it to be. And another thing, I don't ever want to discuss anything related to the FBI or background investigations with you ever again."

Chapter Nine

THE PRESIDENT'S GONE MISSING

Rules for Radicals: "All definitions of words, like everything else, are relative. Definition is to a major degree dependent upon your partisan position. Your leader is always flexible, he has pride in the dignity of his cause, he is unflinching, sincere, an ingenious tactician fighting the good fight. To the opposition he is unprincipled and will go whichever way the wind blows, his arrogance is masked by a fake humility, he is dogmatically stubborn, a hypocrite, unscrupulous and unethical, and he will do anything to win; he is leading the forces of evil. To one side he is a demigod, to the other a demagogue."

George Washington's Rules of Civility and Decent Behaviour: "Let thy ceremonies in courtesy be proper to the dignity of his place with who thou converses, for it is absurd to act the same with a clown and a prince."

One day in the West Wing, I met an interesting woman named Ruby Moy. Moy was working with Alexis Herman, the director of the Office of Public Liaison. I learned that Moy had worked at the White House before. She told me that she had worked in the Johnson administration for Johnson's chief of staff Walter Jenkins. That really got my interest, because Jenkins was the "father" of the FBI SPINs.

I was in my first year as an FBI employee when Walter Jenkins was arrested in the bathroom of the YMCA, having sex with a man he'd just picked up. As it turned out, Jenkins had been caught at least one other time in the same circumstances, but President Johnson claimed he didn't know anything about it.

135

President Johnson and his administration were already, in the summer of 1964, plagued by problems and scandals, not to mention the Vietnam War. He couldn't afford another scandal, especially one that involved a close, personal friend, the man he'd selected to run the White House.

President Johnson had a reputation for excess, especially on the personal side of his life. Many of his associates were not of the highest character, and President Johnson could not allow his loyalty to Jenkins, however strong, do further damage to his administration. He also knew that public confidence in his administration was at an all time low.

President Johnson needed a way to restore confidence in his administration, and fast. To rid the White House and the Executive Branch of any other "ticking personnel bombs" before they exploded in the media, he called J. Edgar Hoover, the FBI director, and ordered him to create a system to investigate the backgrounds of all White House employees and all others who would serve in major posts, such as agency directors and cabinet secretaries. If the FBI investigated the White House staff in the same manner it cleared its own employees, who would think of arguing about the quality of the White House staff?

But the image that the FBI "passed" or "cleared" anybody at the White House was an illusion, a neat trick created by President Johnson and his lawyers. While it was true that the FBI investigated White House staff members, the FBI was prohibited from coming to any final conclusions or recommendations about a candidate. Those conclusions and recommendations were to be made by the White House Counsel's Office to the president. The FBI just gathered the facts. It couldn't even *underline* or otherwise highlight the allegations. If the White House Counsel's Office wanted to ignore problems of character, they could, and the FBI couldn't do a thing about it. So really, one could argue that the weakness of the SPIN process was there from the beginning . . . it just took people like the Clintons to exploit it. And exploit it they did.

Much of the information in this chapter comes from investigations I've conducted since retiring from the FBI. It is included in more detail in the epilogue which is at the end of my background investigation into Bill and Hillary Clinton. It's the sort of information, based on sources who must remain anonymous, that would go into a raw FBI report, or that would help an FBI agent determine if a case is worth pursuing, or that would perhaps be used to obtain search warrants or subpoenas. It is by no means conclusive, but the information is deeply troubling in the issues it raises about the president's irresponsibility and callous disregard for national security.

I have been informed by a well-placed White House source that that there are times when the president, the leader of the free world, is missing—that is, cannot be located by staff—for hours at a time.

Previous presidents have, of course, maintained an unbreakable link twenty-four hours a day between themselves and their key advisers, especially at the Defense Department. But today, late at night, when calls are placed to the president, he sometimes cannot be found. There is a message system, and messages are left. But in a crisis, messages won't be good enough.

On several occasions, the president has called the phone switchboard and "raised hell," claiming that he was in the Residence, but that phone operators had not "tried hard enough" to reach him.

The Secret Service should know where the president is at all times. But this is no longer the case, I have been informed, because the first lady has booted them out of the Residence. Moreover, *she* does not always know where the president is, because the Clintons sleep in separate bedrooms.

All of this raises the question of, "If the president cannot be found, where is he?"

One answer has been given me by another source, a highly educated, well-trained, experienced investigator who is conducting his own investigation into the Clintons. It appears that the president is a frequent late-night visitor to the Marriott Hotel in downtown Washington, which has an underground parking garage with an elevator that allows guests to go to their rooms without passing through the lobby.

The president does not have a room in his name, and the guest who rents the room is known only to the management, though some information indicates this individual is female and may be a celebrity.

The president's driver is believed to be Bruce Lindsey, a high-level White House staffer and longtime friend of the president. The car is parked near the elevator. The driver waits in the car until the president returns, often hours later. The car usually arrives after midnight and sometimes leaves early in the morning, sometimes as late as 4:00 A.M.

I asked my informant about the president's Secret Service protection on these trips. And I should state here that if I had been informed that the president *was* protected, this testimony would take on lesser importance. But to my dismay, I was informed that the president's midnight travels are unaccompanied by *any* security agents— even at a distance.

How could this be? My informant himself investigated how Mr. Clinton may avoid Secret Service protection during these late-night liaisons.

My source notes a guard shack is located at each White House car gate. The gates are large and electrically driven. The guard opens the gate from within the booth using an electronic switching device.

The guards are usually facing out, to see if somebody is trying to get in to the White House. They are less concerned about cars leaving the White House. The guard observes exiting cars through a convex mirror that is about eighteen inches in diameter.

Seeing the car approach with the intention to exit, the guard opens the gate. When the car has gone by, the guard closes the gate. Rarely, if ever, does a guard attempt to identify who is leaving. Moreover, the tinted windows and curved roof lines of White House sedans make it nearly impossible to see into the back seats.

A sensitive White House source told my informant that the president makes his exit from the White House in the following manner. The president usually leaves late at night, sometimes after midnight. The president leaves alone through the West Executive Lobby exit in such a manner that to the uniformed guard at the desk it would appear the president is walking to the OEOB, which is across the parking lot from the West Wing.

In fact, once out of sight of the guard the president immediately veers left and enters a waiting White House sedan, usually driven by Bruce Lindsey. The president lies down on the back seat, covering himself with a blanket kept there for that purpose. Lindsey then drives the sedan north toward the electric car gate and exits, turning east on Pennsylvania, en route to the Marriott.

Not content with this information, I pursued it further with another source—a senior law enforcement officer with more than twenty years' service in a federal agency—who recently has been assigned to the White House.

I questioned this source about the ramifications of the president's jaunts in the event something were to happen to him while he was unguarded. I was told that the Secret Service had a procedure to account for such events and indeed to protect itself. Every time one of the members of the first family countermands efforts to guard him or her, an agent prepares a memo noting the event. The memo goes into a Secret Service file so that the agents, and the agency, are covered. It's called the CYA, or "cover your ass," file.

My source used the term "the first family" rather than simply "the president" because he says Hillary Clinton is as bad as the president. She has told her Secret Service Protective Detail agents in public to "Stay the f--k back, stay the f--k away from me! Don't come within ten yards of me, or else!" When the agents have tried to explain to the first lady that they cannot effectively guard her if they must remain so far away, her reply is, "Just f--king do as I say, okay?" The first lady has even bragged publicly, in her newspaper column, about evading the Secret Service to go on a joy ride.

This behavior may help explain why the Clinton administration appears to regard the Secret Service as the "enemy," in the same way that drug dealers are always on the lookout for "narcs."

I remember a conversation about the Secret Service I had with Craig Livingstone after Congress started sniffing around about the White House pass issue. Craig was clearly upset, "Who's leaking all this new sh-t to Congress? Do you know?"

"Leaking what, Craig?"

"You know, this pass stuff, and all that stuff." Livingstone and the Clinton crowd liked the word "stuff." They used the word "stuff" a lot.

"Well, Craig, it could be anyone. Have you considered it could be the media? After all, they see your people every day, walking in and out, back and forth. They would see the passes, or the absence of a pass. Most of them worked here during the last administration when things were done differently."

"Nah, it's not the press. It's one of you guys. Somebody in the Secret Service, probably."

"I'm not sure about that," I responded. "There are *hundreds* of permanent employees, aside from the FBI and Secret Service. It could be anyone or a number of people. I would guess there is more than one leak. But who knows?"

Craig said, "Well, I told your director this morning that I was sure it wasn't you or Dennis."

"Look, Craig, Dennis and I have but one wish, and one wish only, and that is that our name *never* be used in any sentence with any higher-up at FBI headquarters, *especially* the director. Don't even praise us, because that will just bring us unwanted attention. Neither one of us wants to be promoted; we like the way our assignments are set up now, and attention or awards just cause the other agents to get jealous. Understand? Would you do me that favor and not use my name when you speak to Director Freeh?"

"Hey, Gary, don't worry. I think it's that damn Secret Service again. They've had it in for me ever since I wrote that memo. They even refused to give me one of their pins to wear so that I could go with the president to events. I called Mack [McLarty] and told him about it, and he ordered the Protective Detail to issue me the pin but they wouldn't do it; they defied McLarty!"

"What memo?"

"Oh, you didn't hear about that? Your Secret Service buddies didn't tell you about that one? Right after the election we had some problems with their agents down in Little Rock. They didn't have a good attitude. Bill and Hillary were complaining about them. And McGaw was not showing proper *respect*. He should have flown down right away after the election to introduce himself to the Clintons and congratulate Bill, but he didn't."

Craig was speaking of John McGaw, former head of the Secret Service, and now head of Alcohol, Tobacco and Firearms (ATF). When the ATF director was forced to retire because of the failed Waco raid, McGaw was moved over to take his place and "clean things up" at ATF. I knew McGaw. He was a good man, a very professional, disciplined, smart man.

He and President Bush were always seen together. In fact, after the inauguration of Bill Clinton, McGaw went with President Bush to Kuwait on a victory visit of sorts. President Bush had made McGaw director of the Secret Service shortly before he was defeated.

I had never seen McGaw fail to show proper respect to the president. Craig couldn't be talking about the same man. "Maybe he was waiting for an invitation," I said.

"Nah, he was loyal to Bush," Craig retorted. "Anyway, I wrote this memo, this four-page memo, and I recommended that the Secret Service be dumped in favor of the FBI. I thought the FBI could do a better job of guarding the president. Someone got hold of the memo, leaked it to the Secret Service, and they went ballistic. They have been on my ass ever since."

He wanted to get rid of the Secret Service! Why not tear down the White House fences while they were at it? The Secret Service was devoted—and it was good. Secret Service agents were trained to throw themselves in front of the president and the first lady, take a bullet, die for them, even if the first couple detested them. I wasn't sure I'd be up for that.

It was true that the Secret Service agents I talked to had little respect for Craig. They called him "the Sheriff of Nottingham" or "the Mayor of the White House" behind his back. They felt he was into everything he wasn't supposed to be into and wasn't doing the job he was paid to do, which was process the SPINs to allow for the permanent passes. Instead, Craig was turning up at every function, directing them around, and scolding them for doing their jobs.

Craig was on a roll. "You remember when John McGaw was sent over to ATF? I had a piece of that action. I was sitting here watching CNN, and there was Bush over in Kuwait and right next to him was good old John McGaw, just like old times. That was crap! It was nothing more than pure disrespect for Bill Clinton. So when we sat down to decide what to do about ATF, I suggested that McGaw be punished for his disloyalty and sent to ATF. Then when we have ATF merged with the FBI, we'll have McGaw ride off into the sunset. First, he cleans up ATF's image, and then we *dump* him! We called him into the meeting and gave him his options. He had no choice; take ATF or hit the road, Jack."

No wonder Craig was having trouble with the Secret Service. The Clinton administration had been giving the Secret Service a hard time from day one.

So it's no surprise that the Secret Service came up with its CYA file. That file is now a very important national security document, for it would allow Congress, using its oversight authority, to document one of the most serious and irresponsible breaches of security in U.S. history. Nor would an investigation have to rely on this file alone. I asked one of my sources what would happen if even some of the information on these matters was aired publicly. He told me that, of course, the first thing that would happen is that a very large number of people would be fired as suspected leakers, since the Clintons would move to punish the innocent and guilty alike. But, he also told me, the *second* thing to happen would be a wholesale stampede by the fired staff and their supporters up to Congress "with the *rest* of the story," since the permanent staff "have about had it with the antics and poor manners of Bill and Hillary Clinton."

When I was in the White House, I heard enough stories to confirm that assessment. One day I got a call from a friend named Carol, who had worked in the Speechwriter's Research Office for the Bush administration.

Carol telephoned me about worrisome stories she was hearing from a friend inside the Clinton White House.

"Gary, I can hardly believe how nasty Bill Clinton is toward his staff!"

"What do you mean?"

"Well, the Filipino staff threatened to quit."

"What?"

"I'm serious." She mentioned the Filipino staffer who'd told her. That staffer was a good enough source for me.

There are about a dozen men who are from the Philippines, or whose parents were, who serve the president and vice president. As distinguished U.S. Navy personnel, they work in the OEOB and the West Wing, and they run the Navy Mess. They are part of the permanent staff and are renowned for their dedicated, discreet, intelligent, and loyal service. They are, of course, investigated by the military or by the FBI through the SPIN process. And they're proud of their positions. The Filipino stewards are a White House tradition, marking the long-standing friendship between the Philippines, the United States in general, and the U.S. Navy in particular. The positions are a badge of honor, and these staffers had trained for and looked forward to holding these positions. For them to "quit" was unthinkable.

I knew that the White House's prize French chef had walked. So had others in the kitchen staff, because of what they considered the outrageous demands and rude behavior of the Clintons—such as giving the staff an hour's notice for luncheons with numerous guests, and then throwing a fit if the food wasn't ready on time. In the chef's case, an additional factor was the president's preference for fried food over haute cuisine.

But the Filipino stewards resigning en masse was a different thing entirely—more like the Beefeaters threatening to leave the Tower of London or the Swiss Guards threatening to abandon the Vatican.

"Carol, what happened?"

After five years on the job as an FBI Agent, I was pleased to meet FBI Director Clarence Kelly at FBI Headquarters—1973.

Every FBI Agent is required to undergo regular firearms training—even when assigned to the White House. I am firing a high powered rifle with a scope for long distance effectiveness.

With Dennis Sculimbrene in the East Room of the White House during a Bush-era Christmas party.

Dennis presenting my FBI retirement award in August 1995. Dennis, a decorated Vietnam Veteran and career FBI agent, who had worked at the White House from Carter to Clinton, lived the FBI motto of fidelity, bravery, and integrity. Unwilling to compromise his principles, he retired with his head held high and his self-respect intact.

The celebrated gingerbread man. At first glance one wonders what this has to do with Hillary's theme, "An Artist's Interpretation of the Twelve Days of Christmas," until the five golden rings are discovered: his ear lobe, nose, nipple, belly button, and...

On a ladder hanging Hillary's ornaments—still in shock. Martha Stewart commented, "Gary, I'm going to make you famous with this interview." If she had only known what was going to happen later...

Displaying the "dangerous" Rush Limbaugh ornament. Hillary's social secretary said she checked each ornament twice. It's doubtful she saw this one. Needless to say, "Rush" did not go on the tree. Condoms were "okay," but a Rush ornament was strictly verboten.

Signing books.

With my wife Nina in Atlanta, appearing on the very popular Neal Boortz Show. Mr. Boortz had only two guests on his show in 1996. I was one.

Talk radio gave me a chance to refute the lies being pushed by the Clinton White House "Masters of Disaster," and their liberal media allies. *Unlimited Access* sold more than 500,000 copies. Truth really does win out.

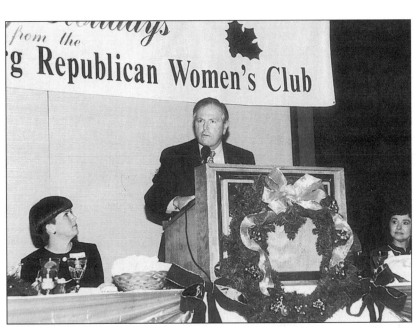

Speaking to the Charlotte-Mecklenburg Republican Women's Club in December 1996. Left to right, Raymoth Campbell, President of CMRWC; me; and Congresswoman Sue Myrick (R-NC).

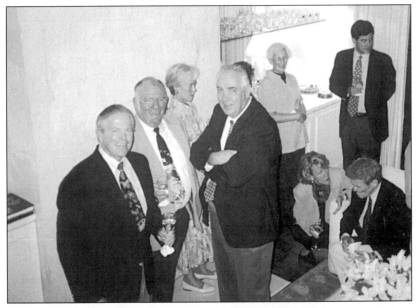

I was proud to defend the beleaguered Billy Dale and his colleagues from the Travel Office. I am with Billy Dale (right, arms crossed) and other former Bush staffers at a Christmas party in 1996.

At the gala celebration hosted by the Southeastern Legal Foundation. Here Speaker of the House Newt Gingrich poses for a photograph with me, my sister Karen, and wife Nina.

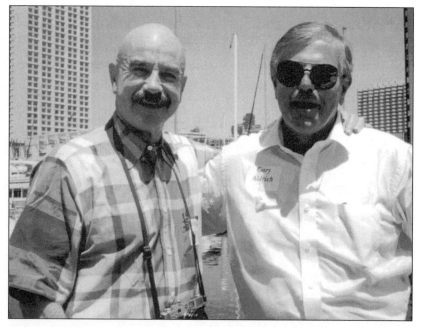

Unlimited Access was number one on virtually every bestseller list during the GOP presidential convention in San Diego, August 1996. I'm with G. Gordon Liddy, former FBI agent and popular talk show host.

"He's treated them like dirt, Gary. And they're not used to that. I heard that for the first few months he just ignored them."

I would have thought this odd, because Bill Clinton had struck me as gregarious to the point of being unpresidential. I once passed him in a White House hallway, and he nodded to me and said, "Hello, sir," as though he were *class* president and I was the school principal. For him to ignore people would be like him passing a basket of french fries and not trying to bury his face in it (as documented by Hunter S. Thompson)—almost unthinkable. But I had heard many similar stories about his coldness to permanent staff.

"What do you mean, he 'ignored' them?" I asked.

"Gary, he didn't even acknowledge they existed. It was as if they were just inanimate objects that took up space. So they did the only thing they could do under the circumstances. They glared at him. They pretended they didn't hear him when he called. They pretended they didn't understand him when he asked for things. You know, the usual drill—what anyone would do to punish a jerk. They played dumb. They brought him a Coke if he asked for a Pepsi, mustard instead of ketchup, chips instead of fries, that kind of thing. Can you picture that?"

Yes, I certainly could, and I had to chuckle. I could just imagine the scene. "I asked for chicken salad, not tuna, damn it! This is tuna!"

"Yes, Mr. President, *of course* you did. *Sorry,* Mr. President, sir. I'll get the correct sandwich right away, Mr. President." And as the little man in the white jacket turns away, a barely perceptible grin momentarily creases his face. I could just see it.

"So, what happened? Did they ask for a transfer?"

"No. Somebody with a brain got wind of what was happening, maybe Mark Gearan, and finally told the president that he was royally tweaking off the stewards. So he apologized to them, but, frankly, they didn't buy his apology. He said he was real sorry, but that he was really busy and had a lot on his mind. Like George Bush didn't? The stewards have seen presidents come and go. They know better. They know when they're respected."

What Carol told me about "the man" lined up with what I was hearing lately from Secret Service agents, Residence staff, and other permanent staff. Usually, Bill Clinton was not overtly abusive like Hillary, but he could appear just as haughty and arrogant. The Residence staff told me that Bill Clinton walked right by them every day and looked right through them as if they didn't exist. When he did speak to them, it was in tones they thought were insulting. They felt the Clintons—and their staffs—didn't appreciate the White House and didn't appreciate them, the ones who kept the White House running. What gave their complaints added weight was that the staff rarely, if ever, complained in the Reagan–Bush days.

The permanent staff was getting fed up with the President's behavior; so was I—even while I was still at the White House.

I remember one incident in particular. On 19 April 1993 I was working at the White House on some investigative reports, when my wife called and told me to turn on the television. I asked what channel. She said any channel.

I turned on the TV and watched as FBI agents in armored personnel carriers pushed in windows and walls and sprayed tear gas inside the Branch Davidian compound in Waco, Texas.

Smoke and flames burst out of the building. I knew there were children inside. I waited impatiently to see FBI agents lead them to safety. But there was no safe place. More than twenty children died that day.

As soon as the initial shock was over, I listened in disbelief as the White House and Janet Reno claimed we'd just witnessed a "mass suicide." That's not what it looked like to me.

On 23 April, four days after the burning of the Branch Davidian compound, I again listened to President Clinton try to explain to the nation why and how such a nightmare had occurred. He steered attention away from the White House, which had approved the plan of attack on cult leader David Koresh, and focused on the FBI for having developed the harebrained scheme in the first place. But knowing the FBI as I did, I was virtually certain that Janet Reno had been presented with a variety of options.

I was sitting in Deborah Coyle's office when the president walked around the corner.

"Well, Deborah, who's this? Hiya." President Clinton had a wide grin on his face, but I was still thinking about all those kids being burned to death.

"Hello, Mr. President. I'm Gary Aldrich, one of the two FBI agents assigned here at the White House."

"Well, FBI, huh? Howdja like the way I defended the FBI just now—did you hear the press conference I just gave?"

What was I supposed to say? That I had just about gagged when I heard him lay the entire mess at the FBI's door? "Mr. President, since you asked, I must say I'm just a little confused at the characterization of this as a mass suicide. I can't see how children can make a decision to commit suicide."

"Well, hmm, ah, well, these kids were badly abused. Reminds me of a similar circumstance in Roman times, when the forces of . . ."

Obviously, his knowledge of Roman history exceeded mine, but whether it was relevant or merely a verbal smoke screen is a pertinent question.

"Well, Agent Aldrich, I'm sure glad to meetcha. I've heard about you guys. You're doing a good job. Keep it up!"

"Yes sir, thank you, Mr. President." He walked on. Deborah was grinning.

"Deborah, does he do this often? You know, just walk around and talk to total strangers? How does he find the time?"

"Yes, Gary. I've worked for him for years, and he'll never change—he's always *on*."

Well, the president's "act," if that's what it was, was starting to wear thin on me.

Chapter Ten

SO WHAT?
(PART TWO)

Rules for Radicals: "Change means movement. Movement means friction. Only in the frictionless vacuum of a nonexistent abstract world can movement or change occur without that abrasive friction of conflict."

George Washington's Rules of Civility and Decent Behaviour: "Artificers and persons of low degree ought not to use many ceremonies to Lords or others of high degree, but respect and highly honor them; and those of high degree ought to treat them with affability and courtesy, without arrogance."

By the summer of 1993, almost three years to the day I first entered the White House, I went to my supervisor and threw my White House pass on his desk. I told him that I was disgusted and wanted out. I was the first FBI agent assigned to the White House who had ever asked to be transferred.

It was time to go while I could still look at myself in the mirror. I didn't want to become just another victim of the Clintons, used to suit their political agenda, used to torment the innocent, used to provide cover to the guilty. But the FBI would not let me leave the White House. The case load was too high. I was stuck, but I no longer had to investigate the Clinton political staff. I would be in charge of reinvestigating the permanent staff, and that job had always been a pleasure.

Our periodic inspection was just around the corner. Dennis learned through his friends at headquarters that he and I were to be targeted by the inspectors—blamed for the late cases. We were being set up as scapegoats. I pulled out all my old case logs and began to prepare my defense. Dennis did the same.

My accounting background came in handy whenever I needed to make charts, graphs, or schedules, and this time was no exception. I proved with my schedules that, from the very beginning of the Clinton administration straight through to the fall of 1993, the FBI SPIN requests had come in fits and starts with no apparent relationship to who was being investigated or how long the particular person had been inside the White House.

Even after the violent death of Vince Foster, which should have been the White House counsel's wake-up call, nothing had changed. After the forms that enabled the FBI to conduct an investigation were filled out, dated, and signed, they were sent somewhere to gather dust.

My study revealed that some forms that eventually ended up on my desk had been sitting somewhere for months for no apparent reason. Dennis and I were receiving many forms a full seven months after they had been filled out and signed. We could easily determine the extent of the delay from the dated signatures on the form.

In some cases, the date was scratched through with a pen, and a current date was penned in next to it, and I guess someone in the Counsel's Office thought that made it okay. The effect of these tardy submissions to the FBI was manifold. Six months is a long time in the life of a new White House employee. That time might include a change of residence and a change of office or agency within the Clinton administration. That made the cases more difficult to close.

Since initially no apparent thought was given by the Clintons to matching experience and education with particular job vacancies, there was a lot of reshuffling of White House jobs. In addition, more than a few people were already quitting.

The FBI had agreed to finish the cases within a specified time frame, but of course that agreement was based on the assumption that the forms would be turned in on time, complete and current. A lot of them were late, and most were neither complete nor current. Because additional information was needed to conduct a full investigation, it was necessary for Dennis and me to find the staffer under investigation and help him update the forms. This was "holding their hands" as far as I was concerned, and I resented having to do it.

What I gathered as evidence to protect myself was absolute proof of what I had seen all along. Of seventy-eight cases that I surveyed, sixty had been delayed by negligence on the part of the Counsel's Office. Of those sixty, forty-two of the staffers had in fact filled out their forms on or about 20 January 1993, the day of the inauguration.

The Counsel's Office held on to the forms as long as seven months, while these staffers—whose backgrounds were unknown to the Secret Service—wandered the hallways of the White House and the NSC, where piles of top secret documents were the rule, not the exception.

These "mystery guests" could and did wander out to the South Lawn and were within handshaking distance of the president, and no security officer or Secret Service agent knew who the hell they *really* were, beyond appearances—and that was a worrisome clue in itself.

The day finally came for the FBI inspector to review my cases. I walked into my appointment with my charts, graphs, and other documents. When he saw I was no pushover, he quickly backed off. I began to tell him of the serious problems that Dennis and I had documented and told him that the FBI was being used. I predicted that there would be more, not less, trouble ahead for the FBI. His response to my warning was, "I'm here to investigate your FBI field office and *your* work—not problems at the White House."

One day I met an interesting fellow named Billy Bert Shaddox, a former Navy and White House photographer and a friend of George Saunders. He shared our dismay about the Clinton administration.

"I came here after the inauguration to help the Photo Office get set up. But this administration is a mess. I've never seen one like it. They have no respect for the White House or for the presidency, or even for the *president*. They call him 'Bill,' for goodness sake! I call them 'kids in cutoffs.' They're a bunch of middle-aged hippies!"

Shaddox explained that he had tried to take some of them aside and explain where they were and what it all meant. But they didn't get it.

Shaddox indicated that the White House photographers were disgusted, too. "They're getting 'assignments' to go over to the OEOB and take pictures of somebody's birthday party and nonsense like that, and they don't like it. These people are paid government employees; they have regular, assigned duties—and here they are walking around taking pictures of Suzy's big day! Geez, don't they know that kind of thing is an abuse? Government employees, government time, government cameras, government film, processing. Don't they know that it's the same as stealing?"

We talked about Shaddox's Navy detail days in the Johnson, Nixon, Ford, Carter, and Reagan White Houses as a photographer. "Gary, each of the administrations was different, but all at least seemed to have respect for the White House and for the presidency. Carter was casual, but these people are off the scale."

"What about Clinton himself? He likes to compare himself to JFK."

"No way is this president like JFK. More like Johnson, if you ask me. President Johnson was the crudest president I've known. And he was a womanizer, too. Johnson used to go out to his friend's house to play poker, or at least that's what he said. His poker story was just cover for what he was really doing, which was meeting lady friends. He'd arrive, and the babes would be there, waiting.

"Johnson was *very* crude. He had no restraint at all. He didn't care where he was, or who saw him, when he decided to relieve himself. He'd just whip 'er out and let 'er go. The Secret Service guys told me that if he got the urge outside the Oval Office, he wouldn't even bother to hold it until he got to the Residence. If nature called, he would just stop at the Rose Garden, walk over to the bushes, and let 'er rip.

"One of the agents told me about when Johnson was waving goodbye to some guests. He could still see their car taillights when Johnson unzipped and whipped old Charlie out. There was a strong wind and it blew his stream all over the leg of the Secret Service agent standing next to him. The agent jumped back, swearing, 'Mr. President, you're peeing on my leg, sir!' Johnson said, 'Son, that's a president's prerogative.' "

Shaddox swore he'd heard that story from the offended agent. According to Shaddox, Johnson also had a drinking problem. "He had a Filipino steward who had the key to a locked liquor cabinet in the Oval Office. Johnson would go over and make two strong drinks. After the second, the steward would lock the cabinet and put the key on a chain he kept around his neck. He was instructed by Johnson to refuse to give up the key, no matter what."

Shaddox would not go so far as to say that he thought Clinton had a drinking problem, but Clinton's constant rosy glow seemed to be caused by something more than just a simple allergy. We agreed that President Clinton had a classic drinking man's face.

George Saunders, the man without a real job, invited me to the Navy Mess in the West Wing to have lunch. It was Mexican day, and he had nachos.

Sitting across from us was Rahm Emanuel, who was notorious for his temper tantrums and garbage mouth. Trained as a ballet dancer, he spent a lot of time, according to Elizabeth Drew in her book *On the Edge*, "gliding" in and out of Stephanopoulos's office. He was also one of the president's senior advisors but could never be accused of knocking himself out in the appearance department. Today, a normal work day in the White House, he was wearing casual slacks, a polo shirt, no jacket, no tie. President Clinton was in Denver meeting the Pope.

"Gary," Saunders said, "I'm doing nothing at all. My contract runs out the end of this month, and I don't think it'll be renewed. I'm just window dressing around here, to make it look like they have a security program; that's all. There's really no one covering security at all. No one's allowed to. Craig Livingstone means well. I know he does. He tries to help, but he's up against it with this Counsel's Office."

"Yeah, I know," I said, and I wondered whether Craig was counting the days like we were.

But Congress was beginning to smell a rat in the White House. On 19 August 1993 in response to an inquiry from Congressman Frank Wolf of the House Appropriations Committee, which oversees the budget for the White House, Mack McLarty wrote, "To our knowledge, there have been no material changes in security procedures at the White House when compared to those of previous administrations."

This was absolute nonsense, of course. There had been wholesale change, and McLarty knew it, or Nussbaum, Foster, Kennedy, and others had lied to him.

Congressman Wolf responded with a letter dated 22 September 1993 that said, in part, "I also understand that many of the staff and volunteers continue to hold 'temporary' passes with many clearances pending and being held in the White House Counsel's Office for further review. I am told that information on many individuals is of a nature that would in previous administrations make them ineligible for clearance. What is the status of these pending clearances?"

But even with Congress's growing interest in the suspected breakdown of White House security, nothing happened, nothing changed. Hundreds of staff roamed far and wide, their background investigations sitting in a pile in a corner of Bill Kennedy's office. Bill and Hillary Clinton, their daughter, national security, and the entire senior staff (for that matter *all* the staff), were subjected to continuing and unreasonable risk as a result of the failed security program.

Persons with the little "t" passes were still driving in, entering with boxes and briefcases, able to avoid the magnetometer and able to avoid body and briefcase searches, even after Vince Foster's tragedy had shown how vulnerable we were.

Of course, the Secret Service had insisted on tight security. They always did. They didn't *want* to allow persons without permanent passes to come and go without being searched. But the Clintons felt that the Secret Service's searches were a "hassle" and unnecessary and just another way for the "disloyal" Secret Service agents to "bug" the Clintons and their friends. So they ordered the Secret Service to modify their security program to fit the petulant and immature demands of the Clinton staff, and there wasn't a damn thing that could be done about it.

I was invited to lunch with Phil Larson. He had been gone from the White House for nine months, and I heard through the grapevine that he was working for Congressman William Clinger on the Government Operations Subcommittee, Minority Staff. In essence, Larson was an investigator for the committee that had oversight responsibilities over the White House.

"Gary, I'm receiving lots of calls from friends of mine down at the White House, and what I'm hearing disturbs me. I just want to make you aware that the Oversight Committee is probably going to look into the White House security problems and the White House pass situation. We may ask GAO to investigate, and that might involve the FBI. I'm telling you this as a friend. Can you confirm that all the Clinton people are walking around without a pass?"

"No, I can't. I can't say that I've looked at *every* person's pass—those that bother to wear them—to see if they have the little 't' or have graduated to a permanent pass. But I can tell you it's a problem."

"According to what I've heard, the Personnel Office is another mess, with lots of people working for months without a presidential appointment or any other documentation that would justify paying them."

I listened to Phil's other concerns. Obviously, he had many sources, but I told him I couldn't comment further.

We parted company, with Phil warning me that Congress was probably going to look into the Clinton administration's handling of background investigations, passes, and other matters that might have an effect on me.

I thanked him for the information and went to the House of Representatives, where I was spending much of each day. It was a relief to go to the House, which was much better organized than the dysfunctional Clinton White House. I still had to go to the White House every day for administrative reasons, and that was a real drag. In fact, I thought that would make a good bumper sticker: "Working in the Clinton White House is a real drag."

I ran into a Secret Service buddy who confirmed that Congress was asking questions about the conduct of the Counsel's Office with regard to White House passes and security clearances. A congressman had apparently sent a letter to Nussbaum asking him to respond to allegations that the White House security program—and the quality of White House staff—had taken a nose-dive.

The Secret Service, my friend told me, would argue, if challenged by Nussbaum, that suitability was the counsel's problem, while the Secret Service was focused on the physical protection of the president. But I wondered. Who was supposed to grant security clearances and maintain national security? Was there *no one* at the gate?

The next day, I ran into some more friends from the Secret Service. We talked for a few minutes. They were very concerned, as I was, about security lapses.

"I wonder if the Department of Justice or Congress knows that what this administration is doing is illegal?" asked one. "To me, it's a clear violation of national security, established standards of conduct, and Executive Orders of the president."

I said, "There are bigger issues here than just what the Department of Justice or Congress thinks about all of this. This conscious downplaying of standards sets legal precedents. Now that they've allowed just about anyone in the White House, they may have no legal means to get rid of real risks. After all, how can they fire someone for serious character problems, when all anyone would have to do is trot out about twenty-five of the president's 'finest' with problems just as bad? That would be about it. They think that standards are set up by 'straights' like us, but they're for the protection of the presidency—and these Clintons are destroying that protection. They're destroying the office by bringing in people who scurry if you shine any light on them." I was obviously nearing the end of my tether. I wouldn't normally have spoken like this.

Another agent struck a lighter tone. "They sure like it loose over there. I wonder why?"

I didn't wonder any more. I knew.

On 9 September 1993 the Clinton administration's long-awaited and highly touted "Reinventing Government" report was released. The project was organized by Vice President Gore. A separate office had been established for it and millions of dollars were spent to produce this 168-page booklet.

The report interested me because it included a plan to merge the FBI, the ATF, and the DEA, something that had been considered and studied and rejected before. Now here it was again.

It took me a while to find the issues that interested me because the booklet wasn't indexed and had no table of contents. My eyes glossed over some of the booklet's exciting advice: "Hold all federal employees accountable for results," "Eliminate what we don't need," and "Streamline background investigations for federal employees." This was interesting. I read on: "The current method of completing background investigations is time-consuming and inefficient."

Yeah, I thought, they sure are inefficient if nobody is reading them.

Dennis and I met Anthony Marceca, a special agent from the Criminal Investigative Division of the U.S. Army, detailed to the Security Office to assist Craig Livingstone.

He explained that his job was to improve the efficiency of the Security Office. But within a few minutes I wondered if he didn't have another possible assignment.

Marceca made openly disparaging remarks about Craig and his operation, which made me suspicious that he was trying to draw us out. Were we the ones blabbing about the Counsel's Office?

"The girls in the Counsel's Security Office are sloppy in their work," he said. "And they're way behind. There's no system. They're completely disorganized."

That sounded like blame-shifting to me, and I wondered whether some more innocent heads were being set up to roll.

Dennis and I just listened. After he left, we laughed. Had Craig sent Marceca to test us? If so, how stupid did Craig think we were? On the other hand, were *we* getting paranoid?

On 1 October 1993 I got my wish and was given a new assignment. I was fully prepared to admit that the Clinton administration had finally "won"; they had gotten to me, and I didn't want to be a party to the mock security program they wanted to run. All of the early attempts to make the best of it, to put a good face on it, came down to a feeling, finally, that the Clinton administration was a corrupt disaster, beyond redemption or repair.

My new assignment included conducting background investigations on House committee staff members and on staff appointed to new positions at the White House, an Executive Branch agency, or any position that required Senate confirmation.

The extensive caseload was just what I needed to keep my mind off the Clinton White House. Starting 1 October my routine would be to drive down to the White House, open the office, and sort through my messages and mail. I'd make a few calls, take care of some paperwork, and set up appointments with congressmen and staff.

Then I'd leave the White House, drive down to the Hill, and spend the rest of my day walking from appointment to appointment, through the Capitol building; the Cannon, Longworth, and Rayburn House Office Buildings; and sometimes the Annex, which was once home to the FBI's fingerprint division. The Annex is where I and hundreds of other FBI agents were trained to take and read fingerprints and photograph crime scenes.

When I did conduct investigations at the White House, the cases involved Residence and permanent staff—secretaries, gardeners, and career staff at the OMB, the NSC, the Council of Economic Advisors, and the U.S. Trade Representative's Office.

I benefited because now I could investigate persons who were *not* closely associated with the Clintons. I figured I'd discover fewer character problems. I was right. It was a relief.

October 1st was also the Secret Service's moment of truth. They had threatened to refuse entry to all temporary White House pass holders on that date. Would they do it? Would they get away with it? I waited to see who would blink, the Secret Service or the Counsel's Office?

On October 5, 1993 I had coffee with a Secret Service pal. Was the Secret Service finally given access to the FBI background investigations?

"Well, yes and no. Yes, Kennedy has promised that we'll be able to see them, but only about fifty a week. So far, we haven't received the fifty we were promised this week, so I don't know what to believe. Plus, the only issue we can comment on is 'dangerousness.' "

He went on to explain that their role had been significantly reduced. "If the Secret Service can't prove that a staffer is dangerous, then we have to issue a permanent pass, even though a staffer might still have a history of theft, drug use, or even mental problems. The drug question comes down to this: Is the staffer using drugs *now, today, inside the White House?* If so, we can bar entry, *unless* they go into some kind of drug rehab program. Otherwise, it makes no difference what they used, when they used it, or how much they used." In other words, hard-core drug users could be White House employees in the Clinton administration if they promised to quit *after* they were caught.

He also explained that if past drug use included the *sale* of illegal drugs, then they might be able to make a case for denying a permanent pass, but even so, that decision could be overridden by a simple one-paragraph memorandum by White House counsel, saying, in effect, "I don't care what the Secret Service says. Issue the pass. We'll take responsibility."

Some security system. The Secret Service wasn't happy with it, but apparently this was coming from above, from the new director of Secret Service or from Ron Noble, a political appointee who was over both the Secret Service and the ATF. Noble was rumored to be a close friend of Margaret Williams, Hillary's powerful chief of staff, and in a battle like that, the Secret Service didn't stand a chance.

On 6 October 1993, George Saunders came by our office. His contract had expired, and he thought that perhaps it might be his last day at the White House. He'd tried to get a heads up from Craig or Bill Kennedy, but neither would say anything definitive. "I've been doing basically *nothing* for nine months now, at least nothing of any real substance. I haven't been able to interview anyone; I haven't seen any of the FBI summaries; and the only matters I've seen are related to credit problems of low-level support staff. I'm not being used. They don't seek my advice. They don't even ask me to lecture the interns or the new staff on security."

"Do you think you're kept here just to maintain a false image of security?" I asked, knowing the answer. George's complaints were familiar by now.

George looked downcast. "What else can I think? I don't know if Livingstone or Kennedy are even reading the FBI summaries, but I have to believe they are. You know, Craig complained to me that many staffers have got to be fired for serious character problems, but Kennedy won't do it. And Craig told me you guys don't even have the paperwork to do background investigations on staffers who have been here from the beginning. That's unbelievable."

Yeah, but it was true.

On 11 March 1994 Ann Devroy of the *Washington Post* reported that a few White House staff members *still* did not have passes. In fact, *hundreds* still didn't have passes, and many had even avoided filling out the forms to enable an investigation. Dee Dee Myers, one of the worst offenders, was finally grilled by the White House press corps about the issue and had to admit her own delinquent status.

Over the next several days, Dee Dee released additional facts about the security mess, probably intending to limit the shock at the extent of this national security disaster. Dee Dee was quick to assure the media that "steps were being taken" to clear up the problem.

But there *weren't* any positive steps being taken. If anything, one could argue that things were getting worse, as official Clinton administration edicts about "lifestyles" and other issues inhibited our inves-

AGAIN
THRIFT & MORE
706 NORTH VICTORY DR.
MANKATO, MN. 56001
PHONE (507) 345-2409

>>>>>>>>>>>>>>>>><<<<<<<<<<<<<<<

DATE 06/29/2013 SAT   TIME 10:47

3X	@ 0.50	
BOOKS T1		$1.50
TAX1		$0.11
TOTAL		$1.61
CASH		$20.00
CHANGE		$18.39

** THANK YOU! **

CLERK 1   019900   00001

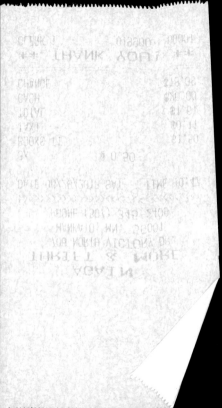

tigations. Lies like this passed easily from the lips of Clinton staffers. The great mystery to me was how anyone could still believe them. There were no hardball questions for Dee Dee, nor did the press follow up to see what "steps" the administration took to address the issue.

On 23 March Bill Kennedy was "demoted" by Lloyd Cutler. He was going to be the designated scapegoat for the disabled/failed security program, even though he was just doing what he had been told to do. It was another "twofer," because while Kennedy was no longer the gatekeeper in charge of vetting and background investigations, he could now spend 100 percent of his time on Hillary's Whitewater legal problems, filling a void left when Foster died. Kennedy was making $125,000 a year in taxpayer dollars, plus benefits.

It was soon revealed, however, that Kennedy had legal problems of his own for failing to pay his full federal income taxes in 1991 and 1992. When he was first asked to come to the White House by Hillary Clinton and Vince Foster, Kennedy did repair some of his tax problems, but not all of them. Kennedy was another Nannygater. Like so many of the Clintons' friends, the Kennedys were wealthy enough to have a nanny; they just didn't want to have to pay for her.

Now Kennedy had a new problem. His wife was leaving him. He was afraid that she would disclose his problems to the media or that her allegations would show up in civil divorce proceedings. So he tried to quick-fix his tax problems. Once again, however, like so many times before, Kennedy could not do it honestly, could not bring himself to be a "straight." He structured his IRS payment so that it might be concealed from investigators. Kennedy told his estranged wife to write a check to pay for the missing tax money, using her old checkbook and her *former married name.*

Kennedy was making $600,000 a year in Little Rock *and* trying to save a couple thousand dollars at the nanny's expense. Until he was found out, he insisted he was entirely innocent. He told the media that his estranged wife occasionally liked to use her "old" married name, while at other times, she used her maiden name. It was a whimsical thing, not an attempt to deceive. Right.

When Kennedy was interviewed by Dennis, did he confess his federal tax-dodging? Kennedy came to the White House shortly after the Zoe Baird and Kimba Wood debacles. He knew the potential impact that his own Nannygate problems could have on the Clinton administration. When caught, Kennedy claimed that he had alerted his supervisor to his Nannygate problem. Who was that supervisor? None other than the late Vince Foster.

Kennedy, drowning in character problems of his own, was supposed to maintain standards at the White House and help vet various cabinet level applicants. It was ludicrous. He had ignored the Secret Service, the FBI, and anyone else who had an interest in protecting President Clinton and national security. He had even ignored his own security director's pleas to take action. Now we know why. Kennedy *himself* was a security risk.

In spite of claims that White House security was enhanced by the replacement of Kennedy with Beth Nolan, nothing much happened. After all, Nolan had been an attorney in the Counsel's Office from the beginning and had worked with Kennedy. In February 1993 she had met with Greg Walden, President Bush's ethics czar, and had learned all about the security system. She knew how it was supposed to run, and surely she must have seen how Kennedy was dismantling the system.

I wondered if there had been a ceremony, a "passing of the baton," with Kennedy carrying hundreds of unread, unadjudicated FBI case files that had been stacked up in a corner of his office over to a corner of *her* office, where they could be restacked, not to be disturbed until the Clinton Library would open years hence.

There was no wholesale enhancement of security. How could there be? After all, hundreds of uncleared staff members had worked in the White House for more than a year. This was a staff composed of many who would never have been approved for a permanent pass in anyone else's White House. *Now* they were going to be dismissed? How could that possibly be accomplished without enormous disruption and embarrassment to the White House?

Nobody was fired except for poor, single moms working in support positions who admitted they were behind in their rent payments. Firing them was George Saunders's job. A "threefer." Fire the moms, give George something to do, and make everyone believe they were cleaning up the place.

All the rest—the drug users, the tax scofflaws, the bankrupts, the liars—remained in, except for this one famous guy named Watkins who used the presidential helicopter as his personal golf cart. But then, Watkins wasn't really fired. He was merely transferred down the street to become a highly paid consultant for the Campaign to Reelect Bill and Hillary Clinton.

Did some people with serious character problems leave? Sure, but not because of anything developed in any of my FBI investigations. They left because they chose to become lobbyists, or they were promoted, or they were tired, or they were just plain disgusted by what they themselves did or what they saw others doing. And if they left for that last reason, I knew exactly how they felt.

On 24 January 1995 Dennis arrived, looking gloomy. He had a hard time hiding his emotions. He jokingly chalked it up to being Italian.

"What's up, buddy? You don't look like you're having a good day. What's happening? Go by the RA?" RA was short for Resident Agency, our Tyson's Corner office in northern Virginia.

"Yes, I did, and that was my big mistake. I got into an argument with Tom about conditions down here and the fact that we aren't getting any backing from him."

"Dennis, that's an old story. We've been on our own ever since Clinton took office. There hasn't been one debate, one issue, one fight that we've won."

"Yeah, I know. I guess I just keep thinking that they'll get wise to what this administration is doing one of these days. The FBI that I know, the one I *think* I'm working for, wouldn't put up with this kind of thing. Would they?"

"You're asking me? Look, Tom Renagahan and Jim Bourke pretty much control the SPIN process, and they seem to have little interest in anything but meeting deadlines. They don't care about anything else. It doesn't matter if a case is complex and we're turning up good stuff; they push to close the case to make the deadline. Even if we could convince Tom there's a big problem, he's only a supervisor. He wouldn't be able to change anything. As unit chief, Bourke would step in and stop him. And don't forget the fact that they tried to set us up, pal."

Making war with FBI headquarters Unit chiefs was always a loser, even if you were totally right, because the thinking was, "If there is a good idea, we at FBI headquarters have already thought of it," and, "If something goes wrong, it must have happened out in the field; it couldn't possibly be FBI headquarters's fault." The bureau wasn't much different from any other bureaucracy in that respect. We were top-heavy, and the heavies at the top had the power.

"Dennis, you're wasting too much time wishing that the FBI would rise to meet your expectations. The bureau's changed. What *doesn't* change is the work we have to do. In our jobs, character still counts for something, even if President Clinton and his wife don't think so."

"Oh yeah, sure. How does character count in our jobs, if this administration has thrown character, standards, the law, everything out the window? Nobody cares. Gary, people higher up, people in Congress—I think they all know this is happening. Clinton's abolished security here for a whole year now, and the Secret Service, the FBI, the military, Congress—nobody's willing to challenge the way the Clintons are staffing the government or endangering *national* security. I mean this whole Inman case is typical of how screwed up things still are."

I had to agree. Admiral Bobby Inman had been announced to replace the stumbling, bumbling Les Aspin as Secretary of Defense on 16 December 1993. Thanks to the abysmal vetting by the Clintons and their staff, exactly one month later the president announced that Inman was withdrawing his name from consideration. There seemed to be issues in his past, you see.

"Look, Dennis, why don't you take the rest of the day off. Believe me, the Clintons will never notice you aren't here trying to protect them or national security. They don't seem to care, so why do you?"

"Gary, you're absolutely right! I'm the fool for thinking that this garbage is important. Damn it, I'm going on leave, if anyone cares."

"Come on, buddy. You just need a break. I'll call the office and have you put on leave, how's that?"

Dennis thanked me, closed his briefcase, and walked out the door. It was about 1:00 P.M. At about 5:00 P.M. I was standing in the snow at the Fairfax Hospital Trauma Unit helicopter pad as the chopper carrying Dennis gently set down.

I had gone out to the RA to deliver some reports, as Dennis could not do it for me, and between the time I left the White House and arrived at the RA, a call had come in from the Manassas Airport security office, wanting to know if we had a Dennis Sculimbrene working for us. They had found him underneath the front of his Cessna airplane, with the back of his head crushed in, the apparent victim of a freak accident caused when the engine of his plane backfired as he was trying to turn the prop by hand. Dennis was airlifted by a Life-Flight helicopter to the county's best trauma unit.

I didn't know if Dennis was alive or dead, but I rushed to the hospital to assist him and his family, if I could. I was the first to get there, but soon several other members of the SPIN squad rolled up. We got on the phones to notify Dennis's friends and relatives.

Greg Schwarz, the agent who had been shunned and kicked out of the vice president's office, brought Dennis's wife Katy to the hospital.

We were by the hospital door as they wheeled Dennis in, and in spite of the tremendous blow he had received (it had broken his skull and driven pieces of it into his brain), he was conscious. We misinterpreted this to mean that he would be all right. They wheeled him into an MRI and then right into surgery.

At about 1:00 A.M. the surgeon came out with the good news/bad news. Dennis was alive, but just barely. He was in a coma; the doctor had to remove a small portion of the back of his brain that had been damaged by the blow and was full of skull fragments.

The doctor said that if he was alive in the morning, then maybe he would make it, but the doctor could not predict exactly what Dennis would be like, if he survived. I stayed with his wife until the rest of the family arrived.

Thankfully, our supervisor, Tom Renagahan, who couldn't seem to help us with our problems at the White House, was a great comfort at this tragedy. Indeed, the goodness of the FBI came through in full force with FBI Director Louis Freeh and Assistant Director Anthony Daniels joining us at the hospital. Unlimited support was given to Dennis and his family as we all waited to see if he could survive. He did, and he returned to the White House, still doing the work of two agents, but without his sense of taste, the loss of which has been somewhat helpful, all things considered.

But on that day in January, I lost my buddy, my sounding board, and it got mighty lonely for me at the Clinton White House. Agents were sent down to fill in for Dennis—they needed three!—but when they questioned me about how the Clinton White House worked, I didn't feel like trying to catch them up on how things *didn't* work. My mind was on Dennis. The Clinton administration was irrelevant. We had tried to alert the powers that be to the White House's dismantled security, and we had failed in our attempt to fix it. Our job was done. The problem belonged to someone else.

Chapter Eleven

AND THE BEAT GOES ON

Rules for Radicals: "Our rebels have contemptuously rejected the values and way of life of the middle class. They have stigmatized it as materialistic, decadent, bourgeois, degenerate, imperialistic, war-mongering, brutalized, and corrupt. They are right."

George Washington's Rules of Civility and Decent Behaviour: "Labour to keep alive in your breast that little celestial fire called conscience."

I'd had enough. Not only would I leave the White House, but I'd decided to retire early from the FBI.

Still, it was no easy slide to June 1995—to coffee, donuts, a gold pin, and a congratulatory letter signed by Director Freeh. No, it had to be tough right up to the end.

In early December 1994 President Clinton announced that outgoing Congressman Dan Glickman would replace Mike Espy as secretary of Agriculture. At a Rose Garden ceremony to make the announcement formal, the president gave Espy credit for doing "a superb job" and for "taking charge" to implement major reforms.

The president didn't mention that Espy's idea of "taking charge" included an apparent weakness for taking things that didn't belong to him. Espy was under criminal investigation for wrongdoing while in a Cabinet position.

The FBI had yet to begin its background investigation into Congressman Glickman, but already congressmen from both parties

—including the new Republican majority—stepped forward to praise him. Again, it seemed as though our investigation would be superfluous.

Special Agent Tim Traylor visited Glickman's residence for the usual formal interview. It was a midmorning, workday appointment. He was greeted at the door by an unshaven, sleepy-eyed, bathrobed Glickman, a halo of powdered donut crumbs around his mouth. Traylor said that Glickman seemed surprised, looked at his watch, and said, "Oh yeah, the FBI thing. I forgot about that."

Between chews and swallows, Glickman invited agent Traylor in, his slippers clip-clopping as he led him to the kitchen.

Traylor was appalled at Glickman's lack of professionalism, which was ironic, because Agent Traylor was one of the last to condemn the administration. Unlike most agents, Traylor was vocal about his politics and loudly proclaimed his support for Clinton and the Democratic party. But even Tim had come to believe that the FBI was no longer being used to screen appointees who would be granted enormous power, great benefits, and a big salary. We merely provided political cover.

While Traylor investigated Glickman's neighborhood, Special Agent Greg Schwarz investigated through his connections on the Senate side, and I handled the House side.

Privacy Act provisions prevent me from providing details about Congressman Glickman's background investigation. But news accounts, mostly generated by the White House, claimed that Senate confirmation hearings for a well-scrubbed Glickman were being held up by the FBI SPIN process.

This delay came at a bad time for the Clintons. Henry Foster, the Clintons' nominee to replace Joycelyn Elders as surgeon general, was under heavy fire for lying about the number of abortions he had performed: Was it 2, 20, or 700? The Clintons might believe that truth is relative, but some people keep records, and FBI agents can read and add. The Foster nomination was in serious trouble, and he soon became another "victim" of a thorough FBI SPIN investigation that somebody actually read.

When Glickman's case wasn't finished in the usual thirty days because of serious questions that needed answers, the White House pressured the FBI to complete the probe. Calls were placed several times a day by the White House Counsel's Office asking why the

Glickman case was not finished. About this time, Security Director Livingstone, who must have read my Glickman reports or heard about them, stopped being friendly. I guess I wasn't going to be the Clinton security consultant after all.

The FBI, feeling the heat, forced us to spend more and more time explaining why we needed to continue the investigation, and less and less time actually investigating.

The supervisor of our squad began calling us into his office for conferences. He asked us to explain every action we took, to justify each interview, to prove the necessity of finding all the documents we sought to examine.

Soon the conferences turned into major arguments, and on more than one occasion the four of us, three senior agents and one bureaucrat, stood nose-to-nose in a circle, shouting. One of us, not me, threatened to go to the *Washington Post* if the pressure from the White House didn't stop. The FBI insisted we close the Glickman case. But we didn't budge.

I told my supervisor to order me, *on paper*, to cease my investigation, or shut up. I knew full well that he would never officially command me to close a complex investigation with a written order that would make him responsible if things went wrong.

I also knew that if the serious questions about Glickman were not resolved, we might see yet another independent counsel appointed, costing millions of dollars and further tarnishing the presidency.

If we proved Glickman to be honest and ethical, the FBI SPIN would document that. If we found problems, the White House and the Senate would be responsible for going forward, not the FBI. What we couldn't do—ethically or professionally—was submit a half-completed report just to get the White House and FBI management off our backs.

Meanwhile, the media began its own investigation and reported that there were some questions about bad checks Glickman had written on the House Bank and about dependents of Glickman using congressional credit cards. The media unearthed that Glickman, a millionaire whose wife worked for Congress as chairperson of the Arts Subcommittee, was alleged to have misused congressional funds for personal business. There was some talk of "traffic tickets."

More shocking were reports that Glickman's administrative assistant had committed suicide, but not before accusing him, in writing, of misuse of funds. She left instructions to submit these allegations to the House Ethics Committee in the event of her death. The House Ethics Committee, however, apparently took no action.

Nevertheless, the Senate—the *Republican* Senate—stood by its former congressional colleague and confirmed Glickman the day before April Fools' Day by a vote of ninety-four to zero. I felt the world had been turned upside down. I was disgusted and disheartened.

But fate wasn't done with me yet. Next in my in box was the Anthony Coelho investigation. It was then I realized, too late, that Buzzard's Point hadn't been so bad after all.

Again, the Privacy Act will not allow a disclosure of anything from Coelho's SPIN, but there is a phone-book–thick collection of media reports on the antics of Coelho that would keep any investigator busy for a long, long time.

On the heels of the Aldrich Ames spy case, the Clintons announced a presidential commission to study "Roles and Capabilities of the Intelligence Community" and to recommend fundamental changes for the CIA, the FBI, and other agencies.

The members of the commission would need to know the most secret activities of the most secret agencies in order to perform their function. So it was vital that all members of this important commission be of the highest caliber and have spotless backgrounds.

Departing Speaker of the House Tom Foley appointed former Congressman Tony Coelho to the commission. He was an odd choice. Coelho had left Congress under a cloud and had gone to New York and made millions in the commodities markets.

He had also taken a presidential appointment to a commission on the handicapped. Coelho's disability was epilepsy, acquired in his youth from head injuries when a pickup truck he was in flipped over.

To control his mental and emotional handicap, Coelho received a daily dose of methaqualone, or Phenobarbital.

What effect would such a drug, taken daily, have on a man with extraordinary access to our nation's most carefully guarded secrets, a man expected to make sober and reasoned decisions? It was a fair question. Would we now grant security clearances to persons whose minds were chemically altered, even for alleged medical reasons?

Tony Coelho was nothing if not an interesting character. He had been in so much trouble as a congressman that more than one book and many articles had been written about him. He had been the subject of several, albeit unsuccessful, federal criminal probes. Hiring Coelho to serve on the Intelligence commission was taking the protection of national security to a new low.

The Coelho investigation was received on 7 March 1995. It was to be completed by 27 March "without fail." To order that we finish this investigation in what amounted to fifteen working days was an outrage and impossible—and that's what I advised my supervisor, in writing, the very day I got the assignment. I made sure that he, in the presence of witnesses, acknowledged the receipt of my memorandum. It would be too easy to throw my memo in the round file; it had been done before. I kept a copy for my own protection. But he still harangued me with calls to meet the deadline.

When the deadline passed, I let his increasingly panicked calls go directly to the message machine, and I turned off my beeper, which was going off so often I couldn't keep fresh batteries in it. The FBI SPIN management knew I was investigating serious allegations, but their attitude seemed to be, "Yes, yes, Gary, we know about that, but what about the *deadline?*"

As far as I was concerned, the deadline would have to wait. Among the allegations against Coelho—some of which he freely confessed—were the following:

- Taking daily doses of methaqualone or phenobarbital for medical reasons.
- Prior alcoholism and considerations of suicide.
- Illegal, unethical, or inappropriate lobbying of the new Clinton administration.
- Potential conflicts of interest.
- Resigning from Congress on 15 June 1989 after multiple accusations of serious wrongdoing, including violations of federal laws.
- Failing to correctly report income on a federal income tax return.

- Failing to report a loan of $50,000 in violation of House ethics reporting requirements.
- Issuing, in less than one year, 316 personal checks—for a total of more than $293,000—all drawn on a bank account for which there were insufficient funds.
- Accepting a "sweetheart" junk bond deal from Michael Milkin (later convicted and sentenced by U.S. Federal Judge *Kimba Wood*).
- Accepting a $4,000 gift from a savings and loan banker later indicted and convicted of federal violations.
- Using inappropriate influence to protect owners of failing savings and loans.
- Accepting illegal political contributions aboard a 112-foot yacht owned by a savings and loan businessman who was later indicted and convicted of fraud.
- Improperly appointing a friend and large contributor to the finance chair of the DNC (the friend owned a failing Texas savings and loan).
- Alleged improper contacts with employees of the Clinton Department of Agriculture for the purpose of influencing decisions made with respect to farm chemicals being produced by a leading manufacturer, also a big contributor to politicians.

This list is by no means complete. These are just some of the *public,* media-reported allegations against Coelho, most of which have never been investigated fully for one reason or another. Now there *was* a reason to fully investigate these allegations, but I wasn't being allowed to. While it was true that Coelho was never charged with of any crime, the Department of Justice Office of Public Integrity only *declined* to prosecute him, and anyone in law enforcement and the political arena knows that declining to prosecute is not the same as declaring someone innocent.

The deeper I dug, the more cynical were the questions I posed to myself. How much were Coelho's chances for an important position enhanced by the fact that he was engaged in fundraising for the president's defense against the sexual harassment lawsuit brought by Paula Jones? Could Coelho's opportunity to join the commission have anything to do with the fact that he defended Hillary Clinton's celebrated windfall profits in cattle futures? What about the public speculation that the Clintons wanted Coelho "cleared" to work on the commission in order to rehabilitate him so he could run the president's reelection campaign?

I was not in charge of standards, nor was I in charge of the Coelho investigation; I was just asking questions, and I was only the lead agent covering the U.S. House of Representatives. Ultimately, Coelho got his security clearance from the Clinton administration and gained access to some of the most sensitive information our government has. If you ask me why, I don't know.

At the end of my assignment at the White House I concluded that the Clintons might as well hitch a trailer to the White House and tow it to Little Rock; they had soiled the place. The U.S. Park Service hedge clipper in the Rose Garden had a finer character than the president of the United States. The sad thing was, the clipper knew it.

On my last day, I took one last stroll around the White House. I walked past the Rose Garden. As the Park Service employee clipped a hedge in front of the Oval Office, glancing occasionally at "the man" who was sitting behind the big desk, I wondered what might be going through the hedge clipper's mind. I think I know because so many of the permanent employees were thinking the same thing: "There's been a big mistake, a whopper of a mistake. How the heck did it happen, and what the heck are we going to do about it now?"

Chapter Twelve

HANGING UP THE BADGE, AND PICKING UP THE PEN

Rules for Radicals: "There is a difference between honesty and rude disrespect of another's tradition. The organizer will err far less by being himself than by engaging in 'professional techniques' when the people really know better."

George Washington's Rules of Civility and Decent Behaviour:
"Undertake not what you cannot perform, but be careful to keep your promise"

I drove down to Washington, D.C., early one morning in June 1995. It was a sunny day but otherwise unremarkable. Except, of course, that it was the last day of my more than thirty-year career with the FBI—having served the last five years in the White House, more than two years in the Clinton administration.

I angled my FBI sedan into its usual space, west of the Old Executive Office Building, or OEOB. I walked the twenty steps to the West gate, and the Secret Service guard standing in the little white security booth waved a greeting as I brushed my blue access pass against the sensor.

As I went through the elaborate entry procedures to gain unlimited access one last time, I realized how ironic my situation was. I was a thirty-year veteran of the FBI, twenty-six years as a special agent, and yet *my* access to the White House was being carefully controlled. All permanent White House employees were required to go through identical Secret Service checkpoints. Access could be denied with a single keystroke by a Secret Service employee looking at a computer screen deep within the recesses of the OEOB. Yet the Clinton Administration had thrown off all access restrictions for favored political "friends," allowing them to roam through the nation's most secure workplace. While the "small fries" who had been fully investigated were treated to continual scrutiny, a potential "Beijing Rose" or a possible "John Wilkes Booth" could come and go, perhaps stroll past the Oval Office, perhaps overhear a careless staffer discussing a highly sensitive matter in an elevator, or perhaps read mail left open on a careless National Security Council staff member's desk. These opportunities and more were available to high dollar donors—providing they brought along their checkbooks.

For friends of Bill, or Hillary, or Al Gore, the security checkpoints had become mere annoyances, something to be tolerated. The iron gates were really more like token-taking turnstiles for those who were willing to help the Clinton administration maintain power with lots and lots of green money. The old security rules, invoked by six presidents before Clinton, did apply, but only to those people offering the least dangers to the president and national security. To people like me, charged with the responsibility of protecting national security, it was the world turned upside down.

It was this bizarre and dangerous turn of events that compelled me to write *Unlimited Access*. To some, my writing a book was a reckless overreaction, an absurd idea. But for others, a whistleblower like me was performing a necessary act—ethical dissent in the best tradition of our Founding Fathers.

After all, the dominant liberal media didn't seem at all interested in what was going on. Congress, charged with the responsibility of overseeing White House security, had naively accepted up to that point Clinton administration assurances that everything was "okay." Well, I worked inside the Clinton White House security system, and it *wasn't* okay, whatever Dee Dee Meyers and George Stephanopoulos said. And they could be brazen in their lies, even asserting that security was better than it was under the Bush administration. At the time they said that—one year into the administration—their own permanent passes still hadn't been issued.

My own agency was mysteriously deaf, dumb, and blind to the obviously dangerous breaches in White House security, preferring instead to question the motives of their own senior investigators on the scene. No one wanted to know the bad news. But the bad news was the truth—and the American people had a right to know how their national security was being endangered by a corrupt and reckless administration. I was resolved that the truth had to be known so that the system could be fixed, our national security protected, and the integrity of the White House restored.

Walking into the OEOB and down to the cafeteria, I made my way to the coffee machine, and then carried my cup to Bernice, who rang up the purchase. "Bernice, this is goodbye. I'm retiring, so I won't be seeing you for a while. Maybe quite a while," I said as I collected my change.

"Why, Mr. Aldrich? I didn't know you were leaving us! Gosh, well, I will be missing you. You FBI guys have been pleasant to us. Not like this new crowd." Bernice looked around. It seemed everyone was afraid. Many believed that Clinton staff members reported any negative comments, no matter how trivial.

The White House atmosphere was guarded, and staff not directly connected to the Clintons were wary. Travelgate and other Clinton excesses and abuses had done that to the permanent White House staff. Everyone seemed intimidated and afraid.

"It's been nice, but time to do something else, Bernice. I'm still young enough to start a new career," I said, making my way to the door. I was in a hurry. I had a lot to do. I had to pack up five years worth of my life spent at the White House into two cardboard boxes.

"Well, good luck to you, Mr. Aldrich. What are you going to be doing next?" she asked.

"Bernice, I'm not sure, but maybe you'll read about it in the newspaper someday," and I winked as I walked away. I was determined to surface the wrongdoing I had witnessed at the White House—I just hadn't determined how to do it. But right now, I had to pack. I walked to the elevator that would take me to the fifth floor of the OEOB.

I had wondered how I would feel on my last day at work, as a special agent of the FBI, assigned to the White House Liaison Office. It turned out I didn't feel much of anything at all. In the last months I had joked with my FBI buddies that I might be suffering from "Clinton Traumatic Distress Syndrome."

Often, when I made such a joking reference to a fine security program that had become a joke, a mockery, a few managed quiet chuckles—dark humor to help survive bad times. It was the law enforcement officer's way to cope with matters beyond his control.

The wide range of emotions that had come with my unique assignment had merged into one long feeling of sadness and, near the end, dull pain. It became hard to get up in the morning, hard to drive down to what had once been a fantastic assignment.

Now, working in the White House was a burden, and my wife had complained that my mood—even at home—had changed dramatically for the worse. She was right about that.

The sense of accomplishment that came with success, acceptance, productivity, excellence, decency, and patriotism had been replaced with a sense of failure and hostility, generated from pointless interviewing, from filing documents that nobody read, cared about, or acted on. The sharp Bush staff and many permanent staff members had been replaced by shabby personnel, working in a shabby environment, often exhibiting crude, abusive, and offensive behavior. Evidence was everywhere that these were people who had no real love for our country or the constitution that holds it together. I finally had to conclude that these people were not "New Democrats," as advertised, but were the children of the 1960s—the radicals—and they had just grown older, not wiser. These were the relativists, who believed the ends justified the means. These were "New-Left Democrats" and I wondered how many others had discovered this truth.

Left or Right, new or old, the Clinton administration certainly had something against honesty. They avoided truth at all costs, sometimes lying under oath if it served their purposes.

I was alarmed at the brand of "spin" they used over and over again, to bend, twist, and break the truth, always at someone else's expense. Surprisingly, the dominant liberal media went right along with this constant deception, apparently uninterested in holding the White House to the same ethical standards they would have demanded of George Bush (and which George Bush exceeded).

But much of my sadness had come from the realization that I could not continue to be employed with the FBI and assigned to the White House. I would not allow myself to be an actor in a "mock" security drama. I had to leave. My own agency, the agency that had consumed more than thirty years of my life's work, was beginning to betray its own ideals, and the public was beginning to notice. It wasn't the first time a president had brought the FBI down a notch or two in reputation. But the FBI is supposed to be an objective, truth-seeking, investigative agency—that was the FBI I joined and served.

Now I was forced to concede, in my own mind, that I could do nothing about the FBI's troubles. But I could do something about the security disaster at the White House. I could expose it to the cleansing light of public scrutiny.

On this, my last day at work, I made a promise to myself. I could not imagine simply ignoring what I had seen at the Clinton White House. I was leaving the FBI, but I would still be investigating. It was my mission to report what I knew to the people who had been paying my salary all these years—the citizens of this country.

I had always kept that in the back of my mind—I was working for the American people. I refused to be a timeserving bureaucrat in a mindless government machine. I knew, however prideful it sounds, that I wouldn't have been a "good German," prepared to ignore the obvious. I took my cue from Patrick Henry.

As I packed the second brown cardboard carton with my knick-knacks and my photos of five years at the White House, I wondered what would become of my partner, Dennis.

Dennis had returned to work after a long period of rehabilitation following his airplane accident, only to find the White House in worse shape than when he left it. I worried for him and how he would reconcile himself to the bad things that were going on—some of which were happening to him.

According to formal statements made by Dennis, before the Billy Dale trial Dennis had been offered a promotion and a raise by the Clinton administration. Needless to say, the offer was angrily withdrawn after he was called as a witness for the defense. The Clinton White House had no use for a law enforcement agent who couldn't be bought. The Clintons had their way with some of the Arkansas Troopers. Now they were simply trying to do the same to us. Dennis's job situation would soon deteriorate from bad to worse.

They sent two agents to the White House to replace me, but lacking any White House experience, they could only imagine what a well-staffed, well-run White House might be, and the FBI had no interest in teaching them. From my experience, I knew the agency wouldn't support the agents if they found wrongdoing. The FBI had lost sight of its mission to protect national security.

After loading the boxes into my car, I took one last stroll around the White House.

The Secret Service guard, who had just looked through my outgoing cartons, said, "Have fun, and say goodbye to Hillary—don't forget, now." He knew it was my last day, and he had seen many staffers' last days lately. He couldn't resist the joke. Many good folks were getting out, including many of his fellow Secret Service agents. This was his way of coping, since he was not in a position to leave. Yet.

I spent about an hour walking and bidding goodbye to many friends. From the East Wing, through the Residence, out to the South Lawn, back into the West Wing, the West Wing Lobby, past the Marine Guard, down the stairs to the West Executive Parking lot, and then through the many offices in the OEOB where some friends still worked.

I walked into the Clerk's Office. I said goodbye to the staff who had been so helpful to me, and I asked Tim Saunders for permission to sit in John F. Kennedy's rocking chair "one more time." The Kennedy rocking chair had been given to the Clerk's Office after Kennedy's death, and they were proud to have it. President Kennedy had several rockers, scattered around the White House for his use, and this had been one of them.

I looked around the room and saw many new faces. For a moment I considered that perhaps the Clintons were right. Maybe they were the new way. Maybe this was the new direction of our country—a significant downward drift. But ending where?

I said my final goodbyes and drove west on I-66 to Tyson's Corner, to the FBI's Special Inquiry Squad, the group that I had once supervised.

There was little traffic, and I pulled into the FBI lot within fifteen minutes of departing the White House. I knew the squad had been planning a "donuts and coffee" farewell for me, and the agent-in-charge would probably come to visit, read a letter from the director—of course too busy to attend—and mingle a bit with the squad.

There wasn't much for me to celebrate. My good friends in the office knew that. I made no secret of my disappointment with the agency, of my strong feelings about what the Clintons had done to the White House and what they were now doing to the FBI and other Executive Branch agencies.

FBI special agents and support employees gathered in the squad's area. Someone said a few words about my career. It was mostly a blur. Dennis came by and looked a bit forlorn. He was losing his sounding board, his soul-mate in the war to maintain some kind of standard in our nation's White House.

The agent-in-charge did come by, and he read the letter from Director Freeh. Then his beeper went off, and he wandered away, leaving me holding the letter and a promise of a wooden plaque that would hold my old badge and credentials: coming someday... the exhibit section was backed up... lots of agents retiring.

Still, it was not much of a ceremony, considering that for more than thirty years I had served my country through this agency. I didn't take it personally. The many agents who had retired since Clinton came to Washington were not given much of a sendoff. Morale in the agency had hit a new low.

I said my goodbyes to my fellow agents, signed forms that promised I would never reveal anything unless I checked with the director first, and then headed for the door. My wife Nina was waiting for me in the parking lot to give me a lift home. We drove past my parked FBI car, waiting there for its new occupant. I wondered, "Will the next agent to drive that car have the excitement I had in my FBI career?" I doubted it.

"How did it go?" asked Nina, who had retired from the FBI ten years earlier. She knew something of what I was feeling.

"Oh, okay, I guess, hon. The usual coffee and donut thing. Some nice words. You know the drill. Just as we expected, no gold watch," I joked.

We rode home in silence, and I think Nina knew what I was thinking. She knew what we were about to do if I could find a lawyer to give me a green light, and if I could find a publisher to buy my book. Then again, could I actually write a book? Certainly not without Nina's support and approval.

We were both excited, but worried. We had reason to be. I was determined to take on my own government. The White House, the

Department of Justice, the FBI and all the other enforcement agencies might become my "enemies" overnight. And I knew Clinton had a reputation for treating critics and defectors harshly.

Jay Stephens had his law offices within an easy walk from the White House. In fact, his office was in the building on K Street that housed Secret Service Headquarters. I set up an appointment with Jay soon after I retired. He was one of the few attorneys who were qualified, in my view, to take on my very unusual case.

As I took the elevator to his office, I held my breath each time the car stopped to let on passengers. Would any of my Secret Service chums get on? Nobody in the White House had any idea what I wanted to do, and I didn't want to be asked about it. The car reached the penthouse level.

I sat in the law firm's reception area for a few minutes. Then a young-looking man with dark hair and elegant, conservative clothes walked up to greet me. "Hi, Gary. Glad you could come in today. Let's walk down to my office."

Jay closed the door. I explained some of what I experienced at the White House, and what I thought I wanted to do about it. He listened, and asked questions.

Jay Stephens knew how the White House was supposed to run. He had held the same position that Vince Foster had—Deputy Counsel. And he had been fired by Clinton's Justice Department, along with about a hundred other United States attorneys, when Clinton took office. I knew that Jay would understand that my complaints were not baseless—were not overblown. I had seen a pattern of serious misconduct and abuse of power, as well as major threats to national security.

I didn't tell Jay everything. I couldn't, because he had not yet agreed to represent me, and there were many things I couldn't tell him without special authority from the FBI.

I told Jay I wanted to write a book. I asked whether his firm could represent me in the inevitable legal battles to come. He was reserved, but I could tell he was excited about the project. "Gary, are you sure you want to do this? Are you sure you can stand up to the Clintons? They seem to have quite an ability to take out detractors."

I told him I knew the risks. I also told him that I couldn't be blind-sided by Clinton character assassination. My record at the FBI was spotless. In fact, for the last several years I had received top ratings and no criticism whatsoever.

We talked for at least two hours before Jay noticed the time. "Gary, I like your project, and I think you can write a book about some of the things you know, but I need to do some research on this. Before I agree to represent you, I'll need to run this past my partners. You understand that this firm's fees are high, and I doubt we could give you any real break?"

My wife had agreed that a certain amount of our savings could be spent on Jay's legal work to see if the project was feasible. If I couldn't legally write the book, I had other things to do. I had already qualified to open my own private investigative agency.

Jay walked me to the door and reminded me how sensitive our conversation was. He promised to call in a week. "Be careful," he said, and I knew he meant it.

A week later I talked to Jay. "Gary, I have completed my review of the law and the applicable policies, and I think I have good news for you. I think you can write a book, within certain guidelines, and the FBI would have no legal reason to prevent it."

We discussed his research at length—and what the likely implications were if I went forward.

I asked Jay to call Alfred Regnery, president of a Washington-based publishing house. It was time to take the next step. I had legal assurance and could go ahead. Now I needed to find out if there was a publisher willing to take a chance on me—and willing to take the heat that would come with my book.

On my short list of possible publishers, Alfred Regnery was at the top. In fact, we never talked to another.

I had never met Al, but I knew he was well regarded in Washington. His publishing house (founded by his father, Henry Regnery) had a fifty-year tradition of publishing serious, conservative, and controversial books. Al was also a lawyer who had served in the Reagan administration. I knew he would appreciate the importance of what I had to say.

In late July 1995, Jay and I walked over to the University Club to have lunch as Al's guest. He did not know who Jay was bringing to the table or why we were meeting.

Al is a dapper, worldly man, about fifty years old. He'd weathered a few wars of his own. I liked him immediately, and we talked for hours.

I told Al I wanted to expose wrongdoing in the Clinton White House. But there was a catch. Until the FBI had reviewed and approved the manuscript, Al would have to take it on faith that I had a serious book to write. I couldn't show him anything—or tell him anything.

I needed an advance big enough to cover my legal fees and other expenses while I wrote the book. Moreover, I had to be the actual writer. I couldn't share my information with a ghost writer. That would have breached the FBI's rules. And anyway, I didn't want one. No one knew my story better or would understand the security implications better than I did.

Al told me he was interested and would call back with more questions and some ideas of how we might proceed. A week later we had another meeting—this time at Regnery's offices on Capitol Hill. I met other members of the staff. They all seemed eager to proceed but were understandably worried about the blind trust they had to give me as a witness and as a writer. I assured them that everything in my book could be backed up by witnesses or documents, and that I was willing to testify, under a sworn oath, that everything in the book was true. Publishing a book like this meant a big investment for Regnery, and publishers know that most of their gambles fail. Nevertheless, by August we had a contract.

Now came the hard part. I wrote day and night, weekends and holidays included, until I was able to submit a more than three-hundred-page manuscript to the FBI. My deadline was December 1, and I nearly made it. But then, because of the budget impasse, the government shut down—including the unit at the FBI reviewing book manuscripts. So the FBI didn't become aware of my book until the first week in January 1996.

Instead of being reviewed by the usual lawyers at the Bureau, my book became a special project to be studied by Director Freeh's general counsel, Howard Shapiro, and his close staff. Jay reported that he found Shapiro polite and professional, and since there was nothing in the manuscript to prevent agency approval, he thought that aside from a few minor alterations to please anticipated agency nit-picking, we could get the book approved—and soon.

But we were wrong about Shapiro, the director, and sadly even some of the assistant directors of the FBI, who agreed, or sat silent when the Bureau decided to leak my manuscript to the White House, to give the Clintons a political heads-up. This was a clear violation not only of the FBI's own regulations, but of an explicit agreement Jay Stephens had reached with Shapiro and Freeh that the FBI would not let the manuscript outside the Bureau.

Instead of dealing with us in good faith, the FBI turned the manuscript over to White House Counsel Jack Quinn, and attempted to kill it—not because my manuscript violated the law, but because the Bureau had become a political instrument of a corrupted White House.

My troubles were only beginning—and so were Dennis's. After I submitted my manuscript to Director Freeh and Howard Shapiro, the FBI and the White House went after Dennis. They sent a team of agents to try to convice him to discredit me. Not only did he refuse, he also backed up my allegations.

Suddenly, Dennis found himself the subject of unfounded and anonymous rumors. The Bureau responded by taking away his White House pass, returning him to the FBI office with no assignments. They told him to come to work, sit as his desk, and do nothing, while they investigated rumors that Dennis parked his car in the wrong space or came to work late. Dennis had a special schedule, as did I, and FBI management knew that. These ridiculous rumors turned out to be totally false, but the FBI wouldn't return him to his White House job.

When he objected to this treatment, they told him he needed psychological evaluation. As the Filegate scandal mushroomed, and Dennis's reports became central to the question of who hired Craig Livingstone, high-level FBI agents, hand-picked by Howard Shapiro, visited Dennis at his home to further intimidate him. Meanwhile Shapiro and White House Counsel Jack Quinn worked in concert to produce a White House press release designed to discredit Dennis.

Dennis had a "smoking gun" document—contemporaneous notes of a conversation with White House Counsel Bernard Nussbaum that credited Hillary Clinton with ordering Craig Livingstone's hire. Amazingly, the FBI, on Shapiro's orders, leaked this document to the White House, which promptly turned it over to Bernard Nussbaum, who was about to go before a federal grand jury. When I worked at the FBI, there was a name for this: obstruction of justice.

Under continued attack from the FBI, Dennis finally reached his limit. He retired, and seeking peace, moved deep into the Virginia countryside. He was trying to put Washington behind him. It was a feeling I sometimes shared.

When, after months of continual delay, frustration, and many rewrites, an opportunity came for a quick weekend getaway, I seized it.

June 1, 1996, was a sunny Saturday morning. I was driving my family from our Northern Virginia home to a Bull Run Park campground, west of Washington. It was a much needed break, not only for me, but also for my family.

We needed to get out of the house and away—as far away as possible—from phones, newspapers, radio talk shows, and television—and away from the word processor, the devilish device that had lately come to rule my life.

Jay and I were fighting the FBI. Howard Shapiro, the FBI's lead counsel, had told Jay my book could never be printed. Jay knew the law, and knew the Bureau's position was clearly unconstitutional. We tried to compromise. We agreed to numerous deletions. But we could never delete enough.

The FBI continued to review and re-review the manuscript, and I continued to polish it over and over and over. Meanwhile, the legal clock kept running, Jay's fees kept getting higher and higher, and the financial and emotional toll on my family was mounting.

By the first of May the FBI had defeated me. Our savings were exhausted. To make our mortgage payment I had to sell a prized, and much loved, classic car I'd spent years restoring.

But just when things looked their bleakest, Jay was contacted by the Southeastern Legal Foundation. The Foundation had heard of my first amendment fight with the FBI and wanted to help.

The foundation agreed that if I were sued by the government for publishing the book, they would defend me. That was a relief. But still, if we lost, I knew my family faced the prospect of financial ruin. The FBI could garnishee any earnings from my book, and also freeze my assets and seize my possessions. The financial stakes for my family were as dire as they could possibly be.

So our camping trip was supposed to be a temporary release from a troubled present and a dangerous future. Nevertheless, I could not take my mind off the book. Al Regnery warned me that because of the FBI's delays, it might be mid-August before the book would hit the shelves, and the later it hit, the fewer sales we would have before the November election.

I forced myself to think of campfires and roasted marshmallows, starry skies and lawn chairs, and a hot toddy before turning in.

Then my pager began to squeal.

I saw the phone number for the House Government Reform and Oversight Committee. I knew it was probably Barbara Comstock. Barbara was dedicated and extremely hardworking. She was at the Rayburn House Office Building on this beautiful weekend morning, looking at dusty White House documents.

Nina reacted as I knew she would, "Who is it now, Gary? Can't we get a weekend? Can't we get a life?"

I tried a small lie, "Hon, this will just take a second."

My young son said, "Yeah, sure Dad." I'd missed too many soccer games and school events to have any credibility with him.

"Hello, Barbara, were you trying to reach me? This is Gary Aldrich."

Barbara's breathless voice answered, "Gary! Good. Listen, I have this piece of paper in my hand and I don't know what it means. Maybe you can help. It's a form—looks like a form—and it was sent over to the FBI, from the White House. It has Bernie Nussbaum's name on it, asking for a file on Billy Dale. But it's dated long after Dale left the White House. Can they do that?"

"Barbara, wait a minute. Where is the form going?"

"Well it seems to be going to the FBI Special Inquiry unit, Gary. Can they do that?"

"No, Barbara, they can't do that. They can't get a file on an employee who no longer works at the White House. I mean, they probably could try, but the FBI would not send the Dale file; it would be a violation of the Privacy Act."

"Well, it looks like your 'buddies' over at the FBI may have sent the file anyway."

"Barbara, I think you have it in your hand!" I shouted into the cell phone. My family was staring at me. "The last time somebody did this they went to jail! Do you remember Chuck Colson? He went to prison for having just one FBI background file. And now, Barbara, you've found it, you found the smoking gun!" The Filegate scandal was about to be uncovered.

"Let me get this to the Chairman," she said excitedly. "There may be more stuff here. We just got these boxes from the White House Thursday night, and there's a lot of material to go through."

As we pulled into the campground, I wondered if the Oversight Committee had at long last found the evidence they needed to prove that 1600 Pennsylvania Avenue had become debased by abuses of power, corruption, and illegal activity. Was there finally a crack in Clinton's stone wall?

After I had retired, I contacted the House Government Reform and Oversight Committee, then-chaired by Congressman William Clinger of Pennsylvania, because I knew the committee could reveal some information to journalists and researchers like me, as it became available. In turn, I was one of the committee's many sources of information about White House security snafus, though I could never discuss—and never did discuss—material from confidential FBI files. The investigators and I weren't friends (I didn't know them that well), but we did have something in common. We shared the same deep concern for our nation's security.

I'd known committe aides Phil Larsen and Barbara Comstock—and of their good work—before I retired. It was Phil and Barbara who in late 1993 had implored me to meet with my own member of Congress, Frank Wolf, to express my deep concerns about security at the White House. Wolf, at the time, sat on the Oversight Committee, which was supposed to be one of the congressional watchdogs on the White House.

Because of the restrictions on me as a serving FBI agent, I was reluctant to meet with Wolf. In contacting a member of Congress, I risked the wrath of some of my fellow FBI agents for "going outside the agency" and possible discipline from my supervisors. But my concerns about national security overrode my fear of personal consequences. I agreed to meet him in his offices at the Cannon House Office Building. Wolf expressed his "deep concern" for national security and made it clear he felt he had been lied to by the White House. He indicated he had talked to other federal law enforcement officers who were assigned to the Clinton White House.

I confirmed that in my opinion the White House had tremendous security problems, but I could only speak in generalities, because I did not have permission from the Bureau to say more.

Congressman Wolf promised to keep our visit confidential and agreed not to press me with questions I thought were inappropriate, but he also assured me that not only did I have a legal right to report my concerns to Congress, I also had a moral obligation to do so.

Still, when he asked me who else might be willing to talk to him, I refused to name anyone. I was protecting myself, certainly, but also my fellow law enforcement officers. My instincts told me it wasn't a good idea to urge others to come forward under circumstances that, despite Congressman Wolf's assurances, could cost them their jobs.

I met with Congressman Wolf again, more than a year after I retired from the FBI and a week or two before the 1996 election. Wolf was no longer on the Oversight Committee, but he was still interested in the FBI, Secret Service, and White House security issues.

He again asked me if I knew of any other FBI agents or Secret Service agents who might want to step forward. Frankly, after the thrashing I had taken from the Clinton White House and the dominant liberal media, I was speechless. After my book came out, when I needed support the most, few members of Congress expressed any interest in defending me. The Oversight Committee had clearly distanced itself, worried about the controversy. I told the congressman that as long as witnesses like me were left standing alone against such odds, it was highly unlikely anyone else would come forward.

I left the Hill wondering why I had not been supported more, knowing full well that congressional investigators already knew much of what my book made public; they knew the truth, but wouldn't act, and were content to let the truth-teller catch all the flak. It was discouraging to say the least.

Shortly thereafter, my partner Dennis, now retired, was summoned to Capitol Hill for a similar session. A member of Congress—Dennis has requested that I leave him anonymous—asked him for names of other agents who might come forward. Dennis demurred.

The congressman then told Dennis he didn't like my book because it was flawed. In his view, it contained too much personal and sensational information about the Clintons and their staff, and therefore had no serious impact on the Clinton administration. Dennis asked him if he had actually read it. The congressman admitted he hadn't.

Dennis was angry. He told the congressman that he had known me for more than ten years and had never heard me tell a lie. He said he

could confirm many stories in my book and had his own examples of
Clinton administration wrongdoing that supported my points. He
strongly recommended that the congressman actually read the book
before he continued to condemn it.

As I pursued my post-retirement investigations into the Clinton
White House, I kept crossing paths with David Brock. Phil Larsen
informed me Brock was also writing a book on the Clintons—sure to
be very explosive. Though we had never met, I regarded Brock as
someone who knew a lot about the Clintons's Arkansas days. Brock's
stories in the *American Spectator* had been a revelation, bringing to
light Paula Jones and the Arkansas State Troopers who had been
asked to pimp for then-Governor Clinton.

I eventually met Brock at his office, and told him I wanted to interview the Arkansas State Troopers. I wanted to see if there was anything they hadn't told Brock that they might share with a former
fellow law enforcement officer.

From what Brock told me, it was clear he was not on good terms
with the troopers. The troopers had spoken to Brock "on the
record," but then had serious second thoughts about going public.

Brock laughed as he told me how they had tried to back out of
their story. He was obviously proud that he had forced them into the
public limelight as named sources. The troopers feared retribution.
But Brock was doing very well for himself. His investigations for the
nonprofit *American Spectator* were earning him nearly $200,000 a
year.

After hearing how he treated the troopers, I decided that Brock was
not my kind of "compadre," using people as stepping stones to an
astronomical book advance for an opus on Hillary Clinton. I agreed to
meet him again, but wouldn't share sources or information with him.
I didn't want my friends treated the way he'd treated the troopers.

I saw another, a darker side of Brock at a subsequent meeting. He
told me he knew a high-level Clinton appointee, a supposedly very
eligible bachelor, who was actually a closet homosexual. But Brock
wouldn't out him, because Brock himself was a homosexual and it
would not be appreciated in the "community." The appointee was
close to a man with whom Brock was now involved, which was how
Brock found out about the appointee's secret lifestyle.

It was certainly not my interest to out anybody, but Brock apparently sized me up that way. I told Brock that I had no interest in using his information. (In fact, it only underlined for me the twisted ways of Washington.) Brock seemed disappointed. Then Brock tried to tell me about another Clinton employee, this time a high-level female, who was supposed to be a notorious lush. Again, I demurred, telling him my focus was the breakdown of the security system at the White House. Unless these people lied to the FBI on their FBI background checks or unless he had evidence that their behavior endangered national security or violated White House rules or standards, their stories were of no interest to me. Again, he seemed disappointed.

Brock's *American Spectator* pieces had focused on Governor Clinton's alleged extramarital affairs. It seemed to be his primary interest. But it was certainly not mine.

As an investigative journalist, Brock made regular stops at the House Government Reform and Oversight Committee, keeping them advised on the "blockbuster" book he was writing on the Clintons.

I have been told by several high-level sources on the committee that everyone there had high hopes for "the Brock and Aldrich books." Apparently they knew, as I did, that the dominant liberal media was hiding the Clinton administration's scandals and abuses. If we could get the truth out in the open, the committee's job would be easier, politically safer.

High-level sources on the committee told me that investigators were already outlining areas where I might be called to testify. But the committee would soon back off.

I made the mistake of giving Brock an advance copy of my book. Brock's own book was still months away from completion. I had no problem with his using some of my material as background, but evidently he had a problem with what he saw as a rival book.

Brock attacked me on the Marriott Hotel story (see Chapter 9). Brock had worked on this promising lead, and had been telling anyone who would listen to him, including me, that his information and his sources were very strong. When he related the allegation, he never included qualifiers, or caveats, or passed the buck to third- or fourth-hand sources. I even called him before the book went to press and asked him if he would object to my using the story. Not only did he not object, he didn't back off from the story. I told him I had developed additional evidence that the president was slipping away from his Secret Service detail, and I was satisfied there was enough to include the story in my book.

Brock had a reputation as a good investigator, and he had given me many details. He identified the location of the hotel, and told me where the cars were parked, and which elevators were used. Brock said he took the same elevator, and confirmed that it could be used to bypass the hotel lobby.

My interest in the story, however, was quite different than Brock's. He wanted to catch the president with some bimbo. My interest was what it meant, from a security point of view, if the president was essentially missing for hours at a time. I was aghast—and could hardly believe—the president might be without his secret service protective detail. So I tried to "knock down" the story by proving the secret service was always with Clinton. But what I found shocked me. Several witnesses confirmed that Clinton left the White House without his secret service detail. I also uncovered—through my own investigations and interviews—how the president could slip out of the White House without the knowledge of the Secret Service. Other sources appeared to corroborate other important aspects of Brock's story.[1] I had come to a point where the weight of evidence indicated it was true. Still, I was careful to couch the story in terms of what "would go into a raw FBI report." My point in surfacing the story was to spur further investigation by the proper authorities—by the FBI, or by the next Bob Woodward for that matter. The national security implications, after all, were enormous.

---

[1] How could the president elude the ever-vigilant, ever-present White House press corps? Helen Thomas, a long-time White House correspondent provided the answer in her nationally syndicated column of July 4, 1997:

"Reporters have counted on straight information from the White House press office when it comes to the president's activities, but lately they are beginning to wonder if 'straight' is subject to interpretation.

"When a press aide says there is a 'lid on,' it means the president is inside, usually in the White House quarters, and is staying put for the night. That means reporters and photographers on the 'body watch' or so-called protective coverage, can leave.

"But lately, the press corps has found that within minutes of leaving the White House, that lid somehow comes 'off' and the president is on his way to a restaurant or a friend's home.

"When members of the media protested about such incidents, an aide said, 'He's the president, he ought to be able to do what he wants to do.'

"But that isn't exactly playing straight. When a president is in public, the public should know. And given the security concerns when the president is out and about, it is even more important that the 'body watchers' are around."

But Brock turned the Marriott story into a landmine for me, claiming he was "shocked, shocked" that I had printed a mere "rumor." Brock apparently wanted to position himself as a media darling—a "right-wing" critic of *Unlimited Access*—perhaps to set up liberal media approval for his own book. But it wasn't only liberals who applauded Brock. He provided convenient cover for conservatives who wanted to "prove" their moderation or bipartisanship by distancing themselves from me. I became a useful lightning rod to deflect criticism from themselves and their own investigations. George Will, for one, pounced on Brock's repudiation of the Marriott story (a repudiation that had not yet gone public) and blindsided me with it on *This Week with David Brinkley*.

Another surprise was having my accuracy questioned by Phil Larsen, now retired. He unwittingly helped the media discredit me, blurting out to a *Newsweek* reporter that one quotation I attributed to him wasn't *exactly* as he recalled it. I hadn't taken notes. I didn't record our conversations. I used my best recollection to recreate Larsen's remarks, which had been made to me three years before I wrote the book. I was stunned that Larsen would allow such a minor mistake—if mistake it was—to be turned into a major issue with a news reporter. The reporter—no friend to conservative causes—was gleeful to get such a remark from a former committee investigator. Larsen's claim of a single inaccurate quote had grave consequences in terms of my credibility.

Ironically, it was Larsen who had played a major role in convincing me to come forward. He knew I had put my job on the line by providing such cooperation. Moreover, he was experienced at handling the media; he knew their rules and their prejudices. I was stunned that he would undercut me without so much as a phone call.

I called Larsen and he quickly apologized, telling me he wished he hadn't been named and quoted in the book, but claiming the reporter had caught him "off guard." But it was too late. The damage was done.

Now the wolf pack press began to tear into me. Reporters fanned out to find additional witnesses who could hammer my credibility. All they found was more and more confirmation that my book was accurate. But that wasn't "news."

Even the more conservative press—which looks to the dominant liberal press for approval—was reluctant to support me or to follow up on leads that could have confirmed the Marriott story. One former Clinton White House employee independently, but not for attribution, confirmed the main outline of the story to my publisher, though this person knew of only one incident. Another source said my only error was that I had the wrong hotel.

Let me be categorical: I stand by the Marriott story, and even if we have to wait thirty years to get the truth from the mainstream media—as we've had to wait to get the truth about the Kennedy White House—I am absolutely certain that the truth will emerge and that the entire story will be completely confirmed. I am *that* confident about the comprehensiveness of my sources beyond David Brock.

In the end, not knowing whether to believe me or Brock, the Oversight Committee decided I was too "hot," too controversial to be used as a prime witness, and they swiftly abandoned plans to have me appear in front of television cameras before the committee. I'm sure some rationalized that they had Brock's book coming as a backup. If so, they quickly found out how wrong they were about that. Publishing sources told me that Brock's book, the *Seduction of Hillary Rodham,* was having serious editorial problems. When the book was finally released, it was an enormous flop, a veritable *Titanic* disaster for his publisher, the Free Press. The Oversight Committee investigators rapidly turned their backs on Brock.

Many went on to describe Brock's book as a love letter to Hillary Clinton. I didn't think it was that bad. But he certainly didn't do me, or the truth, any favors. My goal was to alert the American people to the wrongdoings of the Clinton White House and the massive implications for our national security—and I did it at grave risk to the financial well-being of my family. But for Brock, it appears that fame and fortune were everything, and that the truth was subordinate to promoting his book and "dissing" the competition.

Brock's relationship with the *American Spectator* predictably soured, and he was eventually stripped of his six-figure salary and told he would now be paid per article. Though defended to the end by his loyal editor R. Emmett Tyrrell, Jr., Brock attacked his patrons on the right as "homophobic." No doubt he thought that was good marketing, too.

Of course, David Brock wasn't much of an assailant—or even the most prominent. That honor must go to George Stephanopoulos, the crown prince of the Clinton administration's "masters of disaster"—who had managed to spin every Clinton scandal into an assault on the whistle-blower. Stephanopoulos made a concerted effort to convince national network news shows to drop me as a guest—and in large part, he succeeded.

What was especially galling about this was not so much the dominant liberal media's craven capitulation to Clinton White House pressure, but the fact that no one called Stephanopoulos on his rhetorical overkill. Stephanopoulos called me a "pathological liar," which certainly qualifies as slander and was demonstrably untrue given my record in the FBI. But Stephanopoulos got respectful air time and I didn't. He even refused to concede that *anything* in my book was true—something that even my harshest critic, if at all fair-minded, couldn't say. In other words, it was an obvious lie. But no one accused Stephanopoulos of being irresponsible, as I was accused of being. And, no, ABC News didn't offer me a regular seat on the *Brinkley* show as they did for Stephanopoulos, nor was I invited to teach a class at Harvard, as Stephanopoulos was. How the media managed to convince itself that a professional spin doctor had more credibility that a thirty-year FBI veteran whose account of the White House was backed up in sworn testimony by his FBI partner—Dennis Sculimbrene—says volumes, to my mind, about the amazing bias of the dominant liberal media.

Most people know that the work of a trained law enforcement officer and that of an investigative journalist is very much the same—except that a law enforcement officer is chosen for good character, has more investigative training, knows how to gather evidence for a court of law, has higher standards, and is always held to a higher standard. Admittedly, journalists are usually better educated. But skill with the written word is one thing. Ethics and honesty are another—and something that's not often learned or even emphasized at Harvard, Berkeley, or Yale where political correctness is the only "truth" lately recognized.

When even the media had to concede security breeches—with the Clinton "coffees" and "sleep overs" and other events with shady characters, some of whom actually had outstanding warrants for their arrest—I kept waiting for the liberal media to write the stories and air the broadcasts about how the White House security system had broken down, how Gary Aldrich and Dennis Sculimbrene had tried to warn them about it, how I had been unjustly criticized, and how Dennis had been hounded into retirement. I'm still waiting.

My initial contact with the press was actually positive. On June 13, about three weeks before *Unlimited Access*'s publication date, I had an editorial published in the *Wall Street Journal* outlining some of the security problems I came across at the White House.

Almost immediately, my phone started ringing. Although my number was unlisted, the media managed to get it. I received calls from almost every major news agency in the world, continuously, all day long, and late into the night.

Around lunchtime, after I had logged more than one hundred calls, several cars arrived at my residence. Soon reporters and television network representatives, waving hand-written notes from producers or media stars, were coming to the front door and ringing the bell incessantly. I was not taking calls, nor was I inclined to answer the door, but they would not go away. Finally, I went outside, talked to each reporter, took their cards and told them I would call them when I had something to say. They accepted my response, and were friendly and cooperative. But the Clinton "masters of disaster" had not yet gone into overdrive. When they did, the media readily accepted their character assassination of me.

The "masters of disaster" were created by Harold Ickes, the president's then-Deputy Chief of Staff, and the former attorney of record for at least one allegedly "mobbed-up" union leader. Ickes's solution to the scandal-a-week problem at the White House was brilliant: move the scandal response to another, lesser level, away from the Oval office, and as far away from the press secretary and the president as possible.

Ickes choose a former Reno Justice Department lawyer, Jane Sherburne, to head up the unit, which would report not to the press office, but directly to Ickes. It was eventually staffed by more than twenty full-time government employees, including lawyer Mark Fabiani who had done similar damage control for ethically-challenged Tom Bradley, mayor of Los Angeles.

This had never been done before. Press inquiries were always handled by the Press Office. Likewise, legal matters had always been handled by the Counsel's Office. Ickes's "masters of disaster" usurped both these functions and turned them into something else. The "MOD Squad," as I began to call it, existed, and still exists, for the sole purpose of taking witnesses like me "out" and "killing" scandals—and does so, I might add, at taxpayers' expense.

The Ickes unit was housed in Room 488 of the OEOB, well away from the more formal activities of the president, but close to resources that would come in very handy, such as the recording studios of the White House Communications Agency, which the Clintons converted from a largely national-security-focused media monitoring operation—it is staffed, in fact, by military personnel—to a political enemy media monitoring system.

Ickes's symbolic message: "Important issues, such as the president's agenda, are handled by the press secretary. Less important matters, such as scandals, subpoenas, and other messy business are handled by our munchkins in the OEOB."

The first order of business was to identify the scandals so the "masters of disaster" could formulate a plan of counterattack for each. Ickes tasked Sherburne to come up with the list of scandals. She identified thirty-nine separate, significant Clinton scandals—a list that has been obtained by the House Oversight Committee.

The MOD Squad's counterattacks were not confined to digging up dirt on potential witnesses against the president, or providing misinformation to the compliant media. During congressional investigations, Sherburne and her lieutenants from this home-grown "ministry of misinformation" would be seen meeting with important witnesses, going behind closed doors with Democratic Congressmen, hustling around reporters, and spinning, spinning, spinning. Some investigators believed their activities came close to obstruction of justice.

When a new scandal or new witness showed up on their radar screens, they would swing into action. They got so good at destroying witnesses and bringing doubt on important evidence via the dominant liberal media, that they began to call the media their "Arsenal of Democracy."

The "masters of disaster" became so bold that when they had a little down time, they crafted a 332-page report entitled, "Communication Stream of Conspiracy Commerce," a masterpiece of paranoia—or sincerely meant disinformation—that tried to portray the Clintons as the victims of a right-wing conspiracy. You could have fooled me. Indeed, from my experience, the conspiracies all appeared to be in the other direction.

The day after Shapiro gave my book to Jack Quinn, a very curious thing happened. A middle-aged white male parked across the street from my house and watched my wife and children as they walked the fifty yards to the bus stop.

Other mothers at the bus stop noticed him. He had a decidedly menacing appearance, and one mother decided to note his tag number and call the police if he kept hanging around.

My wife, who had been an FBI agent, thought he fit the profile of a retired law enforcement officer. She "made him" as a private investigator, and meant to confront him on the way back to our house. But after our children boarded the school bus, he drove away, following it.

My wife and I searched the area where the car had been parked. He had been there long enough to smoke several cigarettes.

We checked with each neighbor to determine if they were expecting a visitor, or knew the car. Nobody knew him. Our street ends in a cul de sac, and is not used as a shortcut to any other street. People who come to our street have a purpose for being there.

Naturally, we didn't know then that Shapiro had given my book to the Clinton White House exactly one day before this very unsettling incident. I had the car's tag checked, but a PI friend told me the tag came back "unlisted." Somebody didn't want us to trace that car.

Still later, somebody set off a cherry bomb or M-80 or some other explosive inside our mail box, late at night. I saved the evidence. Nothing like this had happened to us before—except when dirty tricksters threw Clinton/Gore campaign signs on our lawn. But I suppose the "masters of disaster" would tell me I should feel lucky it was only my mailbox that blew up.

Chapter Thirteen

RADIO FREE AMERICA

Rules for Radicals: "No organization, including organized religion, can live up to the letter of its own book. You can club them to death with their 'book' of rules and regulations. This is what that great revolutionary, Paul of Tarsus, knew when he wrote to the Corinthians: 'Who also hath made us able ministers of the New Testament; not of the letter, but of the spirit; for the letter killeth.'"

George Washington's Rules of Civility and Decent Behaviour: "When a man does all he can though it succeeds not well blame him not that did it."

In order to get to the ABC studios, I needed to get up very early Sunday morning. It was not helpful that I had stayed up late Saturday night, preparing for my first major network appearance, and had trouble sleeping on top of that.

Unlimited Access had exploded in the media on Thursday. Since then, we had received frantic invitations from *Meet the Press* and the other major Sunday morning talk shows. I had wanted to go on Tony Snow's program, but was overruled by the public relations team my publisher and I had assembled to help market the book. Snow had worked in the White House, and seemed more friendly to conservative causes. Snow was fair, balanced, and, in my view, more interesting. But we eventually selected ABC's *This Week with David Brinkley* because it had a larger audience.

Two long sessions with a television media consultant were fresh in my mind, but appearing on the *Brinkley* show would unnerve anyone about to launch a verbal carpet-bombing of the Clinton administration. I understood my book was an accusation against the president of the United States, and I knew the gravity of what I was about to do. I respected the office, but, knowing what I knew, I couldn't respect the man who now held it.

Everyone was nervous. I was getting plenty of advice—from my publisher, from my lawyers, from the media consultants, from my family and friends. Everyone was giving advice like crazy, because everyone was as nervous as I was. Lots of folks had reputations riding on this effort, but no one so much as I.

Nina looked me over, straightened my tie, brushed my hair, and pronounced me a fit enough warrior for an appearance before fifty million people, on a Sunday morning—taking on the Clinton White House.

I looked out the front window and saw the blue Lincoln Continental idling in the driveway. For a moment I thought, "Go away, leave me alone." I swallowed hard and realized that I'd rather be in Mexico or any place but here. Still, I'd made a commitment.

The *Brinkley* executives really knew how to treat a guest. For the first time in my life, somebody opened a door for me, and then got behind the wheel wearing a black brimmed cap.

I punched the electric window button, and lowered the darkened glass, grinning a little too foolishly at my family, standing there in the driveway, camera up to save that Kodak moment. My children ran over, not really clear about what I was about to do, but sensing that it must be important. They crowded around the window and "oohed and aahed" at the black interior of the leather-lined Lincoln Town Car.

Then we sped off, heading east toward Washington—a ride that would take about thirty minutes. We stopped by the Embassy Suites Hotel in downtown Washington to pick up Matt Glavin. Glavin was president of the Southeastern Legal Foundation, the group that backed me up, and was the only one I would allow near me on this most important morning.

The others—the PR people—had been making me nervous lately, as they pushed and pulled, tugged and advised, as if *their* lives depended on it. It was not their life.

I knew they were only trying to help, but it was unnerving, and the more they were around, the more it was a reminder that I was about to launch myself into an enormous controversy, the likes of which my family and I could not fully appreciate until many months later—after I had survived the media assaults and the Department of Justice threats.

Only then could I bear to play the videotape of the *Brinkley* program—the one that simultaneously boosted me into the stratosphere, while nicking my trajectory enough to send me and my book spinning wildly, almost out of control.

The PR people pretended that they knew what was going to happen, but they didn't. In truth, no one could have predicted it. Most of the time, I was running on instinct, the instincts of an FBI agent, honed over the course of twenty-six years of being attacked by defense attorneys, and dodging real bullets. The Clinton White House was a virtual nest of defense attorneys—that was what I was up against.

It's a very good thing I didn't know that the White House had been given a copy of my manuscript more than four months before the *Brinkley* program. I was nervous enough as it was.

We pulled up to the front of the ABC studios. The car was immediately surrounded by waiting news cameramen and "anchor" personalities shoving microphones, all trying to get tape of our arrival. Matt asked the driver if there was some back entrance that we might use. The driver thought there was, and alerted the appropriate people with his cell phone.

We went around the block, cameramen chasing the car for a short distance. I saw several speak into walkie-talkies as the Lincoln sped away. The reason for the hand-held radios became clear, as we rounded the corner and headed into the alley behind ABC's studios. There was a wall of cameramen in the alley, anticipating the maneuver. The car went forward, nearly running over a few, as we drove toward a gated wire fence, complete with security guard.

The gate closed behind us, and the guard and a few helpers prevented the news media from rushing inside. Cameras were trained on me anyway, as I got out of the car and made my way to the studio. Questions were shouted, but I have no recollection of anything they asked. I can't even recall if I responded, but their frenzy was early evidence we might have a bestseller on our hands.

We were escorted to the "Green Room" by friendly staff, but the room was already filled with members of the White House "masters of disaster"—George Stephanopoulos and others sent down to "do" Gary Aldrich. As we walked into the room, a hush came over the Clinton crowd. As fast as we had entered, we quickly exited. I had no interest in being in the same room with Stephanopoulos—then, now, or ever.

An ABC staffer allowed us to use a nearby empty control room, where I was joined by the PR team and barraged by advice, as if I was a fighter about to go into the ring.

There was a knock at the door, and I saw a friendly face through the window. It was Dorrance Smith, a high-level Bush administration appointee, now executive director of the *Brinkley* show. I was glad to see Dorrance; his friendliness was an oasis in an otherwise bleak and hostile environment.

We chatted for a few minutes about the "good old Bush days" and then I was taken away to the makeup department. Dorrance wished me "good luck," and I was led off.

Entering the brightly lit room, two barber-like chairs at the ready, I sat down, feeling like a man having his head shaved in anticipation of the electric chair. I wasn't too far off in my assessment of the circumstances. A sense of dread came over me, even as the makeup artist transformed my face into something worthy for the TV cameras.

I was led back to the control booth. The program had already started, and Defense Secretary William Perry was being questioned— long distance—about a huge terrorist bomb that had killed many American soldiers. Many were wondering if American soldiers lay dead on foreign soil because of someone's stupidity or incompetence, but the *Brinkley* group treated Clinton's Defense Secretary with the utmost politeness. Would I get the same velvet glove treatment for surfacing serious wrongdoing in the federal government? Not likely.

Commercials came on, and attendants appeared at the door. "Are you ready, Mr. Aldrich?"

Yes, no, maybe, I don't know. "Yes, let's do it."

Matt shook my hand. "Good luck, my friend. No matter how this comes out, you're doing the right thing, Gary."

Matt and I had become close. We had already been through many print media interviews, most of which had been confrontational: *Newsweek, Time, U.S. News & World Report,* the *Weekly Standard,* the *New York Times,* the *Washington Times,* the *Washington Post,* the *New York Post,* and many more.

Matt and I, assisted by Craig Shirley, had covered a lot of ground in a few days. I was used to answering questions. But this was much bigger. Craig, a seasoned and savvy PR expert from Alexandria, had distinguished himself as an informed, mature man with good instincts. Obviously Shirley had seen a lot of political combat, and he had friends on both sides of the political aisle. Craig and Matt worked well together, and I knew they were trying to keep my interests in mind.

I was led onto the set. David Brinkley, George Will, and Sam Donaldson looked up at me. I said, "Good morning." Brinkley said, "Welcome to the program."

Will nodded, as did Donaldson. Otherwise nothing was said. There was no attempt to put me at ease. No friendly patter. It wasn't exactly hostile, but close.

As we sat there in silence, microphones being adjusted and tested, staffers checking coats and ties and hiding wires, I heard the commercial running. Someone said, "Stand by." Here we go.

My segment started with a three- or four-minute pre-recorded video by Bob Zelnick, a White House correspondent for ABC news. He talked about the FBI file scandal and Craig Livingstone. He described my book as "a collection of gamy, raunchy, salacious details of life in the Clinton White House," never mentioning the national security issues. Zelnick continued, "A quite sensational book. The White House denied it all, angrily, bitterly," as a picture of the White House popped up on the monitor. There was videotape of Craig Livingstone testifying in front of the House Oversight Committee, trying to explain away hundreds of illegally obtained FBI files on political "enemies."

Next, President Clinton. Then a picture of me walking—B-roll tape, filmed days earlier—followed by a picture of my book. There was a video clip of Tony Coehlo saying: "I know there is a group of right-wing extremists who will do anything to destroy this president." Zelnick then reported in a "voice over" that Coehlo intended to sue me, a threat that quickly evaporated when my book no longer threatened Clinton's reelection.

Then there was a clip of a Marriott employee denying that Clinton could have visited a Marriott hotel without being seen. What was left unsaid is that there are three Marriott hotels near the White House. For security reasons, I didn't identify which hotel was involved, and Brinkley's team evidently didn't do much investigative reporting to check out the hotel's claims, or they would have found what I found.

I thought I heard someone counting down, "5, 4, 3, 2," and then David Brinkley said: "It was almost as if someone opened a trunk in the attic that should have been kept closed."

He described *Unlimited Access* as "a book that oozes contempt for the social, cultural, and political mores of the Clinton White House." His tone verged on the contemptuous—not contemptuous of the Clintons, but of me.

I have watched the videotape of the program many times. It was months before I could watch it; I found it that traumatic. That may sound odd coming from a seasoned FBI agent who testified many times in many trials. But this was the "big one"—a jury trial with millions of members on a collective jury, but with no prosecutor present to make sure my side was heard.

This was a very important case, but there was only one witness— me—and *three* "defense attorneys."

Brinkley asked me about "who hired Craig Livingstone." I tried to answer, but he cut me off. I guess I exceeded my soundbite, and it was clear he didn't really want to hear me out anyway. The questioners wanted to draw blood, not get answers.

George Will was next: "The heart of your book, and what makes you think it's important—the security provisions at the White House—but, before people can get to that, they have to answer a threshold question of, 'Can you be believed?'"

He then announced that he had spoken to David Brock. Brock had said he was my source for the Marriott Hotel story, and that it had been merely a rumor. Brock, Will said, "was appalled to see it in print." Will asked me to explain, and to admit Brock was my only source.

I said I could not confirm or deny that Brock was a source, and that I would not reveal my sources any more than any other journalist would. I described Brock's statement and behavior as "bizarre," as I could not find any other explanation for his broadside attacks.

I tried to explain why I included the Marriott Hotel story in the book. I didn't care, really, if the president was seeing a woman who was not his wife. My issue was that he was out of range of the White House protective umbrella—without his Secret Service protection.

Will then asked about Hillary's Christmas tree. Will said that Ann Stock, the first lady's social secretary, flatly denied my allegations. The insinuation was that my own first-hand account of the obscene Christmas decorations was a lie. Apparently, Will had no problem accepting the word of a Clinton staff member against the word of a career FBI agent.

Will challenged me to take a polygraph about the Christmas tree story. In retrospect, I should have accepted the challenge—it would have made things more clear-cut. Instead, in a distinction that was probably missed by many, I upped the ante and said I was willing to testify under oath to the truth of everything in my book. I knew that polygraphs had mixed results, but you could be sent to prison for lying under oath.

Before the segment ended, Will took another run at me, "Did you put the [Christmas tree] stuff in there promiscuously just to make sure it got read?" That was an absurd question to ask any writer. Of course I wanted people to read my book. Of course I wanted to provide them with news that was important—as I judged the security and the character of the president and first lady to be.

Next, Donaldson took the point: "But sir! When you make a serious charge against someone, a court of law might require," the naming of sources. I told the panel that I would not name my White House sources because they would be punished by the Clintons.

Donaldson reminded me that Tony Coelho was intending to sue me. I reminded Donaldson that a civil suit would give me unlimited discovery abilities, a legal process available to defendants in any lawsuit, and that Coelho had a lot to lose if he gave me that power.

Donaldson then asked me about the meeting I had in the safe with Livingstone, bearing down on the story Craig told me regarding Foster's state of mind.

How could Livingstone have known whether Vince Foster and Hillary had an affair? Donaldson asked. It was another ridiculous question, designed to set up a straw man. The point was that Livingstone believed it to be true and presented the information as if it were common knowledge.

"Did Livingstone catch them *in flagrante delicto?*" was Donaldson's real question. But of course nobody had claimed that they had been seen in bed together. Many credible witnesses, however, had seen them holding hands, kissing passionately, grabbing intimate body parts, and otherwise acting in very indiscreet and telling ways. At least one Arkansas Trooper confessed he had driven the pair to a lonely mountain cabin getaway, and left them there for quite awhile. Did anybody see them in the actual act? The simple answer was "No." Was there plenty of circumstantial evidence, enough to convict them in most any civil court of having an extramarital affair? The answer appeared to be

"Yes." But Donaldson wanted me to recite the entire case in a ten-second sound bite, which was impossible.

That didn't seem to matter to Donaldson. Instead, he exclaimed: "So you don't know that story is true!" which was a non sequitor, given that I was quoting Livingstone and never claimed to have a confession from Hillary or incriminating videotapes.

Brinkley then asked me if a single person had stepped forward to back up anything I said.

I was ready for that question, "Yes, as a matter of fact...."

"Who? Name one!"

I named Special Agent Dennis Sculimbrene, my partner, who had worked at the White House since Jimmy Carter.

Dennis had testified under oath to much of what I wrote in my book, but Brinkley dismissed him as simply someone who might be in cahoots with me.

And so it went. It was an almost unremittingly hostile grilling. I still managed to get a few good points in, and amazingly, Sam Donaldson actually asked me some intelligent questions. Donaldson was the only one, in my view, who was at all interested in the material in my book that was more important—the national security issues.

George Will had one last parting shot for me: "But it's reputations presented to the country!" He mischaracterized my book as a "raw" FBI file, and demeaned FBI agents as investigators who traded in "rumors and nonsense."

I did, however, get the last word. "Ninety-eight percent of my book," I reminded Brinkley and his panel, "is my own first-hand observations and investigations, and the issue here is national security!"

I guess Mr. Will and the others had forgotten that far less evidence than mine had been used by the Clintons to fire seven men, ruin their reputations, and even try to put them in prison. And while Billy Dale and his friends waited for FBI agents who might arrive with search warrants, subpoenas, or even handcuffs, they were each treated to visits from the IRS audit squad. When it came to trashing reputations—or trashing the White House and its traditions—no one could do a better job than the Clintons.

My segment—my chance to tell the world about the Clinton administration, at least on television—was over. The Clintons had managed to get commitments from all the other networks to keep me off the air. So, as I stood up and took off the microphone I pondered what might lie ahead.

"Mr. Aldrich, I think you held up well. You stood up well under the circumstances, and I thank you." I looked over at the person talking to me—it was not George Will or David Brinkley, but Sam Donaldson.

I muttered my appreciation, as Brinkley and Will looked at their shoelaces. Time to go. I turned, and headed off the set. Coming right at me was Mr. Spin Control himself, the Brinkley group's next interview, George Stephanopoulos, with "documents" in hand. I stared at him. As we passed, he glared at me, shouting, "Liar!"

He was loud enough for others to hear, and the incident was duly reported in some newspapers.

Brinkley welcomed Stephanopoulos, and asked him if he was present to represent the White House. Stephanopoulos acknowledged that he was, and soon gave the Brinkley group the collaborators' compliment they richly deserved, "I think that you all did more than an adequate job of destroying his credibility."

Will reminded Stephanopoulos that the White House had pulled out all the stops to keep me off this program, and all the others.

"Someone should pass a bare threshold of credibility before they are invited to speak to millions of Americans," Stephanopoulos said. "His story couldn't get past the fact checker at the *National Enquirer*."

Stephanopoulos scolded the panel. "If ABC news put him on, then there should be some questions asked." I took that to be a veiled threat that the Clinton administration would punish ABC, denying them access to presidential interviews.

Stephanopoulos went on: "We must look behind Gary Aldrich. It's no accident that in the studio today, with Gary Aldrich, is an advisor to the Dole Campaign, a paid agent of the tobacco lobby, a paid agent of the gun lobby, a representative of a group that is closely tied to Speaker Gingrich, a spokesperson in the Buchanan presidential campaign."

Stephanopoulos had nearly doubled the number of people who were actually with me in the studio. There were three people with me—all PR people I had met *after* writing the book. I was representing no one but myself—and the truth.

On it went, with Will and Brinkley asking soft-ball questions. Only Donaldson was willing to ask Stephanopoulos the tough questions. Hadn't I put my finger on some real concerns? Weren't there national security problems at the White House?

Stephanopoulos said the problems had been "fixed," which would have been news to Charlie Trie, John Huang, Jorge "Gordito" Cabrera—a famous South Florida cocaine dealer—and the other shady characters who were traipsing through the Clinton White House.

Stephanopoulos was getting frisky. When asked how an FBI agent with more than thirty years' experience could write such an "unbelievable" book, he sniffed, "Well, thirty years of service in the FBI is no evidence in and of itself of credibility... after all, J. Edgar Hoover had more than thirty years in the FBI as well."

Stephanopoulos described me as a "tool," and compared me to the "Willie Horton" ads that took out candidate Michael Dukakis. "In a sad way and in a strange way, ABC has also become a tool," Stephanapoulos said, sounding disappointed. "This is nothing but a smear campaign by operatives of the Republican Party."

Stephanopoulos finished by waving papers around, "Dozens of people have disputed Gary Aldrich," insinuating that he had statements from those "dozens" in his hand. Nobody asked to see these so called "statements."

The papers were later given to us, and were allegedly from seven individuals, not dozens, and were on plain bond, consisting of one paragraph each. They were undated, unsigned "statements" from such giants of credibility as Dee Dee Meyers—a person who had lied straight-faced to the media for years.

Dee Dee eventually left the White House—just another shameless flack for a corrupt administration. But like George Stephanopoulos, she promptly took a job with the mainstream media—the Clinton White House's "arsenal of democracy."

Weeks later, when revelations about the surprising White House access of Trie, Huang, Cabrera, and others were being reported daily, George Will managed a rather anemic apology confessing that the general thrust of my book about security problems at the White House appeared to be correct.

There were few other television opportunities available to me. The "masters of disaster" had bullied the networks to cancel several major appearances. *Larry King Live* and *Dateline* were just two shows that abruptly canceled my appearances.

At the White House, George Stephanopoulos was crowing that his success in keeping me off the networks would destroy the book. "We killed it!" he was quoted as saying.

But my team didn't skip a beat. If we couldn't get on television, we would use any other means available to get the word out. Craig Shirley had logged more than four hundred requests from talk radio hosts all over the nation. We had always planned to have me on talk radio, but these numbers amazed even Craig. Al Regnery went on *Larry King Live* and on radio shows where I wasn't welcome to defend myself and the book. And Regnery's PR staff, including the office of their PR consultant, Greg Mueller, were frantically "blast-faxing" responses to every false allegation made by the White House and the liberal media pundits. At one point, the PR group commissioned a poll to determine who the general public believed: me or the White House. I won the poll 2 to 1. The results of the poll were also blast-faxed to hundreds of locations.

My first radio talk show was Oliver North's program, which reaches millions of listeners. As we drove to the studios of the Salem Radio Network in Rosslyn, Virginia, we spotted a crowd of television cameramen and reporters. This was one of my first public events after Brinkley. Matt and I knew a back way in and managed to avoid the cameramen. In hindsight, I don't really know why I was trying to avoid the cameras except that the Brinkley show had made me very suspicious of television and the way television reporters try to "package" a story, setting up a fall-guy, dealing in sound bites, and ignoring inconvenient facts.

After the North program, we drove to G. Gordon Liddy's show. The "G" Man was very welcoming, and we enjoyed talking for an hour about the Clinton White House, and our mutual concerns about the FBI. Several million people listen to Liddy, and I was happy to field callers' questions. The questions they asked were hard, but fair. Liddy didn't cut me off, the way Brinkley's people did, and given time to explain my position, I found that listeners could be won over. Talk radio was much freer than network television, and serious issues could be debated at the appropriate length.

After the first radio shows, which were in person, I set up a small studio in my home, complete with headphones to begin the process of being a regular radio talk show guest, interviewed over the telephone.

I did show after show, taking many calls from concerned listeners. The audiences were friendly and well informed, and the shows became easier as I went along. The PR staff set up a fax line to me, and sent me daily schedules, listing as many as twelve shows a day. Many days I would begin my morning with headphones securely positioned, coffee on my desk, ready to talk to audiences numbering in the millions.

I blanketed major listening areas all across the country, on conservative talk shows as well as Christian broadcasting stations, and even some liberal shows. And the best part was, not a single person had to listen to me if they didn't choose to—it was the essence of free speech.

I recall one particular hour when I learned I was talking live on more than 1,300 local stations around the country, and 119 stations worldwide. It was awe-inspiring.

There were two keys to my success on talk radio. One was that I was telling the truth. With fair-minded hosts—and without the pressure of having to think in television soundbites—I could relax and make a detailed argument, which I was happy to do, because I didn't have the problem liars often face of having to remember their last lie.

Another important component of my success was the fact that most every host was well informed about the Clintons and my book. On the Brinkley show I had the impression that at least one of the panelists hadn't even read my book. Not so with the talk show hosts, who are in a highly competitive business where to be misinformed means to lose your audience.

As even more Clinton scandals unfolded, media giants like Paul Harvey and Rush Limbaugh recommended my book to millions more listeners as the truth about what was really going on in the White House. They credited my book with being an early warning signal that was being vindicated day after day. Book sales took off.

Within a month, *Unlimited Access* was on the *New York Times* bestseller list, and by August 5, 1997, it had reached number one on the *New York Times,* UPI, the *Wall Street Journal,* and other bestseller lists. My publishers could not print and ship the book fast enough.

But by early August, a new shiver went up my spine. Just as my wife and I were congratulating ourselves that we could now buy those braces for the kids, and send them to college without worrying about tuition costs, the FBI and the Department of Justice announced that they would file a lawsuit to recover all the book's proceeds, because we printed the book without FBI approval.

A federal lawsuit meant years of litigation, endless legal maneuvering, and fighting Janet Reno's Department of Justice, with its limitless resources, teams of lawyers, and the power of the FBI. Matt Glavin's Southeastern Legal Foundation would provide the lawyers, but could we actually fight the entire U.S. government and win?

I knew the stories in my book were true, and I knew it was just a matter of time before I would be fully vindicated. But the "masters of disaster" had frightened many conservatives (and all the moderates) from coming to my defense. My wife and I were enormously disappointed by this. With the threat from the FBI and the Justice Department now so high—and with so few allies in sight—Nina and I were actually discussing pulling the plug on the book and shutting down our promotion efforts.

Then the telephone rang. A total stranger introduced herself, and invited me and my family to come to San Diego the Saturday before the Republican Convention to speak to a group of six hundred high-profile conservatives, some of whom had served in the Reagan and Bush White Houses.

I have since joined this wonderful organization—the Council for National Policy, or CNP—and found a home with persons who love our country as I do. Founded by longtime Virginia conservative Morton Blackwell, CNP members are heads of major conservative organizations or major donors who support them. The rules of the organization do not allow the disclosure of membership. But the fellowship and warmth of these patriotic, God-fearing, honest, hardworking, and successful people provided desperately needed validation and moral support for Nina and me. I have been working hard with the CNP and other such groups to promote conservative causes ever since.

In San Diego, with my family looking on, I took the stage in front of the most dynamic group I had ever seen. This was my first major public address, so naturally I was a little nervous. When I looked around the room at these giants of industry, public service, and conservative volunteer organizations, I realized that we had broken through. My story had been accepted.

Before I spoke, the then-president of CNP, former Attorney

General Edwin Meese, a personal hero of mine, made an eloquent speech about how things had been, not so long ago, in a White House occupied by two men of decency—Ronald Reagan and George Bush.

Meese had managed a tremendous Department of Justice, and had contributed greatly to a reenergized, reinvigorated, and proud FBI. All the agents loved this guy and knew him to be decent, honorable, and trustworthy. General Meese would have made a great FBI director.

After complimenting me, my book, and Nina's support of it, he motioned me to the microphone.

Everyone rose from their seats. The clapping, cheering, and whistles went on and on and on. I had not seen such enthusiasm in my lifetime, and I was greatly moved. I tried to speak, but they just would not stop. It was embarrassing. I didn't feel worthy of it.

Finally I was able to speak, voice cracking at first, overcome by emotion. I asked Nina to stand. I could never have done the book without her support, encouragement, and courage. The crowd of six hundred rose again, and Nina received a standing ovation. I was moved to tears, and for a time I could not find my voice. When I was able to talk, I told the group about my days in the FBI and at the White House—the "people's house" that the Clintons had sullied and demeaned.

In the weeks and months that followed, as new evidence made headlines about security breaches at the White House, with the Lincoln bedroom for sale and suspected Chinese agents running amuck, reporters sometimes asked if I now felt vindicated.

I usually answered "yes" to be polite. But vindication really happened for me that night in San Diego, when six hundred people with sterling reputations, took the risk and joined their reputations with mine. Thank you, members of the Council for National Policy.

That night I was finally sure I could agree with everyone who said, "Gary, you did the right thing." Nina and I knew the worst was over. We had found the allies we sought. We had friends who would see us through.

The Republican National Convention was just plain fun for us. I did many radio shows day and night, and autographed books whenever there was a spare moment. People wearing "I believe Gary Aldrich" buttons, supplied in the thousands by my publisher, waited in long lines to get my signature or get a picture standing next to me. Congressmen, senators, governors, and even some former presidential candidates stopped to chat with me, and show their support and encouragement for what I was trying to do.

Regnery Publishing had a large boat for parties, and they hosted a cruise in my honor. Tom Phillips, president and founder of the parent corporation that owns Regnery Publishing, presented me with a commemorative, leather-bound copy of *Unlimited Access,* signed by all on board, including many media celebrities who I'm sure would rather remain anonymous.

Back at the dock, a group of Navy SEALs, there to check for terrorist bombs on passing boats, took my three children out for a fast ride on their high-speed chase cruiser. They *insisted* on doing so as soon as they realized who the children belonged to: "That's the guy who wrote the book about Clinton."

When we passed a group of Secret Service agents, my young son stopped to talk. I was out of earshot and couldn't hear the conversation, but then my boy shouted, "Hey dad! Turn around!" I turned and smiled as I saw the grinning agents giving me the thumbs up.

And then there was Congressman Bob Dornan. He took me under his wing. He was one of the first Republicans, in national office who was willing to support me enthusiastically and without reservation. After Congressman Dornan, many more followed, some even reading whole portions of my book on the floor of the United States House of Representatives.

The PR people were now having trouble keeping up with invitations for me to speak. Event after event was offered to me, and I went from city to city, trying to get the word out. My family did not see much of me from the time the convention ended to election day in November. But they knew I was working for a good cause—for the restoration of integrity in the White House.

I still had a full radio schedule, and did the shows from hotel rooms, or from phone booths at airports in between flights. At many of the events, FBI agents would stand up and announce to the crowd that they knew me, or knew of me, and believed I was telling the truth. At event after event, federal, state, and local law enforcement officers and members of the military would come as a show of support, often asking me to autograph the book.

Perhaps my capstone vindication came on May 30, 1997, when hundreds gathered in Atlanta, Georgia, for the Southeastern Legal Foundation's "Celebrate America" dinner. There, I had an opportunity to publicly thank the thousands of dedicated and hardworking people who contributed their time, money, and support—often through the Foundation—to help me in my first amendment battle.

Ironically, sitting next to me at the dinner was Griffin Bell, Attorney General in the Carter administration, and the man who crafted the legislation giving the FBI the power to review agents' manuscripts. He told me the law was meant to protect national security, not muzzle whistle-blowers like me, who have uncovered government wrongdoing.

Just as gratifying for me were the words of one of the featured speakers that night, Speaker of the House Newt Gingrich, who put my story in what I think is the proper context:

> When you think about what happened to Gary Aldrich, there are a couple of points I need to put into context. First of all, people tend to join the FBI and work for the FBI because they really have a deep commitment to an orderly, systematic process of criminal investigation and of protecting people through the rule of law. Second, the Bureau—while they still had an office in the White House, which has been abolished by the Clinton administration as one of their responses [to Aldrich's exposé]—tended to pick among its best, most mature and most reliable people. Third, someone [was chosen] who had for 26 years enforced the law in the Federal Bureau of Investigation and someone who normally would have a remarkable record as an expert witness, who would have appeared in many court situations, and who would have, in fact, understood how to gather information. It think it's a terrible commentary on the way the Washington news media operates, that it was given information which has for all practical purposes been borne out. John Huang was in the White House, I don't know how many times, gathering information—when there is reason to believe he was also going into the Chinese communist embassy; when in fact the National Security Agency was engaged in tracking the Chinese communists trying to bribe the American political system; when in fact we now know the Attorney General had been informed the FBI thought the Chinese communists were trying to corrupt our system and she placed one

call to the National Security Advisor and forgot to call back. Now, I just want you to think about that. You've been informed by the Federal Bureau of Investigation that a foreign government may be trying to bribe your system. You make one call to tell the National Security Advisor and he doesn't return the call and you forget *for a year* to suggest to him that this is a problem? We now know that a Paraguayan lobbyist was in the National Security Offices the day the United States Government made a decision about a coup in Paraguay—the day that same lobbyist wrote a $50,000 check.

The evidence is overwhelming and... if you go back and look at the news coverage of 1973 and 1974, the willingness of the news media to take each leaf and repaint the forest of that era compared with the unwillingness of the news media in the last two years to even put together the forest is astonishing.

I have no doubt that when history records the difference between George Stephanopoulos and Gary Aldrich, they will record which one enforced the law, which one systematically was dishonest, and Gary Aldrich will come out remarkably well.

In the end, of course, *Unlimited Access* didn't change the course of the election. But what it did do for the more than 500,000 people who bought the book, and the millions more who read it and talked about it, was to lift the lid on White House corruption. Sunlight is the best disinfectant, and at long last, there is evidence that the sun is beginning to shine on 1600 Pennsylvania Avenue.

Chapter Fourteen

POSTSCRIPT ON FILEGATE

Rules for Radicals: "The Declaration of Independence, as a declaration of war, had to be what it was, a 100 percent statement of the justice of the cause of the colonists and a 100 percent denunciation of the role of the British government as evil and unjust... in no war has the enemy or the cause ever been gray."

George Washington's Rules of Civility and Decent Behaviour: "Read no letters, books or papers in company; but when there is a necessity for the doing of it, you must ask leave. Come not near the books or writings of another so as to read them or give your opinion of them unasked; also look not nigh when another is writing a letter."

In late 1994, I received a call from Craig Livingstone about my FBI SPIN investigation of a close White House associate of his. Livingstone's associate apparently wanted to change her report—in effect, to recant her previous recollections about a significant character issue she had confessed to me. Her request was made more than a year after my report was sent to the White House. I told Craig there was no way I could simply "change" information in an FBI report after a year had passed. I offered to conduct a second interview to allow her to answer the same questions again. I told Livingstone I could point out the inconsistencies between my first and my final reports. This was the best I could do—that is, if I wanted to be ethical, protect national security, and obey the law. The ultimate judge of her character issue and the truth of the matter would be the officer who had to make an adjudication about the discrepancy and the facts. This would best be done at the agency that was considering her as an employee.

211

Craig, apparently taking a cue from his supervisor, Associate Counsel William Kennedy, did not want me to "stand on ceremony."

I checked both my report and my notes of her interview, and was satisfied the report was accurate. There was always a chance a witness would remember something new, so that was not an issue for me. The issue was Craig's request that I alter a document in an FBI file, which was a violation of federal law. Of course I refused.

I later learned that another agent was sent down to reinterview Livingstone's associate only days after I refused to go along with Livingstone's scheme to rewrite history. The reinterview was done in such a way that I was intended not to learn about it. The agency's records and my own accuracy and veracity were being questioned, and I should have had a chance to be part of any subsequent interview, or at least to be made aware that it was being conducted. Not only was this kept "hush-hush" within the FBI office, but the interview report was crafted by the new agent as if it were the very first interview of Livingstone's friend. Was this done so that the *real* first report—my report—could simply be tossed away?

I was deeply concerned that Craig might have waltzed a number of otherwise innocent people right into violations of federal law, with yet another of his stupid schemes. After all, he allowed his sidekick, Tony Marceca, illegal access to Marceca's own security file, which contained unfavorable witness testimony. As a result, Marceca was able to identify the persons causing him "trouble." Marceca promptly sued them.

After my book was released and I learned of this misadventure, I reported my concerns to the Independent Counsel investigators. As of yet, there has been no criminal prosecution.

I have recently discovered that my former partner Dennis had also complained that Clinton White House staff were returning to his office, directed by Livingstone, demanding to be reinterviewed and claiming that they too had different or "better" recollections about what they had first confessed to Dennis in a first interview. In each case, they wanted to downscale their confessed drug use to match what the Clinton White House announced could be tolerated. In this way they could continue to work at the White House and obtain a permanent pass. Dennis suspected they were simply recanting that which they wished they hadn't revealed in the first place. I have since talked to Dennis about this. Sadly, the FBI appears to have become a too willing party to these relativist alterations of Clinton staff background investigative reports. There is no evidence FBI headquarters ever complained about Livingstone's tactics, or for that matter, anything else the ethically-challenged Livingstone had in mind to make sure those Clinton and Gore friends got their security passes without interference from any "straight" FBI or Secret Service agents. How many other files were altered in this manner? How many other agents were ordered to go back and change their reports?

FBI management has acted as though its agents were incapable of conducting accurate interviews and writing accurate reports, when those reports ruffled the Clinton administration. FBI Counsel Howard Shapiro certainly took that position regarding my book and when he advised Freeh to have agents interview Dennis about his background investigation on Craig Livingstone, whose subpoenaed background investigation proved embarrassing to Hillary Clinton. Dennis's report clearly documented Hillary Clinton's interest in having Livingstone placed in charge of White House security. How Director Freeh could even entertain the allegation that agents would lie about such routine matters was inexplicable when contrasted with the mountain of evidence of the flawed characters of Clinton administration staff contained in his own agency files. This real evidence, not rumor or innuendo, was developed by his own experienced, educated, and throughly trained agents—graduates of the very same FBI academy that once produced a young special agent named Louie Freeh.

Most people with any knowledge of criminal investigations agree that FBI agents are the best investigators in the world. How could Freeh ignore this reality and the documentary evidence in his own files? The Clinton staffers' serious character flaws filled volumes of files. Did Freeh or Shapiro ever bother to read any of these files before they decided career FBI agents would unprofessionally— indeed, illegally—make things up?

The FBI had dealt with the Bush administration in a very businesslike and professional manner. That changed under Clinton. The informality of the Clinton administration leeched into the office of the FBI and led to a dangerously compliant relationship that made it appear that the FBI's focus had shifted from protecting national security to acting as political go-fers for the White House. One egregious example was of this was the all too cozy relationship between

Director Freeh and the hapless Craig Livingstone. I just couldn't believe the director of the FBI would actually have anything to do with Craig, a low-level staffer, let alone send him "Dear Craig" letters, signed "Louie." Of course, if Director Freeh had been told that Craig was a friend of Hillary or Bill Clinton, I could understand his deference to Craig on those grounds. But I could barely stand to be around an obvious lowlife like Craig, and I was *paid* to be the FBI's liaison with his office.

This was merely a small symptom of a large problem—the overly compliant posture of FBI Headquarters to the White House; or put another way, the politicization of the FBI.

I had no idea how deep relationships ran between the White House and the front office of the FBI, until after my book was released. What I learned was shocking. On July 30, 1996—exactly one month after my first appearance on national television—FBI Counsel Howard Shapiro appeared before the House Committee investigating Travelgate, Filegate, and other matters. It was here that Shapiro confessed under oath that he had given an advance copy of my book to the White House, in violation of the Bureau's—indeed, the *entire* federal government's—policies and procedures.

Although Shapiro claimed to be only "somewhat" knowledgeable about the contents of my book, he advised questioners that at the time he reviewed it, he doubted its serious allegations were true. This was Shapiro's fig leaf. He had absolutely no grounds to make this claim. The FBI never made any attempt that I am aware of to find out if there really *was* a White House national security problem. In fact, we now know there was significant evidence reposing in the FBI's own criminal, background, and counterintelligence files to confirm beyond any doubt the national security problem at the White House.

Shapiro testified that he took my book to White House Counsel Jack Quinn in the presence of Kathy Wallman and "possibly" Beth Nolan, both assistants to Quinn. Shapiro testfied that, "Frankly, it was—I was just in and out. I might have been in for two or three minutes but it was pretty much a drop." Shapiro expected the committee to believe that he thought my unedited manuscript was important enough to leak it—delivering it personally—to the counsel to the president of the United States, but he didn't have the time to wait for a reaction. I, for one, find that hard to believe. In fact, there is evidence of further FBI–White House complicity.

Shapiro admitted many more close contacts with the White House. His testimony provided a rare opportunity to view the operations of upper management at FBI headquarters in Washington.

In later testimony, Shapiro revealed that Quinn directed him to work with Jane Sherburne, the head of the "masters of disaster." Shapiro testified that he thought Sherburne worked for Quinn in the Counsel's office. So all the time that the FBI's chief counsel worked with Jane Sherburne, and reported back to the FBI director, he didn't know who she worked for, nor what her job really was?

Knowingly or not, Shapiro became part of the White House damage control team. The real question now is just how closely did Howard Shapiro and the FBI work with the White House "masters of disaster," whose work was essentially political, geared to Clinton's reelection?

Shapiro, it should be remembered, was advertised by Director Freeh as the best person to work with the Clinton White House "to get to the bottom" of how and why the FBI had illegally provided nine hundred highly sensitive background investigation files of former White House staffers to Craig Livingstone.

Predictably, the FBI's internal probe, micromanaged by Shapiro, found little. Instead of looking at the Special Inquiry Unit at FBI Headquarters—where the White House requests for the nine hundred files were received, and *approved*—Shapiro and his investigators concentrated on interviewing employees in the file and duplication unit, as if key answers could ever be found there. It was at best unproductive; at worst, it was a politically inspired coverup to hide what really happened. The FBI Special Inquiry Unit— which, amazingly, was never investigated by the internal probe— not only controlled which files might be approved for dissemination, but also knew of the poor characters of both Craig Livingstone and Anthony Marceca, who had requested the files and who were apparently trying to dig up dirt on former White House employees now considered political "enemies" by the Clinton administration. The SPIN unit had the power—and should have used it—to deny Livingstone and Marceca access to the files. So the manner in which Shapiro handled the internal FBI probe was a purposeful sham, in my view.

Was Shapiro trying to protect Craig Livingstone and those above him? Or, was Shapiro charged with hiding his own agency's incredible incompetence—an incompetence that quickly became complicity in the outrageous Filegate affair and subsequent coverup?

We may never know, because when the FBI's report, written by Howard Shapiro, was submitted to the House Government Reform and Oversight Committee it was publicly accepted at face value. Although Chairman Clinger's committee did do a tremendous job of looking into the Filegate matter, they were up against the clock, and short of personnel. They didn't have the staff or the resources to pursue the matter further. The Clinton administration was certainly not cooperative in the investigation, and my sources on the committee told me the FBI had found creative ways to stall, to run down the clock.

Chairman Clinger, who has since retired, issued an interim report, promising that the investigation would be completed by the 105th Congress. But as I write, no additional congressional investigation is under way or even being contemplated. Kenneth Starr's office, also charged with investigating this monumental blunder, is similarly inactive. Yet contained within those 900 files are the statements of more than 18,000 witnesses, given to FBI agents in the strictest confidence. Every one of those 18,000 witnesses—who are in the files, by name—had their trust violated by the Clinton White House, and, sadly for me, by the FBI, which has now appeared careless and stupid, or worse—a willing tool of a corrupt government, an agency unworthy of the people's trust.

My own recent pleas to committee investigators that the Filegate matter needs to be more fully investigated have been met with blank stares and lame excuses about "more important matters." What could be more important than investigating an apparent enormous abuse of federal power that violated the rights of thousands of private individuals, and that involved the apparent misuse of a federal law enforcement agency?

There is, in fact, a civil, class-action lawsuit pending on behalf of the victims who had their privacy violated. I am one of them. But if Congress cannot act on something as serious as this, what use is Congress for the protection of ordinary citizens? As I've discovered, it's not only the White House that needs reform. The attitude of Congress, however active it might be in passing unnecessary regulations, is strangely passive when it comes to protecting the rights of American citizens. In fact, Congress is culpably inactive when it comes to defending those rights and in prosecuting its oversight of the executive branch.

There are, however, hopeful signs that Congress has finally gotten the message. The Government Reform and Oversight Committee now seems to have enough staff and money to address the mushrooming White House scandals. Other committees are finally addressing their respective areas of oversight responsibility, and not just waiting for the media or independent prosecutor Kenneth Starr to do their jobs for them. It's long past time for our members of Congress to act to restore integrity to our government and its institutions. And it's time that we the people make sure they do.

THE SPIN
BACKGROUND
INVESTIGATION
OF BILL AND
HILLARY CLINTON

"Clinton is an unusually good liar. Unusually good. Do you realize that?"—Bob Kerry, U.S. Senator (D-Neb.), as quoted in *Esquire*, January 1996

The only people at the White House not required to have extensive background investigations conducted by the FBI are the president and vice president and their immediate families, and yet, perhaps under certain circumstances, they are the ones who need a proper vetting most of all.

Presented below is a facsimile of the background investigation summary that I would have prepared on the Clintons and presented to the public if that had been part of my official duties at the White House. All of the information contained herein has been compiled from public documents—newspapers, magazines, and books—with the exception of the exhibits at the end, which are the result of personal investigations conducted since I left the FBI. When I note that the Clintons have refused to release certain records, this is information that has been requested by the media or by other public bodies.

SPECIAL INQUIRY SUMMARY REPORT
15 April 1996

INTRODUCTION

The candidates under investigation are Bill and Hillary Clinton. They have both indicated an interest in continuing to be employed by the federal government and have stated that they believe they are suitable and meet all official requirements for such employment.

What follows is an investigative summary and attachments so that an adjudicator can make an informed decision on whether their employment and access to the White House and the Executive Branch should be continued.

MR. CLINTON'S EDUCATION

William Jefferson Blythe Clinton, a/k/a "Bill," is a white male, aged 49, born 8/19/46 in Hope, Arkansas. It is reported that he graduated from Hot Springs High School, Hot Springs, Arkansas, in 1964. While attending high school, Mr. Clinton ran for class secretary and lost.

It is reported that after graduation, Mr. Clinton attended Georgetown University's School of Foreign Service and graduated in 1968. It is reported that while at Georgetown, Mr. Clinton was very active in campus politics.

It is noted that Mr. Clinton has refused to allow a review of any disciplinary records at Georgetown and has also refused to supply any records related to his attendance or performance as a student while attending classes there.

A degree is claimed by Mr. Clinton, but the investigator has not personally seen a copy, and no objective assessment of his performance as a student while at Georgetown could be established; the investigation of this period of the candidate's life could not be completed due to the failure of the candidate to cooperate in making such records available.

In 1968 Mr. Clinton was selected as a Rhodes Candidate and was given a scholarship to attend Oxford University in Oxford, England.

Mr. Clinton's selection cannot be taken as evidence of outstanding or unique ability; it has been reported that at the time he was selected, there was little if any real competition in the state of Arkansas for this vacancy, which in that state at that time was often determined as much by political connections as by scholarship.

It appears from documents, various interviews, and his own words that he attended Oxford for one full year only and took no degree. There are no records to support a claim that he registered or attended any classes during his second term. Instead, it appears that Mr. Clinton lived with various friends on or near the Oxford campus and spent his time involved in various anti–U.S. and anti–Vietnam War activities.

Investigation reveals that after the winter of 1969, Mr. Clinton embarked on a tour of Europe, and there are suggestions that school officials told Mr. Clinton that he was no longer welcome on campus, but that could not be confirmed. Various friends and classmates of Mr. Clinton, however, have reported that he was uninterested in study and a was lackluster student.

Investigation has determined that when Mr. Clinton returned to Oxford after the first year, he "crashed" with various friends and was described as a moocher who never paid for anything and never seemed to have any money to share or to contribute to the cost of his own subsistence.

During Mr. Clinton's attendance at Oxford, and his subsequent trips around Europe and Asia, he had no apparent source of income aside from his scholarship, and it is unknown how this tour was funded. However, it has been established that he served as a "quasi" ambassador for a leftist organization in Washington, D.C., known as Vietnam Moratorium Committee, or VMC, an organization founded by one Sam Brown, among others. It appears that Mr. Clinton's sole purpose at Oxford in the fall of 1969 was to organize student protests against the United States for the VMC.

There were no grades available for review to prove or disprove claims regarding Clinton's achievement, since the university will not release such records absent the candidate's authority. It is noted that normally a candidate would sign a release so as to allow investigators to confirm or deny educational claims.

In this case, the candidate will neither sign a release form nor will he provide documentation related to his attendance and performance at Oxford. This failure to supply needed documentation is a significant failure to cooperate on the part of the candidate, since much of his claim of "suitability" is pinned to his educational opportunities and experiences.

After his tour of Europe, Mr. Clinton returned to his mother's home in Arkansas before leaving for Yale Law School. Mr. Clinton attended Yale Law School from 1970 to 1973, at which time it is reported that he graduated with a degree in law. Again, no records are available to confirm or deny his performance at the Law School.

It is noted, however, that even if the candidate had signed a release form allowing a review of his transcripts, there would not be the usual information available to determine his grade point average. Yale, at that time, had capitulated to student protests demanding a "pass/fail" system. One student who attended with Mr. Clinton said of the grading system, "You really had to work hard to flunk out."

There is also some indication that Mr. Clinton was again uninterested in study. In one class that Mr. Clinton attended with his future wife, it was reported that Mr. Clinton's performance was considered "mediocre," whereas Hillary Rodham's was "impressive."

Mr. Clinton received course credit for spending a semester working on the presidential campaign of Senator George McGovern. Mr. Clinton did not, however, work as a paralegal or as an assistant to a lawyer on the campaign.

In summary, judging Mr. Clinton's academic performance would be highly speculative because of the absence of objective records available to the public.

There have been claims that Mr. Clinton is "highly intelligent" or "brilliant," but no testing data have been made available to substantiate these claims. He has attended prestigious institutions, though investigation has revealed that Mr. Clinton had important political sponsors who may have helped sway admissions boards, and, again, absent any objective criteria being made available, measures of Mr. Clinton's intellectual achievements are speculative.

With regard to personal conduct, no information has been made available by the candidate regarding his conduct while attending Georgetown, Oxford, or Yale.

Mr. Clinton's financial standing during this time is also a matter of conjecture. It has been reported that his family was of modest means. Nevertheless, aside from his Rhodes scholarship and work on the McGovern campaign and other political activities, there is no record of student employment, loans, or grants. If such loans were made, there is no way to determine if they have been repaid, as the candidate has failed to sign the proper waiver to determine if he obtained student loans.

It is recommended that additional attempts be made to obtain the necessary records and waivers from Mr. Clinton, since the absence of this basic information prevents the completion of this part of the character inquiry and precludes the final determination of suitability, at least with respect to the educational component of this background investigation.

MR. CLINTON'S NEIGHBORHOODS

The scope of this inquiry includes only the adult years of Mr. Clinton. At the time of his graduation from Hot Springs High School, he was living with his mother in Hot Springs, Arkansas.

During the times he attended Georgetown, Oxford, and Yale, he lived on campus or with fellow students in apartments they had secured. There is, however, no documentary evidence that Mr. Clinton ever secured a place of residence on his own behalf. At Yale, Mr. Clinton lived in an off-campus apartment with his future bride, Hillary Rodham. It is reported that Rodham made the arrangements to secure the apartment.

There is no known documentation that Mr. Clinton signed a residential rental agreement. Therefore it is impossible to determine if he lived up to financial obligations during the years he was attending college. This was a nine-year period from 1964 to 1973. When Mr. Clinton was not attending college, he lived with his mother.

One determination of suitability would be the review of police blotters in the areas where Mr. Clinton resided. Since police records are normally not available to the general public, and since Mr. Clinton has not allowed a review of law enforcement agencies, only neighborhood "folklore" about the candidate has been available and no arrests of the candidate are reported.

Mr. Clinton's neighbors described him as "outgoing and gregarious" but report that while living with his mother, the candidate was subjected to a dysfunctional family experience.

Mr. Clinton himself has described his stepfather as abusive and has related a history of his stepfather's alcoholism, spousal abuse, aggressive and hostile behavior, and womanizing. Mr. Clinton's stepfather reportedly fired a pistol at Mrs. Clinton on one occasion, hitting a lamp instead.

There is no evidence that the police were called regarding this incident, although it is conceivable that had they been called, Mr. Clinton's stepfather could have been charged with attempted murder or aggravated assault in addition to the obvious firearms charges.

After marriage to Hillary Rodham, Mr. Clinton lived for a short period in a rented residence. With the exception of one other residence, Mr. Clinton has lived in housing provided by state or federal governments.

As governor of the state of Arkansas for 12 years, Mr. Clinton lived in the Arkansas state mansion, rent free. From 1993 to the present time, Mr. Clinton, as president, has lived in the White House.

At both locations, except for insignificant, largely symbolic, sums paid by Mr. Clinton for purely personal items, all food, services, and transportation for Mr. Clinton and his family have been borne by some government agency; therefore it is virtually impossible to determine if Mr. Clinton is "financially responsible," using the traditional definition of the term.

In both locations, state and federal agencies provided the accountants and recordkeeping to determine whether or not Mr. Clinton "owes" the government minor sums for purely personal needs. These government employees would know if Mr. Clinton has paid these sums. Their interviews, however, have not been permitted under the umbrella of "security concerns." It is noted that these sums, if any, are minor in nature.

MRS. CLINTON'S EDUCATION

Hillary Diane Rodham was born 10/26/47 in Chicago, Illinois, and was raised in the Chicago area. She was described as very active in high school and a high achiever. She graduated from Maine Township High School in 1965 and in the fall began attending Wellesley College.

While in high school she displayed a tendency to speak at inappropriate times and behaved in an irreverent manner during serious moments, often causing her teacher to scold her or send her to stand in the hall. During one incident, while her teacher was playing a recorded speech by General Douglas MacArthur, she and a classmate mocked the general, which was disruptive to the classroom. She was reportedly "read the riot act" by her unamused and disappointed teacher. Her high school classmates voted Mrs. Clinton "most likely to succeed."

At Wellesley it appears from all information available that Mrs. Clinton was a serious student. There are, however, no claims that she exhibited "brilliance." Mrs. Clinton has never allowed any examination of her educational records, academic or disciplinary; therefore no objective determination can be made as to her academic achievement or citizenship while attending Wellesley. It has been noted that in her second year she became active in student causes and became known as a campus activist. There is no evidence that these activities hampered her studies.

Still, given that campus activism and campus unrest in the 1960s often involved serious acts of destruction and illegal activity, it would be important to determine if Mrs. Clinton was the subject of any disciplinary action by the college or came to the attention of nearby police agencies.

Mrs. Clinton was elected student government president and was allowed to give a commencement address after allegedly "twisting the arm" of the president of Wellesley College. The Wellesley president reportedly told others that she did not think it was such a good idea for Mrs. Clinton to participate in the ceremony.

Mrs. Clinton allegedly embarrassed a senior U.S. senator, a black Republican who had spoken before her, with a mocking, insulting, and disrespectful retort to the senator's speech. This act won Mrs. Clinton a certain notoriety, and she appeared on the cover of *Life* magazine as a representative of college radicalism.

Mrs. Clinton went on to attend Yale Law School and worked on George McGovern's presidential campaign, an activity for which she received course credit. Grades and other records are unavailable for Mrs. Clinton because of Yale's "pass/fail" grading system and her unwillingness to allow public scrutiny.

Some individuals who knew both Mr. and Mrs. Clinton at that time suggest that of the two, Mrs. Clinton was the better law student, showing more interest and ability than Mr. Clinton. She was not, however, described as "an outstanding student."

With respect to financial issues, it appears that her family would have had the financial resources to send Mrs. Clinton to Wellesley and Yale.

MRS. CLINTON'S NEIGHBORHOOD

Insufficient information exists to document Mrs. Clinton's early neighborhood experiences. However, from statements made by her and others, she was not well-liked as a child. Mrs. Clinton has complained of other children taunting and physically assaulting her. There is no evidence that Mrs. Clinton's family lived on the "rough" side of town, and no satisfactory explanation has been offered for why she was singled out for such abuse. But apparently, Mrs. Clinton remembers this period of her life with clarity and anger.

Mrs. Clinton's book *It Takes a Village* also hints at familial unhappiness with passages like this one: "Ask those who grew up in the picture-perfect houses about the secrets and desperation they sometimes concealed." Mrs. Clinton does not identify what "secrets" or "desperation" she is talking about.

Mrs. Clinton's childhood experiences bear on this inquiry only insofar as they reveal themselves in emotional distress today. Reports of Mrs. Clinton's frequently explosive temper and "domineering" attitudes may be evidence of such distress, but they are a matter for further investigation by a trained psychologist.

MR. CLINTON'S PRE–WHITE HOUSE EMPLOYMENT

Mr. Clinton has been involved in politics and political campaigns for many years. Mr. Clinton assisted in various political campaigns in his youth, which might be considered part-time employment. For a short period while attending Georgetown he was a student intern with the Senate Foreign Relations Committee.

On the George McGovern presidential campaign, Mr. Clinton was alleged to be poorly organized and a poor manager who effectively cost the senator votes.

In a lesser-known political campaign, Mr. Clinton acted as a driver. Mr. Clinton was "fired," however, for driving erratically, arriving late to events, and parking the car illegally, causing his candidate significant embarrassment.

Through his political connections, Mr. Clinton was once invited to join senior Senator William Fulbright for lunch in the Senate Dining Room. Mr. Clinton arrived so inappropriately dressed and groomed that the senator refused to dine with him and turned him away.

After returning to Little Rock, Arkansas, upon graduation from Yale Law School, Mr. Clinton was given an assistant professorship at the University of Arkansas School of Law.

In 1976 Mr. Clinton was elected attorney general of Arkansas. In 1978 he was elected governor. It is noted that there exists a wealth of information related to Mr. Clinton's performance in these state positions. His ability as governor for the state of Arkansas is in dispute, with supporters claiming that much was accomplished and detractors stating he achieved nothing of much consequence.

The one issue most closely linked to Mr. Clinton's 12 years as governor is "education reform." Examination reveals, however, that Mr. Clinton delegated these efforts to Mrs. Clinton, who was given the task of raising Arkansas's education standards to the level of its neighboring states—which are Texas, Oklahoma, Louisiana, Missouri, Tennessee, and Mississippi. Arkansas has approximately 2.5 million residents, making it smaller in population than metropolitan Washington, D.C.

There are several serious allegations that have not been fully investigated and are still pending related to then-Governor Clinton's professional and personal behavior, including allegations that he abused and misused state assets and personnel. In several documented incidents, Mr. Clinton used personnel for activities which could only be defined as purely personal and used state employees to assist him in engaging in illicit sexual conduct.

In addition, Mr. Clinton is alleged to have paid off female companions who provided sexual favors by giving them state jobs. One major issue yet to be resolved is the allegation that Mr. Clinton sexually harassed one young lady and, when rebuffed, exposed his genitals to her.

Mr. Clinton is currently being sued by this young lady and is expected to testify on this matter in the near future. There is no record to indicate that Mr. Clinton was ever investigated by local police officials about this alleged incident, which would normally be considered a felonious sexual assault.

It should be noted that persistent rumors—many aired in admittedly politically prejudiced books and videos—attempt to connect Mr. Clinton not only with drug use, but even with drug running on a major scale through operations allegedly run out of Mena, Arkansas. Evidence to support these allegations rests heavily on the numerous Clinton aides, friends, and associates who committed suicide or died in accidents during his 12 years as governor. The only hard evidence, however, are the arrests and convictions of Mr. Clinton's half brother and Mr. Clinton's "closest political friend," Dan Lasater, on felony drug charges involving cocaine.

Investigation has determined the Clintons made many serious enemies while serving the state of Arkansas, but both profess innocence and appear baffled when asked why their enemies' "hatred"—as it has often been described—is so intense.

Mr. Clinton has been interviewed several times regarding this phenomenon and has been asked to explain how he amassed so many dedicated enemies. He was unable to explain, stating that people "either hate me or love me—there seems to be no in-between."

So much has been publicly documented regarding Mr. Clinton's employment in Arkansas, that no further investigation of this period was deemed warranted. There are many issues related to financial matters, of which he was a party, but these matters were seemingly initiated by Mrs. Clinton, with Mr. Clinton acting in passive roles. It is true that Mr. Clinton received some financial benefit and suffered financial exposure as a result of Mrs. Clinton's activities.

MRS. CLINTON'S PRE–WHITE HOUSE EMPLOYMENT

As a law student, Mrs. Clinton was a summer intern at a West Coast law firm that was involved in attempting to free jailed members of the Black Panther terrorist organization. Mrs. Clinton also worked on the George McGovern presidential campaign.

After graduating from Yale, Mrs. Clinton was hired as an attorney on the Committee to Impeach President Richard Nixon.

Mrs. Clinton later moved to Little Rock to marry Mr. Clinton and took a position as an associate in the Rose Law Firm. When Mr. Clinton was elected governor, Mrs. Clinton was made a full partner in the Rose Law Firm. While at Rose, Mrs. Clinton entered into financial arrangements, including one which later became known as Whitewater, with the Madison Bank, owned by Mr. James McDougal.

In one poll conducted to rate attorneys, Mrs. Clinton was chosen as one of the nation's "Top 100" lawyers. But it is not known how significant this poll is.

Rose employee records are not available to the general public, and no "scorecard" is available to tally Mrs. Clinton's performance in winning cases. Nor is there sufficient information to assess what role Mr. Vince Foster, a senior partner at Rose, played in Mrs. Clinton's hiring and promotions. Mr. Foster was a close longtime friend of Mr. Clinton.

Questions about this matter have been raised because of Mrs. Clinton's becoming a Rose Law Firm partner coincident with Mr. Clinton's election as governor. As a partner, Mrs. Clinton did develop a reputation as one of Rose's leading "rainmakers," according to published reports. How much of this client retention and generation was caused by Mrs. Clinton's unique legal talents or personal skills, as opposed to her connection to the governor, is unknown. But because of the legal problems into which Mrs. Clinton's activities have placed the Rose Law Firm—including the continuing Whitewater affair—doubts have been raised about her popularity at and value to the firm.

Mrs. Clinton was appointed by President Jimmy Carter to be the director of the Legal Services Corporation (LSC) in 1978. The GAO determined that under Mrs. Clinton's direction, the LSC gave illegal grants and performed illegal acts to support political causes with taxpayer dollars in violation of her oath as a government employee. These charges are regarded as serious. There are also security implications if it is judged that Mrs. Clinton might use or transfer sensitive government documents for ideological purposes. It is noted that Mrs. Clinton has taken political positions regarded by her critics as "extreme," not only in college, but also in her professional life.

For example, Mrs. Clinton has written that children should be put on equal legal footing with parents and that disputes between children and parents should be resolved by attorneys and judges. It is assumed that the parents would bear the cost of such legal proceedings, since the child would have no income. Issues that might be adjudicated in such proceedings range from a 12-year-old's right to a state-funded abortion without a parent's consent, to a minor's desire to attend an all-night party against a parent's wishes.

In addition, in Mrs. Clinton's writings for the left-wing Children's Defense Fund, she has compared today's traditional family to a form of slavery.

Whether these positions are so "extreme" as to put in doubt Mrs. Clinton's "suitability" for continued employment at the White House is an issue to be adjudicated and is outside the proper sphere of this investigation.

BILL AND HILLARY CLINTON'S RECORD OF EMPLOYMENT AT THE WHITE HOUSE

Allegations of incompetence and mismanagement have been many, especially during the first half of the Clinton administration. Since then, even favorably disposed sources have marveled at the Clintons' "economy with the truth," apparent lack of principles, and continual attempts to cover up negative allegations. There have also been endless allegations of the Clintons' lowering moral, professional, and security standards, and using the office of the presidency in inappropriate ways, such as honoring lifelong Communist Pete Seeger and using the bully pulpit to hail as a "genius" the late Jerry Garcia, despite Mr. Garcia's decades of serious illegal drug use and advocacy for the use and legalization of hard drugs (past presidents have rarely praised rock stars that have criminal records). Much of this information has been discussed publicly. Therefore this summary report will focus on a mere representative sampling of allegations to assist the reader in adjudicating this summary.

It is Alleged That, in Brief,
With Regard to National Security

- The Clintons dismantled the existing security system at the White House and throughout the federal government to allow the employment of hundreds of persons who previously would have been considered unsuitable and/or security risks— including persons with histories of serious illegal drug abuse. New standards have been instituted to inhibit background investigations and downgrade their effectiveness by forbidding questions about aberrant lifestyles and mental stability.
- The Clinton administration has refused to adhere to directions from congressional oversight committees to repair the security system and, indeed, has consciously sought to deceive these committees.
- The Clintons have conspired to subvert the effectiveness of the Secret Service, thereby endangering the safety of the president, the first lady, and White House staff.
- To enforce the willful destruction of the security system, numerous Secret Service agents—and the former director of the

Secret Service—have suffered punitive transfers, and many attempts have been made to compromise, intimidate, and abuse agencies such as the FBI.

- Because of the breakdown of the security system, uncleared Clinton employees have handled, read, discussed, and disseminated confidential, secret, top secret, and other sensitive information related to national security.

- Classified material from the NSC and the CIA has been delivered to the United Nations and transferred to various UN agencies without proper protective agreements. Employees protesting this reckless disclosure of sensitive intelligence have been harassed, transferred, and demoted.

- The Clintons have established close ties to Gerry Adams of Sinn Fein, the political arm of the Irish Republican Army (IRA)—a known terrorist organization with links to terrorist organizations worldwide and one that has murdered civilians and political leaders of one of our closest NATO allies. IRA bombings continue this year (1996).

- Many other allegations have been lodged that require further investigation and should be referred to specialists in national security.

With Regard to Government Ethics, Abuse of Power, and Obstruction of Justice

- The Clintons encouraged the coverup of sexual harassment allegations against David Watkins, a senior Clinton campaign official and friend of the president. Campaign funds were illegally used to "pay off" the alleged victim of Watkins's sexual harassment. The Clintons and their senior staff members later refused to provide information to law enforcement about the Watkins allegations, and instead of firing Watkins, they promoted him and placed him in charge, in part, of the White House "mock" security program.

- The Clintons obstructed justice after the death of Vince Foster by ignoring Secret Service pleas to seal Foster's office as a potential crime scene and by preventing the FBI from investigating the incident in favor of the U.S. Park Service.

- The Clinton administration conducted its own search of Foster's office and caused staff members to obstruct justice by hiding documentary evidence.
- The Clintons used White House lawyers to impede the investigation of the death of Vince Foster and conceal the true nature of his duties as deputy counsel.
- The Clintons abused the FBI by forcing it into a 30-month politically motivated criminal investigation of seven innocent citizens in the White House Travel Office. Further, the Clinton administration obstructed justice and failed to adhere to federal law by hiding and destroying documents that would clear the single Travel Office employee against whom false accusations were finally filed and taken to court.
- Congressional testimony proved that the senior Clinton staff and Webster Hubbell played the major role in implementing a rushed plan to resolve the standoff with the Branch Davidian cult in Waco, Texas. After the plan turned to tragedy, the White House shifted blame to Janet Reno and the FBI.
- Senior staff members were ordered to create false employment records in violation of law.
- Executive Branch agencies were compelled to hire unqualified personnel as personal favors or political payoffs.
- The Clintons politicized the Office of Attorney General to the extent of involving the AG in political campaigns.
- The Clintons attempted to compromise the FBI by keeping FBI Director William Sessions's continued employment in doubt for six months.
- While protected by a million-dollar insurance policy to cover legal costs, the Clintons nevertheless made false statements about their financial situation to support a legal defense fund set up to defend Bill Clinton against sexual harassment charges.
- The Clintons tried to sully the reputations of Arkansas law enforcement officers who leveled charges against them and then tried to buy their silence with federal jobs, one of which was indeed filled with a former Arkansas state trooper.
- The Clintons failed to properly pay their federal income taxes and, when caught, lied about the circumstances. At a later time, the Clintons properly repaid their federal taxes in the amount of $14,615.

- The Clintons failed to admonish their own vice president when he solicited and accepted a gift of $8,365 worth of merchandise from a major corporation, in violation of law. When caught, the vice president shifted repayment of this cost to the Democratic National Committee.
- The Clintons have obstructed justice by encouraging senior staff and associates to thwart, discredit, and influence the investigations into Whitewater and other legal problems confronting the president and first lady.
- Numerous allegations of ethical misconduct and abuse of power exist and require further investigation, with the assistance of legal counsel.

With Regard to the Management and Administration of the White House and the Executive Branch

- The Clintons conspired secretly to divide the powers of the presidency in a manner that is unconstitutional. Hillary Clinton, who has not been elected to any office, has assumed presidential authority over the White House Counsel's Office, the Office of Domestic Policy, the Office of Presidential Personnel, and the Office of the Chief of Staff, among others, as well as leading the Health Care Task Force.
- The Clintons failed to properly manage the activities of their subordinates at all levels in the White House and Executive Branch, resulting in chaos, misconduct, and incompetence. Highly qualified permanent staff have been alienated by what they consider the rude and unprofessional behavior of the Clinton administration. In addition, veteran permanent staff have been fired to make way for poorly qualified Clinton cronies.
- Numerous allegations of mismanagement exist that require further investigation.

With Respect to Health Care Reform—the Major Policy Initiative of the Clinton Administration

- The Health Care Task Force was conducted illegally by keeping secret the names of lobbyists, special interest groups, and others who were invited to participate. To maintain this level of secrecy, the meetings were held inside the White House.

- To continue the secrecy, a senior member of the task force presented false testimony to a federal court, under oath. These falsehoods were prepared by lawyers working at the Department of Justice under the supervision of the brother-in-law of the vice president and by members of the White House Counsel's Office.
- False claims were also made to federal agencies to fund this task force. According to Hillary Clinton, the task force would finish its work at a cost of $100,000. It actually cost taxpayers $13.4 million dollars, plus legal costs.
- Numerous accounts of the failure of Hillary Clinton's task force have been published and are publicly available. Nevertheless, further investigation may be required.

EXHIBITS

A number of exhibits are attached as an addendum to this investigation. In view of the new allegations made within these pages, it will be left to the reader as to whether additional investigation of the Clintons should be attempted.

REPORT OF INTERVIEW AND INVESTIGATION

WHI-1 (White House Investigation-1) appeared at the Liaison Office of the FBI and advised that he was not present to discuss anything that was within the jurisdiction of the FBI. WHI-1 stated that he had been aware of something very disturbing and just needed to talk about it with someone.

WHI-1 will be referred to as "he" in this report; however, no inference as to gender should be assumed. WHI-1 stated that he feared for his job and thought that if it was ever known who he was and that he had given such information to the writer, he would surely be punished even though he was not in violation of any law to repeat to the writer what he knew.

WHI-1 stated that there is a West Wing employee, a young attractive blond woman, who was employed by the Clinton administration. In fact, she was hand-picked for her position by the president. She has told numerous coworkers that she was hired by the president after he met her on the campaign jet. According to WHI-1, the president told Bruce Lindsey that he liked her, and instructed Lindsey to "find her a job" in the White House.

WHI-1 repeated that she is a *very* attractive young blond woman, who dresses in a provocative manner. She wears heavy makeup and flirts constantly with the men who come into the West Wing. Most of the Secret Service agents and uniformed officers know her quite well, as her flirtatious manner has become a topic of conversation.

WHI-1 advised that a Secret Service agent has related that this young woman has been the guest of the president in the Residence quarters. WHI-1 advised that he cannot state the purpose of her visit to the Residence quarters, and does not know if she has visited just one time, or if there have been additional visits. WHI-1 advised he does not know the reason for the visit, but was told the first lady was not in residence at the time of the visit.

Many of the Clinton administration female staffers have complained about the behavior of this young friend of the president. There are complaints that she does whatever she pleases, whenever she pleases, and does not appear to answer to any authority. According to WHI-1 she goes wherever she wants within the West Wing, and answers to no one. Her immunity from normal supervision is unexplained.

WHI-1 could provide no further information related to this woman except to say that "she is very attractive, but a little dizzy." WHI-1 revealed the name of this attractive blond to the writer. The writer is aware of her identity and position and the circumstances surrounding her employment at the White House.

Investigation on XX/XX/XX AT Washington, D.C. **File # WHI-#1** (DATE WITHHELD FOR SECURITY REASONS)

This Document contains neither recommendations nor conclusions of the investigator. It is the property of the investigator, and its content is confidential. It is not to be distributed to any third party without the expressed consent and written permission of the investigator.

REPORT OF INTERVIEW AND INVESTIGATION

WHI-2 called the writer to express concern about the security system at the Clinton administration White House. WHI-2 advised that he heard "through the grapevine" that the writer was very concerned as well. WHI-2 stated that he has worked in the FBI headquarters SPIN Unit for years. WHI-2 will be referred to as "he" in this report; however, no inference as to gender should be assumed. WHI-2 stated that he feared for his job. He believes that if it was ever known that he had given such information to the writer, he would surely be punished even though he was not in violation of any law.

WHI-2 stated that people, including the writer, "have no idea just how bad things are" with respect to the Clinton administration, because they only see part of the story. WHI-2 advised that the entire SPIN Unit is aware of the short deadlines demanded by the Clinton Counsel's Office and the incomplete forms submitted by the Clinton administration. The short deadlines, many of which border on being ludicrous, create circumstances designed to ensure missed leads and incomplete or inaccurate summaries, which are then sent to the Counsel's Office.

Regarding the White House, WHI-2 says that the SPIN Unit is aware that these employees continue to work at the White House, regardless of their documented and admitted character flaws, including past documented heavy drug use, and this has led to a feeling of disgust and dismay, since it appears that security is not taken seriously at the White House and that those responsible for White House security are intimidated by the White House Counsel's Office.

Investigation on XX/XX/XX AT Washington, D.C. **File # WHI-#1**
(DATE WITHHELD FOR SECURITY REASONS)

This Document contains neither recommendations nor conclusions of the investigator. It is the property of the investigator, and its content is confidential. It is not to be distributed to any third party without the expressed consent and written permission of the investigator.

REPORT OF INTERVIEW AND INVESTIGATION

WHI-3 met the writer on the South Lawn of the White House. WHI-3 will be referred to as "he" in this report; however, no inference as to gender should be assumed. WHI-3 stated that he feared for his job and thought that if it was ever known who he was and that he had given such information to the writer, he would surely be punished even though he was not in violation of any law to repeat to the writer what he knew.

WHI-3 advised he wished to talk to the writer about some matters that troubled him. He stated that he was "sick and tired" of the fraud that the Clinton administration was perpetrating on the American public. WHI-3 stated he was referring to the fiction that the Clintons were nice people, or the "all-American couple, or the model family and loving couple." WHI-3 stated that this perception was a total fabrication.

WHI-3 was asked to provide examples of such fabrications. WHI-3 referred the writer to the jogging track; he pointed out the potted plants lined along the south edge of the track, which we were walking on. WHI-3 stated that the jog track had been ordered by Hillary Clinton because she wanted a place to jog and she thought that she could "keep Bill at home and out of trouble" if a jog track was available. The potted plants were ordered by Hillary, according to WHI-3, to hide Hillary's jogging from the tourists who gather by the fence.

The track was built, which altered the South Lawn in a significant way, but the president rarely uses it—he still insists on jogging on the Mall, even though this is thought to be very dangerous. WHI-3 said that the Secret Service has tried to reason with the president about this, to no avail.

WHI-3 also stated that the Clintons have been abusive to each other and to the staff, yelling and screaming obscenities. According to WHI-3, they do not live as husband and wife. This is well known within the White House and no secret, although the Clintons have tried to create a public illusion of marriage.

WHI-3 advised that the White House Residence staff has been ordered to never be present in the Residence when any member of the family is at home. This creates a hardship for the staff, since the Clintons have no reliable schedule.

Signals are passed from one Residence employee to another, a sort of "all clear," and then and only then can the staff "rush in" and attempt to get their tasks completed.

WHI-3 advised that this might sound petty, but when the Clintons return, which is usually without notice, at any moment, then the staff have to "rush out" even though they might not be finished with particular tasks, such as making beds or changing sheets and towels.

WHI-3 advised this would not be a significant problem except that the Clintons, particularly Hillary and her personal staff, are very demanding and tend to criticize when they perceive an imperfection. WHI-3 stated that Hillary's personal staff is usually hostile and inconsiderate. Hillary won't even talk to Gary Walters, the chief usher, and sends messages to him through her personal staff member.

WHI-3 advised that everyone in the Residence is in fear of their jobs, especially since the Clintons fired Chris Emery, the assistant usher, for talking on the telephone to Mrs. Bush about her laptop computer. WHI-3 advised that Mrs. Bush had become reliant on Emery for her computer needs, since he was a bit of a computer buff and had taught her how to use it.

WHI-3 also stated that the Residence staff did not miss the clear message that was sent by the Clintons when they fired the Travel Office staff. WHI-3 advised that everyone took this to mean, "not only can we fire you, but we can prosecute you as well, so you'd better shut up."

WHI-3 stated that since the firings of Emery and the Travel Office staff there has been an air of fear and distrust cast over the White House, and "it's made much worse by the fondness the Residence staff had for the Bush family," a presidency that exemplified good manners, according to WHI-3.

WHI-3 stated that the White House, in his opinion, has become a difficult and unhappy place in which to work, and there is an overall sadness and lack of morale on the part of the staff, who are still upset and angry that this could have happened to them and to the White House.

*Investigation on XX/XX/XX AT Washington, D.C. **File # WHI-#1**
(DATE WITHHELD FOR SECURITY REASONS)*

This Document contains neither recommendations nor conclusions of the investigator. It is the property of the investigator, and its content is confidential. It is not to be distributed to any third party without the expressed consent and written permission of the investigator.

REPORT OF INTERVIEW AND INVESTIGATION

WHI-4 will be referred to as "he" in this report; however, no inference as to gender should be assumed. WHI-4 stated that he feared for his job and thought that if it was ever known who he was and that he had given such information to the writer, he would surely be punished even though he was not in violation of any law to repeat to the writer what he knew. WHI-4 stated that he was aware of the retired status of the writer and that the information might be used in a publication at some future date.

WHI-4 advised that he has worked at the White House for many years and knows the Residence staff exceptionally well. He considers the Residence staff to be loyal Americans and exceptionally professional in their daily assignment, which is to maintain the home of the president of the United States.

WHI-4 stated that the Clintons are very suspicious of anyone they did not bring from Arkansas and think that "everyone is trying to do them in."

WHI-4 advised this is unfair and unreasonable. To his knowledge, in the beginning, no one expressed any strong feelings about the Clintons, their friends, or their politics. WHI-4 pointed out that it is part of the culture and training for Residence staff to avoid any political controversy, and he could not recall hearing conversations of a political nature taking place inside the Residence by any member of the Residence staff—until the "outrageous" conduct they observed shocked them into talking to each other.

WHI-4 advised that the Clintons have made everything personal. WHI-4 stated that complaints about the Clintons are not politically based. He stated that it is the Clintons' behavior that has caused so much concern and discussion. WHI-4 stated that the Clintons and their friends are just not acting "presidential."

WHI-4 advised that he believes the reason staff and the Secret Service are forbidden from the Residence when the Clintons are present is simply because of the very bizarre behavior of the Clintons. The Clintons are afraid, according to WHI-4, that staffers will see or hear things that are so salacious or outrageous they will be tempted to tell others about it.

For example, in the early months of the administration it was rumored that Hillary Clinton threw a lamp at the president. WHI-4 stated he had heard of the first lady throwing a book at the president that had instead hit a Secret Service agent.

WHI-4 stated that the efforts to keep staff away so that they cannot hear or see the Clintons has not achieved what the Clintons hoped to achieve. For example, when an article appeared about Mr. Clinton's alleged sexual affairs, President Clinton heard Hillary coming down the hall and he attempted to escape. Allegedly, Hillary Clinton was heard to scream, "Come back here, you a--hole! Where the f--k do you think you're going?" She then proceeded to scream at him about the article.

WHI-4 stated that he was aware of this because even though staff cannot be in the Residence, they do know where the president and first lady are at all times, and they can hear the first lady when she is screaming and yelling.

WHI-4 stated that the inability of the staff to access the Residence has caused problems, especially on some weekends when the first family is at the Residence, because Hillary Clinton often stays in bed until almost noon on the weekend, playing sixties-style music very loudly on a powerful stereo. Her favorite group is Earth, Wind and Fire, according to WHI-4.

WHI-4 confirmed that Mrs. Clinton is very demanding and inconsiderate of White House staff.

WHI-4 stated that at midnight, hours before a lengthy, long-planned trip overseas, Mrs. Clinton called down to the Usher's Office and "ordered" three tubes of Blistex.

The assistant usher tried to explain in a nice way that the White House pantry and supply room did not maintain a "drug store" to take care of the personal needs of the first family.

Hillary would have none of that, so the assistant usher got into his personal vehicle and drove around the District of Columbia looking for an all-night drug store. When he found one, he used his own money to buy the ointment. Hillary did not thank him nor did she offer to reimburse him for the cost of the Blistex.

This was made all the more obnoxious, according to WHI-4, since Hillary Clinton has many personal staff members to assist her in such personal matters. WHI-4 stated that in his opinion, Hillary Clinton misses no opportunity to abuse the Usher's Office, even though the office has bent over backward to please her.

*Investigation on XX/XX/XX AT Washington, D.C. **File** # WHI-#1*
(DATE WITHHELD FOR SECURITY REASONS)

This Document contains neither recommendations nor conclusions of the investigator. It is the property of the investigator, and its content is confidential. It is not to be distributed to any third party without the expressed consent and written permission of the investigator.

REPORT OF INTERVIEW AND INVESTIGATION

WHI-5 will be referred to as "he" in this report; however, no inference as to gender should be assumed. WHI-5 is a highly placed,
highly credible source with impeccable reputation, and he is considered to be an expert in areas of law, politics, and ethics.

WHI-5 was contacted when it was learned that he might be in possession of significant information related to Bill and Hillary Clinton.

WHI-5 advised that he has become aware of a very important meeting that took place during the Clinton presidential campaign in 1992.
This meeting altered the entire course of the Clinton administration.

WHI-5 says Lloyd Cutler met with Hillary Clinton and members
of her staff to persuade Hillary to remain on board and not to
renounce Mr. Clinton because of the Gennifer Flowers allegations.
Flowers claimed she had a 12-year love affair with Governor Bill
Clinton and possessed phone tapes that were proof of the affair.

WHI-5 stated that Cutler concluded the candidacy of Bill Clinton
was fatally injured, unless Hillary Clinton was willing to "stand by her
man" in some national forum. Cutler and others convinced Mrs. Clinton that without her support, Bill Clinton would not win the Democratic party nomination, and without Bill Clinton as the nominee,
President George Bush would win reelection. There was general
agreement that Bush's reelection was not an acceptable outcome.

WHI-5 stated that at a point, Mrs. Clinton asked, "What's in it for
me? What does Hillary Clinton get out of this deal?" Cutler and
others reportedly told her that she could just about call her own
shots, have a blank check, take whatever she wanted. WHI-5 stated
that according to Cutler, Mrs. Clinton then stated, "If that's the case,
then you know I want domestic."

There was general agreement that Mrs. Clinton would take over a
significant portion of the Executive Branch in the event of a Clinton
win, in exchange for playing the role of "victimized wife, nevertheless
standing by her man." Plans were then made to approach Bill Clinton with "Hillary's deal."

WHI-5 stated that the public forum turned out to be *60 Minutes,*
and the program was carefully scripted, with questions approved and
answers rehearsed before airtime.

WHI-5 admitted that his information is third-hand and should be
judged in that light. WHI-5 would not reveal the identity of his

source and stated that his source would suffer scorn and retribution if ever revealed. WHI-5 advised that his source is an educated and reasonable person who was shocked and disappointed to learn of "Hillary's deal." WHI-5 was also shocked that Cutler would reveal such inside information about the Clintons and the 1992 election.

Investigation on XX/XX/XX *AT Washington, D.C.* **File** # WHI-#1
(DATE WITHHELD FOR SECURITY REASONS)

This Document contains neither recommendations nor conclusions of the investigator. It is the property of the investigator, and its content is confidential. It is not to be distributed to any third party without the expressed consent and written permission of the investigator.

REPORT OF INTERVIEW AND INVESTIGATION

WHI-6 will be referred to as "he" in this report; however, no inference as to gender should be assumed. WHI-6 stated that he feared for his job and thought that if it was ever known who he was and that he had given such information to the writer, he would surely be punished even though he was not in violation of any law to repeat to the writer what he knew. WHI-6 advised he knew that the writer was no longer an FBI agent, was retired, and was no longer working at the White House.

WHI-6 advised that he has been conducting his own investigation of the Clinton administration, and at a future time he will reveal the full results of his investigation. WHI-6 advised that he had no objection to the writer's using some of this information in a book. WHI-6 acknowledged the sensational nature of his information.

WHI-6 stated that he has a close friend who works at the Marriott Hotel in downtown Washington, D.C. The Marriott Hotel has an underground parking garage that connects to the hotel lobby. The elevators in the garage go directly to floors in the hotel so that the hotel lobby can be bypassed altogether.

The garage has heavy security and is manned with security personnel. It also has 24-hour camera surveillance. All comings and goings are recorded on videotape, and car license tags are also recorded.

WHI-6 stated that the president of the United States is a frequent visitor to the hotel. The president does not have a room in his name; the guest who rents the room is known only to the hotel management. Some information indicates this individual is female and may have celebrity status.

WHI-6 advised that an individual usually drives the car into the garage with the president in the back seat. The driver is believed to be Bruce Lindsey, a high-level White House staffer and longtime friend of the president.

The car is parked near the elevator. The driver waits in the car until the president returns, usually hours later.

The car usually arrives at the hotel after midnight and sometimes leaves in the early morning, sometimes as late as 4:00 A.M.

WHI-6 was questioned about the absence of any mention of the Secret Service. WHI-6 advised that his source has never made any mention of the president's being accompanied, even at a distance, by Secret Service agents or anyone else.

WHI-6 was asked about the reliability of his source in view of the incredible nature of this information. WHI-6 advised that he has questioned his source very carefully to confirm the reliability of the information. WHI-6 stated that several other hotel staff members have also seen Bill Clinton at the hotel, without any Secret Service agents in attendance.

At a later date, WHI-6 was interviewed again. Further investigation by WHI-6 has provided more information on how Mr. Clinton may avoid Secret Service protection.

WHI-6 notes a guard shack is located at each White House car gate. The gates are large and electrically driven. The guard opens the gate from within the booth using an electronic switching device.

The guards are usually facing out, to see if somebody is trying to get into the White House. They are less concerned about cars leaving the White House. The guard observes exiting cars through a convex mirror that is about 18 inches in diameter.

Seeing the car approach with the intention to exit, the guard opens the gate. When the car has gone by, the guard closes the gate. WHI-6 observed several White House sedans exit through the gate, and never once did he see the guard attempt to identify who was leaving. He also noticed that the tinted windows and curved roof lines of White House sedans make it nearly impossible to see into the back seats.

WHI-6 has been told by a sensitive White House source that the president makes his exit from the White House in the following manner. The president usually leaves late at night, sometimes after midnight. The president leaves alone through the West Executive Lobby exit. The uniformed guard at the desk thinks the president is walking to the OEOB, which is across the parking lot from the West Wing.

In fact, the president immediately veers left and enters a waiting White House sedan, usually driven by Bruce Lindsey. The president gets into the back seat and lays on the seat, covering himself with a blanket kept there for that purpose.

Lindsey then drives the sedan north, toward the electric car gate and exits, turning east on Pennsylvania Avenue, en route to the Marriott. WHI-6 advised that he will continue to attempt to develop more evidence related to this strange behavior. WHI-6 stated that if he knows about this, then he is certain that others know as well.

WHI-6 advised that the more he learns about the Clintons and their friends, the more he is concerned about the president's personal safety.

Investigation on XX/XX/XX AT Washington, D.C. **File** # *WHI-#1*
(DATE WITHHELD FOR SECURITY REASONS)

This Document contains neither recommendations nor conclusions of the investigator. It is the property of the investigator, and its content is confidential. It is not to be distributed to any third party without the expressed consent and written permission of the investigator.

REPORT OF INTERVIEW AND INVESTIGATION

WHI-7 will be referred to as "he" in this report; however, no inference as to gender should be assumed. WHI-7 stated that he feared for his job if it became known that he had disclosed the following information.

WHI-7 acknowledged that White House staff have seen the president walk out of the White House in broad daylight unaccompanied by the Secret Service or anyone else.

WHI-7 stated that during the summer of 1993, White House staff saw the president exit the White House through the gate and then cross Pennsylvania Avenue. The staff members watched Clinton walk into the White House Town House complex that fronts Lafayette Park on the east. They believed he entered one of the Town House offices, but couldn't see from their angle to be sure of that.

They talked among themselves and were satisfied that they had indeed seen the president of the United States, Bill Clinton, alone, walking across Pennsylvania Avenue.

WHI-7 advised that he knew the staff members, and they were not "kids," but persons of exemplary professional and moral standing. He further stated that they had discussed the possibility that they had seen a "Clinton look-alike" hired to assist in the president's protection, but they rejected the idea, certain that they had just seen the president.

Investigation on XX/XX/XX AT Washington, D.C. File # WHI-#1
(DATE WITHHELD FOR SECURITY REASONS)

This Document contains neither recommendations nor conclusions of the investigator. It is the property of the investigator, and its content is confidential. It is not to be distributed to any third party without the expressed consent and written permission of the investigator.

REPORT OF INTERVIEW AND INVESTIGATION

WHI-8 was told the identity of the writer, who was now a retired FBI agent, no longer employed by the White House. WHI-8 was advised of the nature of the inquiry and the fact that at some future time the information given by WHI-8 might appear in a publication. WHI-8 stated that he understood and agreed to be interviewed.

WHI-8 will be referred to as "he" in this report; however, no inference as to gender should be assumed. WHI-8 stated that he feared for his job and thought that if it was ever known who he was and that he had given such information to the writer, he would surely be punished even though he was not in violation of any law to repeat to the writer what he knew.

WHI-8 stated that he has a long-term relationship with someone in the White House communications chain, but he is very reluctant to state who, since the disclosure of this person and this information would cause this person to lose employment.

WHI-8 stated that ever since the prosecution of Billy Dale, permanent employees in the White House have been very careful, fearing that they too might be fired and end up fighting off the FBI or IRS. WHI-8 stated that he does not know if it was the intention of the Clintons to silence the staff by their aggressive actions against the seven in the Travel Office, but even if it was not, the effect was the same. WHI-8 stated that the way things are now, "staffers would probably walk right past a dead body and pretend it's not there."

WHI-8 stated that he was aware that the writer was asking questions about the "antics of our commander-in-chief." He stated that he can confirm through his source in communications that, often, the president cannot be located for hours at a time. Late at night, calls are placed to the president's known phone locations, such as in his bedroom, and he can't be found. There is a message system, and messages are left.

On several occasions the president has called the phone switchboard and "raised hell," claiming that he was in the Residence, but they had not "tried hard enough" to reach him. The phone operators get the blame, even though they know he was not there.

WHI-8 explained that matters are made worse by the fact that the Secret Service agents, who used to be able to place their hands on the president immediately, have been booted out of the Residence by the first lady, who does not want the agents to see or hear what the Clintons are up to. For this reason, the Secret Service cannot say with certainty where the "commander-in-chief" is.

WHI-8 advised there is another dimension to this issue: The first lady doesn't know where he is, either. That is because they do not sleep in the same bedroom.

WHI-8 was asked what would happen if such information was made public. He advised the first thing to happen would be the loss of jobs since the Clintons would move to punish the innocent and guilty alike, but the second thing to happen would be a wholesale stampede by the fired staff and their supporters up to Congress "with the *rest* of the story" since the permanent staff "have about had it with the antics and poor manners of Bill and Hillary Clinton."

Investigation on XX/XX/XX AT Washington, D.C. **File** # *WHI-#1*
(DATE WITHHELD FOR SECURITY REASONS)

This Document contains neither recommendations nor conclusions of the investigator. It is the property of the investigator, and its content is confidential. It is not to be distributed to any third party without the expressed consent and written permission of the investigator.

REPORT OF INTERVIEW AND INVESTIGATION

WHI-9 was told the identity of the writer, who was now a retired FBI agent and no longer employed by the White House. WHI-9 was advised of the nature of the inquiry and the fact that at some future time the information given by WHI-9 might appear in a publication. WHI-9 stated that he understood and agreed to be interviewed.

WHI-9 will be referred to as "he" in this report; however, no inference as to gender should be assumed. WHI-9 stated that he feared for his job and thought that if it was ever known who he was and that he had given such information to the writer, he would surely be punished even though he was not in violation of any law to repeat to the writer what he knew.

WHI-9 advised that he would describe himself as a "senior law enforcement official" having served for more than 20 years in a federal agency in several cities around the country. He recently has been assigned to the White House. WHI-9 requested that the name of his agency (which was not the Secret Service) not be revealed because of the singular nature of the information he was about to relate.

WHI-9 advised that it is well known in the Secret Service and the FBI that security at the Clinton White House has been a mess, especially in the first year. Even today, there have been many changes that make it much harder to protect President Clinton, the White House, and national security. These changes, all negative, have been caused by actions of the Clintons.

WHI-9 stated that Congress is aware of the problems, as well. As evidence, he described a mysterious meeting he had with a U.S. senator.

Shortly after Vince Foster's death, WHI-9's beeper went off and on the message bar was a telephone number. WHI-9 called the number, which turned out to be a cell phone in a vehicle. The vehicle phone was answered by Senator Dennis DeConcini. WHI-9 knew Senator DeConcini personally.

Senator DeConcini asked him if he could step out of the White House on the 17th Street side of the OEOB and talk to him for a moment, and he apologized for the unusual request, but explained he did not want to be seen in the White House. WHI-9 agreed to come out to the car.

WHI-9 walked out and saw the car and an arm waving for him to get into the back seat. He opened the door and was greeted by the senator. There was some small talk before the senator asked, "Tell me, is it as bad in there as everyone is saying it is?"

WHI-9 told Senator DeConcini, "Yes, in my opinion, it's pretty bad, especially when compared with what I've heard about the Bush administration." WHI-9 said that he gave Senator DeConcini a full dose of what he had been witness to and what he knew.

WHI-9 was asked if recent information that Bill Clinton was trying to travel about town without his Secret Service Protective Detail was actually true.

WHI-9 was quick to point out to me that he did not know anything about "*that* mess" at the time he talked to the senator. He then stated, "Let me put it this way: if the president, who tells the Secret Service what to do and when to do it, says, 'You guys stay right here; I'll be back in a little bit,' what do you think the agents can do about it?"

I questioned WHI-9 about the ramifications of such actions in the event something were to happen to Bill Clinton. WHI-9 advised that every time one of the members of the first family countermands efforts to guard them, a memo is prepared, which goes into a Secret Service file so that the agents and the agency are covered. WHI-9 called this the CYA, or "cover your ass," file.

I asked WHI-9 why he had mentioned the first family. He stated that Hillary Clinton was as bad as Bill. She has told her Secret Service Protective Detail agents in public to "Stay the f--k back, stay the f--k away from me! Don't come within ten yards of me, or else!"

The agents have tried to explain to the first lady that they cannot effectively guard her if they must remain so far away. Her reply is, "Just f--king do as I say, okay?" WHI-9 stated that at least with Bill, when he is out at a public event, the agents are allowed to guard him.

WHI-9 reminded the writer that during a recent trip to Little Rock, where "plenty of people are sort of angry" at the first lady, Hillary jumped behind the wheel of a nearby car and drove away. She stayed away for several hours, during which time she would not tell the Secret Service where she was. She later laughed about it, ridiculing the Secret Service agents in her newspaper column.

This fact was confirmed by a review of an article in the *Washington Post* dated 7/24/95, wherein Mrs. Clinton recounted a recent trip to

Arkansas when, "she had a sudden urge to drive and, much to the dismay of her Secret Service agents, 'jumped behind the wheel of a car and . . . drove myself around town. For several hours, I enjoyed a marvelous sensation of personal freedom.' "

Investigation on XX/XX/XX AT Washington, D.C. **File** # *WHI-#1*
(DATE WITHHELD FOR SECURITY REASONS)

This Document contains neither recommendations nor conclusions of the investigator. It is the property of the investigator, and its content is confidential. It is not to be distributed to any third party without the expressed consent and written permission of the investigator.

SUMMARY

RECOMMENDATION

Normally, no suggestions or conclusions are offered to a reader at the end of a summary background investigation. But in view of the evidence, the following recommendation is made:

That the application of Bill Clinton and Hillary Clinton for security clearances, permanent White House passes, and **ACCESS TO THE WHITE HOUSE** *BE DENIED.*

ENVOI

General information about the state of Arkansas that may be of interest to the reader:

State Motto: *Regnat Populus* (The People Rule)

State Bird: *Mimius Polyglottos* (The mockingbird)

Description of the mockingbird: **"A noted mimic that combines its own song with those of other birds; it is gray above, and white below, with flashy markings on its tail."**

Chronology

Rules for Radicals: "It is not a world of peace and beauty and dispassionate rationality, but as Henry James once wrote, Life is, in fact, a battle. Evil is insolent and strong; beauty enchanting but rare; goodness very apt to be weak; folly very apt to be defiant; wickedness to carry the day; imbeciles to be in great places, people of sense in small, and mankind generally unhappy. The life of man upon earth is a warfare."

George Washington's Rules of Civility and Decent Behaviour: "When you see a crime punished, you may be inwardly pleased, but always show pity to the suffering offender."

Major events pertinent to *Unlimited Access,* Gary Aldrich, the FBI, Congress, and the Clinton White House:

- **December 1994–1995** Gary Aldrich helps decorate Hillary's Blue Room Christmas tree. Ornaments sent in by art students made of condoms and drug paraphernalia. One year later, same room—new tree. Hillary decorates room with notorious South Florida drug dealer Jorge "Gordito" Cabrera.

- **January 1996** Howard Shapiro leaks Aldrich typescript to White House Counsel Jack Quinn.

- **January 1996** Howard Shapiro sends two FBI agents to White House FBI Office to interview Dennis Sculimbrene about Aldrich's book.

- **March 1996** After Sculimbrene testifies before Senate and House investigating committees, FBI pulls Sculimbrene from White House and seizes his White House pass.

- **April 1996** FBI closes its White House Liaison Office, ending a more than thirty-year presence that served seven presidents.

- **May 1, 1996** Gary Aldrich abandons book project after FBI refuses to approve the typescript.

- **May 5, 1996** Craig Livingstone hosts fundraiser for President Clinton with Yogesh Gandhi and John Huang at the Sheraton-Carlton hotel in Washington, D.C. Three weeks later the Filegate scandal breaks, and President Clinton and Mrs. Clinton claim they do not know Craig Livingstone. A group photo of Bill Clinton, Craig Livingstone, John Huang, and Yogesh Gandhi is taken, but the DNC can't find the photo, according to news reports. It is later determined by the Senate investigating committee that the funds given to the DNC by Gandhi were first wired to Gandhi from an Asian bank on foreign soil.

- **May 12, 1996** Southeastern Legal Foundation provides Aldrich with legal backstopping, allowing Aldrich to pursue his first amendment rights and go ahead with his book. Further attempts to win FBI approval fail, and the typescript is eventually submitted to Regnery Publishing.

- **May 30, 1996** House Oversight Committee lawyer Barbara Comstock discovers "smoking gun" Billy Dale FBI file request form, signed by Bernard Nussbaum, in box of documents hidden from committee by White House for two years. The FBI Filegate scandal is born.

- **June 1996** Gary Aldrich writes commentary piece for the *Wall Street Journal*, disputing White House and FBI statements on the Filegate scandal. Media hurricane for Aldrich begins. White House "masters of disaster" start negative spin operation to discredit Aldrich.

- **June 17, 1996** The 24th anniversary of the Watergate break-in.

- **June 19, 1996** Dennis Sculimbrene appears before Senate Judiciary Committee and confirms past drug use of Clinton staffers, Hillary's recommendation of Craig Livingstone, and other key allegations made in *Unlimited Access*. White House has no comment.

- **June 28, 1996** Front page *New York Post* headline regarding *Unlimited Access,* "Bill Romped as Hill stomped in wild and crazy White House."

- **June 30, 1996** Almost one year to the day from Aldrich's retirement from the FBI, he appears on *This Week with David Brinkley.* White House sets off firestorm of protest and counterattack.

- **July 2, 1996** Syndicated columnist Maureen Dowd describes *Unlimited Access* as "Civil servants vs. uncivil kids. Starched shirts vs. short skirts. Scotch vs. Bongs. Men with guns vs. men with men."

- **July 4, 1996** Official launch of *Unlimited Access* and of the movie *Independence Day,* which shows White House blown up by space aliens. Cartoon in the *Washington Times:* Little boy holding dad's hand, standing in line to see *Independence Day* asks, "Daddy, is Gary Aldrich an alien?"

- **July 12, 1996** *Unlimited Access* debuts at number five on the *New York Times* bestseller list.

- **July 17, 1996** Two Secret Service agents confirm in sworn testimony before the House Oversight Committee Gary Aldrich's allegations regarding drug use by Clinton White House staff members. White House Press Secretary Michael McCurry comments, "Of course I smoked marijuana."

- **July 20, 1996** Speaker of the House Newt Gingrich blasts Michael McCurry for his casual attitude about using illegal drugs. Speaker Gingrich had accused the White House of illegal drug laxity in late 1994, but was roundly criticized by the White House and the media for making "false allegations." No media apologies to the speaker after McCurry's confession.

- **July 1996** Treasury inspector general opens criminal investigation of two secret Service agents after they testify about Filegate scandal, contradicting White House version of events.

- **August 1, 1996** Dennis Sculimbrene retires after FBI continues nonstop harassment.

- **August 4, 1996** *Unlimited Access* is number 1 on the *New York Times* bestseller list. It remains on the list for more than one hundred days.

- **September 21, 1996** House Oversight Committee reveals that many Clinton staff members had a history of hard drug use, vindicating Aldrich's account in *Unlimited Access.*

- **September 26, 1997** White House Drug Czar Barry McCaffrey defends White House staff members who used hard drugs. McCaffrey is quoted as saying, "No American should be barred from serving their country in any position as long as they now reject all illicit drug use."

- **September 1996** Retiring Chairman of House Oversight Committee William Clinger praises Gary Aldrich at Republican fundraiser for Senator John Warner and Congressmen Tom Davis. He declares Aldrich book to be "highly credible."

- **October 4, 1996** Former FBI special agent Dennis Sculimbrene is interviewed by a reporter for the *Wall Street Journal,* and confirms that *Unlimited Access* is a truthful account of the Clinton White House.

- **October 16, 1996** the *Wall Street Journal* reports Senator Paul Coverdell's discovery that seven drug dealers have received pardons or offers of pardons from President Clinton.

- **November 5, 1996** President Clinton reelected.

- **November 15, 1996** *Human Events* newspaper publishes evidence that George Stephanopoulos annotated his own copy of *Unlimited Access.* The Marriott Hotel section is marked "National Security Breach." In contrast, other sections of the book are marked "fabrication" or "partisan." The White House and Stephanopoulos refused to comment.

- **January 1, 1997** George Stephanopoulos resigns from White House and accepts job as regular member of ABC's *This Week* Sunday morning discussion panel—joining George Will and Sam Donaldson. It is reported that ABC will pay Stephanopoulos many times his White House salary.

- **January 1, 1997** *USA Today* ranks *Unlimited Access* number 36 of the 100 bestselling books—fiction and nonfiction, soft cover and hard cover—published in 1996. *USA Today* also ranks *Unlimited Access* in the top 25 of all nonfiction hard cover books sold in 1996. Meanwhile, *Unlimited Access* continues to sell briskly, defying all conventional wisdom. Regnery declares, "book has a life of its own."

- **March 1, 1997** *Unlimited Access* passes 500,000 copies in sales.

- **March 29, 1997** Department of Justice releases internal report on conduct of FBI lawyer Howard Shapiro, accusing him of "horrific blunders, poor judgment, and serious mistakes." The report recommends no sanctions. Shapiro tells newspaper reporters he is out looking for a job.

- **April 1, 1997** Gary Aldrich logs 500th radio talk-show appearance and 50th personal speaking appearance.

- **April 4, 1997** Congressional investigators learn of a deal struck by convicted drug felon Jorge "Gordito" Cabrera to give $20,000 to the DNC. The money swap was made in Havana, Cuba, at the Copacabana Hotel. In return for the dirty money, Cabrera meets Al Gore in Miami. Eventually Cabrera is invited to the White House for a meeting with President and Hillary Clinton, and a photograph with the first lady in front of her Christmas tree in the Blue Room. This Kodak moment takes place on December 21, 1994, one year after the Blue Room Christmas tree sported condoms and roach-clips.

- **May 7, 1997** Regarding alleged hush money payments to Webster Hubbell, the *Washington Times* asks: what did the Clintons know, and when did they know it? Hubbell reportedly received nearly $500,000 in questionable payments from friends of the Clinton Administration. The payments came after Hubbell's indictment but before his "cooperation" with Kenneth Starr's prosecutors.

- **May 25, 1997** Author Gary Aldrich and Publisher Al Regnery appear on NBC's Sunday morning *Meet the Press* program. Evidently, the Clinton "ban" on having Aldrich on network television, at least as far as NBC is concerned, has been lifted. Tim

Russert announces that Aldrich will not be prosecuted by the FBI and Department of Justice for printing book without FBI approval.

- **June 1997** Congressman Robert Livingstone, Chairman of House Appropriations Committee, demands that Director Freeh fire Howard Shapiro. Livingstone's demand joins chorus of Congressmen and Senators who insist, "Howard Shapiro must go!" Director Freeh tells Congressman Livingstone that Shapiro will leave soon.

- **June 6, 1997** Newspapers report Howard Shapiro resigns as FBI chief counsel and takes a job practicing law with former Clinton White House counsel Lloyd Cutler, where he will earn triple his former FBI salary.

- **June 25, 1997** Hillary blames aides for missing law firm billing records discovered in her personal quarters. Records are believed to have come from the office of Vince Foster the night he died.

- **June 28, 1997** President Clinton claims he cannot remember calling anyone from the White House to ask them to send money for his reelection, though it appears that more than $500,000 was solicited in this fashion.

- **June 30, 1997** Democratic Congressman James A. Traficant, Jr., is quoted in the *Washington Times* criticizing the Department of Justice and the FBI for attempting to block publication of *Unlimited Access*. Regarding the internal investigation of Howard Shapiro, Traficant states, "Something is seriously wrong in our democracy if criminal and unethical behavior at the nation's top law enforcement agency goes unpunished."

- **June 1997** Veteran UPI White House reporter Helen Thomas complains that President Bill Clinton is sneaking out of the White House, "to visit friends." Thomas states that Clinton and his aides lie to the press about the president's whereabouts, and make the press believe the president is home asleep in his bed when he is actually out on the town. Thomas does not confirm the Marriott Hotel as one of the president's destinations.

- **July 1, 1997** Congressman Gerald Solomon, chairman of the House Rules Committee, alleges that top secret documents appear to have been given to the Chinese communist government by John Huang, former DNC fundraiser, Commerce Department employee, and friend of President Clinton. Congressman Solomon stated that he is worried about "economic espionage."

- **July 1, 1997** Rush Limbaugh interviews Gary Aldrich for his monthly newsletter, and applauds Aldrich efforts, stating "There are too many people like you all over the country who are not going to sit idly by and watch freedoms be eroded, and watch standards be declined—on purpose."

- **July 2, 1997** Strengthening the "masters of disaster" team, the Clinton administration announces the hiring of Paul Begala, a Texan who had worked in the 1992 "war room" in Little Rock with George Stephanopoulos and James Carville. Joining Begala is Sidney Blumenthal, a longtime Clinton supporter and journalist for the *New Yorker*, the *New Republic,* and the *Washington Post.*

- **July 8, 1997** Senate Chairman Fred Thompson states that the Chinese may have tried to "buy" the 1996 presidential election, in his opening statement before the Senate committee investigating Clinton fundraising scandals. It is also reported that former "bimbo eruptions" specialist Jack Palladino, a private investigator who worked for the 1992 Clinton campaign, is now working to reelect Ron Carey as president of the Teamsters Union.

- **July 11, 1997** *Human Events* newspaper reports that John Huang was given top secret CIA reports while he was working at the Clinton administration, but lost track of the reports. The CIA admitted that they didn't keep track of the material given to Huang, now suspected of being an agent for the Chinese government.

- **July 20, 1997** Gary Aldrich is appointed Director of Special Events for the Virginia-based Freedom Alliance Foundation. He will also serve as Investigative Research Fellow. His mission is to ferret out and report wrongdoing in the federal government.

- **August 1, 1997** Kathleen E. Willey, a former White House staff member, is subpoenaed after confessing she was groped by President Clinton near the Oval Office.

- **September 10, 1997** Ex-DNC chief Donald Fowler testifies in front of a congressional committee that he cannot recall asking the CIA to help arrange a meeting between President Clinton and Roger Tamraz, a foreign national of highly questionable character. The meeting with President Clinton in the White House was for the purpose of fundraising.

- **September 11, 1997** the *Washington Times* reports that a fired White House chef was paid $37,000 "hush" money from a secret White House slush fund. The chef was in a position to give damaging testimony about how the Clintons abused White House staff.

- **September 12, 1997** Appearing before a congressional committee, Sandy R. Berger, head of the White House National Security Council, fully admitted that the Clinton administration dismantled security procedures, which enabled unsuitable persons to enter the White House. NSC's Burger was quoted as saying the Clinton administration had only an "informal system" to review the backgrounds of foreign nationals, including the infamous Roger Tamraz. Others at NSC tried to keep Tamraz out but were overruled, according to sworn testimony.

- **September 29, 1997** House Speaker Newt Gingrich describes President Bill Clinton and Vice President Al Gore as "Defendants in Chief" and charges that their conduct during the reelection campaign was "a systematic violation of the rule of the law." On the same day, the *Washington Times* reports on alleged IRS harassment of conservative groups through threatened audits.

- **October 12, 1997** Billy Dale's $80 million lawsuit against Harry Thomason is thrown out of court. Meanwhile, the *Washington Times* reports officials of the Paula Jones Legal Defense Fund experiencing break-ins, harassment, and IRS audits.

- **October 1997** David S. Broder writes in a column in the *Washington Post*, "It is maddening to know this kind of cynical manipulation drives our elections." He was commenting on the dishonest actions of George Stephanopoulos, Dick Morris, and others in the 1996 election. Continuing, Broder says, "It is worse to know that we in the press have celebrated these consultants, who are our sources, and in some instances, even installed them in prominent positions in our own business." This was a clear reference to Morris and Stephanopoulos.

- **October 3, 1997** the *Washington Post* describes chaos and serious missteps in the Department of Justice task force investigating the Clinton fundraising scandals. Subsequent articles claim the FBI and DOJ are not working well together. FBI sources charge DOJ lawyers are preventing senior FBI agents from conducting serious investigations.

- **October 1997** President Bill Clinton announces the appointment of several homosexuals to key posts in his administration, continuing to honor his quid pro quo deal with wealthy homosexuals and lesbians who contributed to his '92 and '96 elections.

- **October 8, 1997** *New York Times* columnist William Safire suggests that FBI Director Louis Freeh should do the right thing and submit his resignation, unless the White House allows him to do his job and protect national security. Safire: "That would crack the stonewall—one honorable law officer."

- **October 10, 1997** Kenneth Starr's report on the death of Vince Foster unsealed, and in large part vindicates Gary Aldrich and his claims regarding Foster's state of mind at the time of his death and the events which led up to the discovery of his body in July 1993.

- **October 12, 1997** Attorney General Janet Reno appears on Tim Russert's *Meet the Press* and declares herself "mad" at the White House for withholding key videotape evidence proving that President Clinton conducted illegal fundraising at the White House.

- **November 5, 1997** Congressman Bob Barr and 17 co-sponsors announce House Resolution 304 calling for an "inquiry into whether grounds exist to impeach William Jefferson Clinton, the President of the United States." Speaker of the House Newt Gingrich describes Congressman Barr as "a serious man."

- **November 6, 1997** Former Democratic Senator Dennis De Concini meets Gary and Nina Aldrich at a *Meet the Press* celebration and praises Gary for "doing the right thing" by coming forward and blowing the whistle on the Clinton White House.

- **November 8, 1997** President Clinton becomes the "first sitting president in history to attend and address a major gay and lesbian event." He had provided a campaign videotape message to the same group in May 1992.

- **November 10, 1997** Congressman David M. McIntosh complains the White House hid memos that prove a massive computer database, housed in the New Executive Office Building at the White House, was going to be used by the Democratic National Committee for fundraising and other political activities. According to Congressman McIntosh, this is a clear violation of federal law.

- **November 12, 1997** R. Emmett Tyrrell is honored at the thirtieth anniversary celebration for the *American Spectator* magazine. Guests include Rush Limbaugh, former senior Resolution Trust Corporation investigator Jean Lewis, Gary Aldrich, and hundreds of others. Rush Limbaugh declares Gary Aldrich and Jean Lewis to be "courageous," for standing up to the Clintons and their corrupted administration.

- **November 13, 1997** David Brock learns he's been fired from his six-figure salaried position at the *American Spectator*. Brock promptly declares magazine's management and staff to be "homophobic."

- **November 17, 1997** Craig Livingstone found alive, well, and still a free man, living in Southern California, working for a firm friendly to the Clinton Administration. A $90 million civil lawsuit is pending, charging Livingstone, Anthony Marceca, and Hillary Clinton, among others, with violating the rights of more than nine hundred persons in the Filegate scandal. Gary Aldrich is one of the nine hundred, according to the former chairman of the House Government Reform and Oversight Committee, Congressman Bill Clinger.

- **November 17, 1997** the *Washington Times* changes the name of the FBI to "The Federal Bureau of Incompetence" in a lead editorial, complaining that the FBI could not find key evidence of Communist Chinese attempts to influence American elections, hidden in its own files and "found" only after Senator Fred Thompson announced the suspension of Senate Hearings on the matter. Director Freeh and Attorney General Janet Reno apologized to Thompson. The same day, Pulitzer Prize-winning journalist Seymour Hersh is attacked in "unusually personal terms" for reprinting "the most salacious tidbits about JFK and his frenetic sex life" in his book, the *Dark Side of Camelot*. Hersh also accused President Kennedy of campaign funding abuses and "buying" a presidential election through bribes and illegal acts. Hersh paints a picture of a president cozy with mobsters. Like *Unlimited Access*, Hersh's book links flawed presidential character with the endangerment of national security.

- **December 15, 1997** FBI lawyers assigned to review *Unlimited Access* notify Gary Aldrich that his manuscript for a new paperback edition has been approved. The new manuscript was submitted to the FBI in the very same manner as the first manuscript. But this time approval is granted a mere ten calendar days after submission to the FBI director. The letter, in part, reads as follows: "Based upon our review, it has been determined that the chapters contain no information of a sensitive or classified nature. As a consequence, Mr. Aldrich is free to seek publication of these materials."

- **December 18, 1997** A *New York Times* editorial praises FBI Director Louis Freeh for arguing in favor of an Independent Counsel to investigate President Clinton and Vice President Gore, despite Attorney General Reno's opposition. Headlines announce: "The Federal Bureau of Independence."

- **December 19, 1997** Gary Aldrich begins work on his next book, investigating William Jefferson Clinton.

- **January 1, 1997** Gary Aldrich announces creation of non-profit foundation dedicated to the support of Constitutional government and the Bill of Rights, particularly the first amendment. The Patrick Henry Center for Individual Liberty, based in Virginia, will support witnesses who wish to come forward to expose wrongdoing and corruption in the federal government.

Appendix

December 15, 1997

Mr. Michael A. Carvin
Cooper & Carvin
Suite 401
2000 K Street, N.W.
Washington, D.C. 20006

Dear Mr. Carvin:

The FBI has completed its prepublication review of the materials your submitted on behalf of your client, Mr. Gary Aldrich, on December 5, 1997. Based upon our review, it has been determined that the chapters contain no information of a sensitive or classified nature. As a consequence, Mr. Aldrich is free to seek publication of these materials.

Sincerely,

Patricia G. Solley/EJP

Patricia G. Solley
Unit Chief
Office of Public and
  Congressional Affairs

Amazingly the FBI completed its review of my second manuscript for *Unlimited Access* in ten days. The first time around it took five months and the manuscript was never approved.

U.S. Department of Justice

Civil Division

Deputy Assistant Attorney General

Washington, D.C. 20530

July 1, 1997

Mr. Charles J. Cooper
Cooper & Carvin, PLLC
Suite 401
2000 "K" Street, N.W.
Washington, D.C. 20006

Mr. Matthew J. Glavin
Southeastern Legal Foundation
Suite 2515
3340 Peachtree Road, N.E.
Atlanta, GA 30326

Dear Messrs. Cooper and Glavin:

Thank you for your letter of June 9, 1997 on behalf of Gary Aldrich. This will confirm that, based upon the information known to the Civil Division at this time, the Department of Justice does not intend to bring an action against Mr. Aldrich for civil sanctions relating to the publication of his book, Unlimited Access.

Sincerely,

Gary G. Grindler
Deputy Assistant Attorney General

Official notification that the Department of Justice had backed off on civil sanctions for the publication of *Unlimited Access*.

THE WHITE HOUSE

WASHINGTON

FEBRUARY 17, 1993

MEMORANDUM TO: ALL WHITE HOUSE OFFICE STAFF

FROM: VINCENT W. FOSTER ✔
               DEPUTY COUNSEL TO THE PRESIDENT

               WILLIAM H. KENNEDY III
               ASSOCIATE COUNSEL

As a condition of employment in the White House Office, as well as obtaining a security clearance generally, each member of the White House Office staff must submit a completed Form 86 (Questionnaire for Sensitive Positions) and supplement, and thereafter be interviewed by an FBI agent. Most of you have already submitted the paperwork. You should be receiving a call from Agent Gary Aldrich or Agent Dennis Sculimbrene requesting a meeting with you. It is mandatory that you have a personal interview with one of these agents before you can receive final clearance to work in the White House Office and obtain a permanent badge.

There are a large number of staff members yet to be interviewed and only a few weeks left to complete them before your temporary clearance expires. Please be responsive to the Agent's request for an interview and accommodate his schedule. Avoid the last-week crunch and the risk of expiration of your temporary clearance.

Early concerns by agents Aldrich and Sculimbrene about White House security were adressed by Vince Foster in a memo instructing all White House personnel to corporate with the FBI.

United States Senate

COMMITTEE ON APPROPRIATIONS

WASHINGTON. DC 20510-6025

August 11, 1994

The President
The White House
Washington, D.C.

Dear Mr. President:

Mr. David Watkins of the Office of Administration asked for assistance from the Senate Select Committee on Intelligence (SSCI) to review the White House procedures for the issuance of White House passes and other security-related functions that provide access to sensitive classified information in the Executive Office of the President and to make any recommendations that could possibly enhance those procedures.

Mr. James Wolfe, Director of Security for the SSCI, met with your officials in May to review your procedures and to inform me of his findings. That review is complete and I am forwarding to you my recommendations to refine your current system.

It should be noted that the White House officials Mr. Wolfe met with were candid and forthcoming regarding security procedures at the White House and the issuance of White House passes. These officials did indicate, however, that there were certain operational inefficiencies during the early stages of your Administration that contributed to the severe backlog of the issuance of permanent White House passes for White House employees. Nevertheless, they have taken the appropriate corrective action to remedy the problem and there appears to be a good system in place to monitor the process of all employees undergoing new employment at the White House.

My recommendations are as follows:

1. The White House Office of Administration should be assigned a Secret Service Agent or other appropriate government official in a full-time position to function as the Director of Security. Such a person would be a non-partisan individual responsible for overseeing all security-related functions within the Office of Administration. The person filling this position would be a security professional to provide the White House with broad security-related specialties, to include but not limited to: knowledge of investigative and adjudicative procedures; classified document handling procedures; communication security procedures; and a law enforcement background. This person would be directly involved in the

Even Democrat Senators had serious concerns about the lack of security at the Clinton White House.

The President
August 11, 1994
Page Two

decisionmaking process for final adjudication of White House access passes and Top Secret security clearances. This person could provide the White House with institutional knowledge that would ensure continuity across Administrations.

2. A single office within the White House should coordinate all background investigations. Currently the Executive Office of the President has two separate offices that initiate, track, control, and process background investigations. One office processes political appointees and another processes career employees. In addition to these arrangements, the White House Counsel's Office processes the background investigations of Presidential Appointees who require Senate confirmation. This practice gives the appearance of an enormous amount of redundancy and lack of centralized control. These offices should be combined and headed by a senior security official (preferably the Director of Security identified in item #1) in the White House. It is my understanding that past Administrations functioned in this manner.

3. All security clearance/background investigation paperwork should be completed and turned in on or before the first day of employment with the White House rather than the current procedure of 30 days. This would alleviate any delay in initiating a security background investigation and thus reduce the amount of time, now approximately 120 days, that it takes to process a new employee for a sensitive White House access pass.

4. Currently, new employees are required to undergo an FBI full-field background investigation for employment at the White House, regardless if they have been the subject of a recent full-field investigation from another government agency. I would suggest to you that new employees who have undergone an FBI background investigation within 5 years should not have to undergo another full-field background investigation. The same background investigation that is currently accepted throughout the government should satisfy White House requirements as well. Implementing this recommendation alone would save the American taxpayers a considerable amount of money.

I hope that these recommendations will be of use to you and your Administration.

Sincerely,

Dennis De Concini
Dennis DeConcini
Chairman
Subcommittee on Treasury,
Postal Service, and General Government

THE WHITE HOUSE
WASHINGTON

August 22, 1994

The Honorable Dennis DeConcini
United States Senate
328 Senate Hart Office Building
Washington, D.C.   20510-0302

Dear Senator DeConcini:

On behalf of the President, let me express our sincerest appreciation for your recent correspondence concerning White House security procedures. We very much appreciated your willingness to share the expertise of Mr. Wolfe, the Director of Security for the Senate Select Committee on Intelligence. He was unfailingly courteous and helpful in his review.

We are currently in the process of our own examination and assessment of White House security procedures. At first glance, many of your recommendations appear to dovetail with the modifications currently under consideration. In any event, all of your recommendations will be given the most serious consideration.

When our review is complete, we would be happy to let you know of any changes we may make. In the meanwhile, I hope you would not mind our continuing to call upon Mr. Wolfe as a resource.

Thank you again for your interest in this matter.

Sincerely,

Lloyd N. Cutler
Special Counsel to the President

As late as the fall of 1994 the White House was still claiming that security was in fine condition and there was no need for a senior senator to be concerned.

THE WHITE HOUSE

WASHINGTON

January 15, 1993

Dear Gary:

Thank you so much for your thoughtful message,
and thank you also for your work to ensure high
standards of conduct for the White House staff.
I appreciate your kind words about my staff, and
I agree that they are a terrific group of people.

While another term was not meant to be, I have
the satisfaction of knowing that I did what I
believed was right for America in meeting domestic
challenges and in enhancing United States leadership
in the international community. I hope that history
will judge our Administration's accomplishments as
ones that have benefitted both our country and our
people.

Being President has been a tremendous honor, and
I will always be grateful for the privilege of
having served the American people and of having
had the support of dedicated public servants such
as you.

Best wishes.

Sincerely,

G. Bush

Mr. Gary Warren Aldrich
Special Agent
Federal Bureau of Investigation

Letter of commendation from President George Bush.

is worth pursuing, or that would perhaps be used to obtain search warrants or subpoenas. It is by no means conclusive, but the information is deeply troubling in the issues it raises about the president's irresponsibility and callous disregard for national security.

I have been informed by a well-placed White House source that that there are times when the president, the leader of the free world, is missing—that is, cannot be located by staff—for hours at a time.

Previous presidents have, of course, maintained an unbreakable link twenty-four hours a day between themselves and their key advisers, especially at the Defense Department. But today, late at night, when calls are placed to the president, he sometimes cannot be found. There is a message system, and messages are left. But in a crisis, messages won't be good enough.

On several occasions, the president has called the phone switchboard and "raised hell," claiming that he was in the Residence, but that phone operators had not "tried hard enough" to reach him.

The Secret Service should know where the president is at all times. But this is no longer the case, I have been informed, because the first lady has booted them out of the Residence. Moreover, *she* does not always know where the president is, because the Clintons sleep in separate bedrooms.

All of this raises the question of, "If the president cannot be found, where is he?"

One answer has been given me by another source, a highly educated, well-trained, experienced investigator who is conducting his own investigation into the Clintons. It appears that the president is a frequent late-night visitor to the Marriott Hotel in downtown Washington, which has an underground parking garage with an elevator that allows guests to go to their rooms without passing through the lobby.

The president does not have a room in his name, and the guest who rents the room is known only to the management, though some information indicates this individual is female and may be a celebrity.

The president's driver is believed to be Bruce Lindsey, a high-level White House staffer and longtime friend of the president. The car is parked near the elevator. The driver waits in the car until the president returns, often hours later. The car usually arrives after midnight and sometimes leaves early in the morning, sometimes as late as 4:00 A.M.

I asked my informant about the president's Secret Service protection on these trips. And I should state here that if I had been

NATIONAL SECURITY BREACH

George Stephanopoulos's personal copy of *Unlimited Access* with hand-written margin notes containing the notation: "National Security Breach."

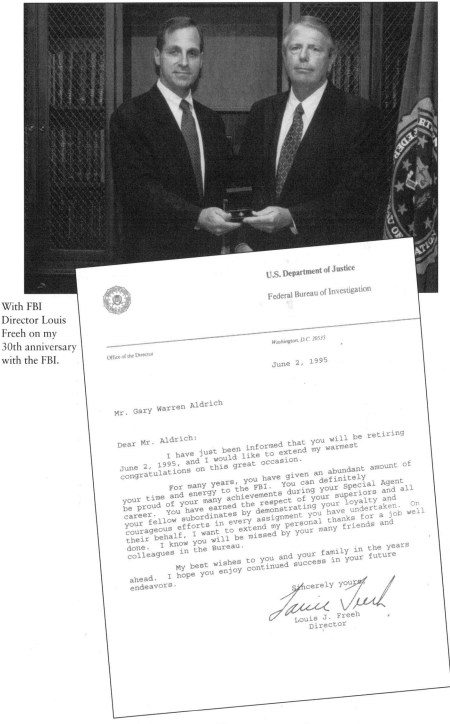

With FBI Director Louis Freeh on my 30th anniversary with the FBI.

U.S. Department of Justice

Federal Bureau of Investigation

Washington, D.C. 20535

Office of the Director

June 2, 1995

Mr. Gary Warren Aldrich

Dear Mr. Aldrich:

I have just been informed that you will be retiring June 2, 1995, and I would like to extend my warmest congratulations on this great occasion.

For many years, you have given an abundant amount of your time and energy to the FBI. You can definitely be proud of your many achievements during your Special Agent career. You have earned the respect of your superiors and all your fellow subordinates by demonstrating your loyalty and courageous efforts in every assignment you have undertaken. On their behalf, I want to extend my personal thanks for a job well done. I know you will be missed by your many friends and colleagues in the Bureau.

My best wishes to you and your family in the years ahead. I hope you enjoy continued success in your future endeavors.

Sincerely yours,

Louis Freeh

Louis J. Freeh
Director

The letter I received from Director Freeh on my retirement.

Author's Note

"The agents . . . were good, loyal men put into an impossible situation."
—*Absolute Power*, David Baldacci

It would be a grave disservice—and unjust—if anything in this book were taken to impugn the dedicated permanent and security staff at the White House—or used to punish them. They are the best of the best, and if I have endangered their jobs by being a whistle-blower, I sincerely apologize. More than that, I will come to their defense.

Further, no one can claim that I left the FBI a disgruntled employee. I love the FBI and treasure my very successful and exciting career there. I will say, however, that I agree with former Director William Sessions that the FBI has become too "politicized"—a trend that has been accelerated by the Clinton administration.

The bottom line is it is not the job of the FBI or the Secret Service or the permanent White House staff to police the Executive Branch. It is Congress that has that oversight authority. It is time they used it. And perhaps it is time, too, for we, the people, to understand the full consequences of what we do when we vote.

Acknowledgments

"I'll bet you could write a heck of a book!" I cannot tell you how many times people said that to me, especially during the last year I worked in the Clinton administration. Then it became, "You should write a book. You should tell what you saw!" And then it became, "Please. You must tell people what you saw!"

How did I get from there to here? It took the help of many friends who were willing to take big risks—and even put their jobs on the line. They know who they are. All I can say is, thank you. And to one special friend, who must also remain anonymous, let me just add that you are a great American.

But there are a few friends I can name.

Thank you, Jay Stephens, former deputy White House counsel, for your guidance and legal advice. I wanted the best legal mind in town, and I got it. But I got much, much more. Jay Stephens is a true patriot, a visionary, and a man who understands the necessity of morality and ethics in government.

To Matthew J. Glavin and Henry D. Granberry and to the organization which they represent, Southeastern Legal Foundation, my deep gratitude for providing legal backstopping at a time when my resources had been exhausted. Your organization's faith in the First Amendment allowed me to continue on. Without it, there would have been no book.

Thank you, Al Regnery, attorney and publisher, and Richard Vigilante, Executive Editor of Regnery Publishing. Al took the great risk of accepting a manuscript that I couldn't show him until just before publication. I assured him he would not be disappointed; he was not. Richard was supportive and encouraging throughout.

Thank you to my researchers, Christopher B. Briggs and Robin Rosen. Without your assistance I could never have met my deadlines.

Thank you to my sister Karen and her husband John for giving me shoulders to cry on—and an old 386 computer to get started on . . . until it crashed.

Thank you to Coleman Rosen, my friendly neighborhood techi who kept the 386 going with scotch tape and chewing gum until I could afford a new one.

A gigantic thank you to Harry Crocker, my editor. For years I had written for juries and lawyers who *had* to read my reports. Harry helped me to understand that we wouldn't necessarily have a captive audience.

And finally, thank you to all the people who live their lives as if there really is a Constitution that gives Americans unique rights—rights that no president can take away from us. If I'm wrong about that, please contact me at whatever Club Fed they eventually send me to.

Select Bibliography

Saul D. Alinsky, *Rules for Radicals: A Practical Primer for Realistic Radicals* (Vintage Press, 1971).

Charles F. Allen and Jonathan Portis, *Bill Clinton: Comeback Kid* (Birch Lane Press, 1992).

Anonymous, *Primary Colors* (Random House, 1996).

John Barron, *Operation Solo* (Regnery Publishing, 1996). An inspiring story of an enormously successful FBI operation.

Stephen M. Bauer, *At Ease in the White House* (Birch Lane Press, 1991).

Michael Jesse Bennett (ed.), *Patrick Henry's Comments on Life, Liberty, and the Pursuit of Happiness* (The Descendant's Branch—Patrick Henry Memorial Foundation, 1991).

Lee Brown, *National Drug Control Strategy—1995* (government publication).

Joseph A. Califano, Jr., *The Triumph and Tragedy of Lyndon Johnson* (Simon and Schuster, 1991).

Robert Carnes, *Don't Call It Love: Recovery from Sexual Addiction* (Bantam, 1992).

George Carpozi, Jr., *Clinton Confidential* (Emery Dalton Books, 1995).

Hillary Rodham Clinton, *It Takes a Village* (Simon and Schuster, 1996).

Alexis de Tocqueville, *Democracy in America* (Mentor Books, 1984).

Cartha D. DeLoach, *Hoover's FBI* (Regnery Publishing, 1995). Good at exposing political misuse of the FBI.

Elizabeth Drew, *On the Edge* (Simon and Schuster, 1994). One of the better books on Clinton.

281

Eric Felten, *The Ruling Class* (Regnery Publishing, 1993).

Paul Flick, *The Dysfunctional President* (Birch Lane Press, 1995). One possible explanation for President Clinton's aberrant behavior.

Gennifer Flowers, *Passion and Betrayal* (Emery Dalton Books, 1995). Offers evidence that Bill Clinton used cocaine.

Todd Gitlin, *The Sixties: Years of Hope, Days of Rage* (Bantam, 1987). Captures the essence of the New Left.

Myron P. Glazer and Penina M. Glazer, *Whistleblowers: Exposing Corruption in Government and Industry* (Basic Books, 1989).

Richard Goldstein, *Reporting the Counterculture* (Unwin-Hyman, 1989).

Alexander Hamilton, James Madison, and John Jay, *The Federalist Papers* (Mentor Books, 1961).

William A. Henry III, *In Defense of Elitism* (Doubleday, 1994). A good book on American society, from a liberal perspective.

Hank Hillin, *Al Gore: His Life and Career* (Birch Lane Press, 1988). A puff piece written by a former FBI agent.

John L. Jackley, *Hill Rat* (Regnery Publishing, 1992). Great depiction of shenanigans at the other end of Pennsylvania Avenue.

Ronald Kessler, *Inside the FBI* (Pocket Books, 1995). Good information on William Sessions's demise.

———, *Inside the White House* (Pocket Books, 1995).

Harvey Kleh and John Earl Haynes, et al., *The Secret World of American Communism* (Yale Press, 1995).

Wayne Kritsberry, *The Adult Children of Alcoholics Syndrome* (Bantam, 1985).

Nicholas Lampert, *Whistle-blowers in the Soviet Union: Complaints and Abuses Under State Socialism* (Shocken, 1985).

Robert Lehrman, *Doing Time* (Hastings House, 1980).

G. Gordon Liddy, *Will* (St. Martin's Press, 1980).

Rush Limbaugh, *See, I Told You So* (Pocket Books, 1993).

———, *The Way Things Ought to Be* (Pocket Books, 1993).

David Maraniss, *First in His Class* (Simon and Schuster, 1995). One of the best books on the Clintons.

Sara Hines Martin, *Healing for Adult Children of Alcoholics* (Bantam, 1989).

Mary Matalin and James Carville, *All's Fair* (Simon and Schuster, 1994).

Allen J. Matusow, *Unraveling of America: History of Liberalism in the 1960s* (Harper-Torch Books, 1984). Excellent description of New Left infiltration of academia, the media, and government.

Peggy Noonan, *What I Saw at the Revolution* (Random House, 1990).

Oliver North and William Novak, *Under Fire* (HarperCollins, 1991).

Meredith L. Oakley, *On the Make* (Regnery Publishing, 1994). Useful on Clinton's days as governor of Arkansas.

Thomas P. O'Neill, Jr., with William Novak, *Man of the House* (Random House, 1987).

Thomas W. Pauken, *The Thirty Years War* (Jameson, 1995). Personal experience of the New Left—with which I could readily identify.

John Podhoretz, *A Hell of a Ride* (Simon and Schuster, 1993).

Gail Sheehy, *Character* (Bantam, 1990). A good book from a liberal perspective; useful on Al Gore.

James Stewart, *Blood Sport* (Simon and Schuster, 1996).

Michael John Sullivan, *Presidential Passions* (Shapolsky Publications, 1990).

Pane Taylor, *See How They Run* (Knopf, 1990).

Cal Thomas, *The Things that Matter Most* (HarperCollins, 1994).

Gregory S. Walden, *On Best Behavior* (Hudson Institute, 1996). A good book, but written mainly for lawyers—about ethical lapses in the Clinton administration.

"Whitewater," *The Wall Street Journal*, 1994. Highly recommended. Better than *Blood Sport*.

George Washington, *George Washington's Rules of Civility and Decent Behaviour in Company and Conversation* (Applewood Books, 1988).

Bob Woodward, *The Agenda* (Simon and Schuster, 1994). A book with its own agenda. It is inaccurate and misses most of the salient characteristics of the Clinton administration.

Index

285

ABOUT THE AUTHOR

GARY ALDRICH worked for the FBI for more than thirty years, twenty-six as a Special Agent, specializing in white-collar crime, especially fraud and political corruption. For the last five years of his distinguished career he was one of two FBI agents assigned to the White House, responsible for performing background checks on White House personnel. He retired in 1995. He is now founder and president of the Patrick Henry Center, which assists government whistleblowers who want to come forward and expose wrongdoing.

Special Gift Offer: See reverse for details

YES, please send ___ gift copies of *Unlimited Access* to my friends, family or colleagues listed, at the special price of $12.50 per copy, a savings of more than 20% off the normal bookstore price of $15.95. **PLUS** send ___ copies free, one for every four paid copies.
I understand you will express ship every copy absolutely **FREE!**

❑ **Enclosed is my check for $** _____ **per copy**
    or
❑ **Charge my:** VISA ❑ Visa MasterCard ❑ MC AMERICAN EXPRESS ❑ Amex

   Name:_____

   Address: _____ City, State, Zip: _____

   Credit card # _____ Signature: _____

   (Maryland and D.C residents add 5% and 6% sales tax, respectively.)   **UNAC GO/01/31**

Mail orders to: Regnery Publishing • 7811 Montrose Road • Potomac Maryland 20854
or call 1-888-219-4747 today and place your rush order

Please send a gift copy of *Unlimited Access* to those listed below:

Name: _____

Address: _____ City, State, Zip: _____

Gift From _____ I prefer to remain anonymous _____

· ·

Name: _____

Address: _____ City, State, Zip: _____

Gift From _____ I prefer to remain anonymous _____

· ·

Name: _____

Address: _____ City, State, Zip: _____

Gift From _____ I prefer to remain anonymous _____

· ·

Name: _____

Address: _____ City, State, Zip: _____

Gift From _____ I prefer to remain anonymous _____

· ·

Special Bonus: This copy FREE!!! (with four paid orders above)

Name: _____

Address: _____ City, State, Zip: _____

Gift From _____ I prefer to remain anonymous _____

USE ORDER COUPON OR CALL: 1-888-219-4747

Special Gift Offer:

Share *Unlimited Access* with friends, family, or colleagues

"I urge you to read this book, and to buy extra copies and give it to friends. Spread the word, spread the truth."— **Michael Reagan on *Unlimited Access***

Now for just $12.50 per copy (that's more than 20% off the bookstore price of $15.95) we will express ship this brand new paperback edition of Gary Aldrich's *Unlimited Access* to as many friends, family, and colleagues as you like.

PLUS we'll express ship every copy absolutely free.

PLUS for every 4 gift copies you order we'll send one more absolutely **FREE!** That's 5 books, express delivered, for $50; you save more than $49.

Just fill in below the names and addresses of those you want to receive Gary's book, and fill out the order coupon on the reverse. Then mail this entire page along with a check (or use your credit card) for $12.50 per copy to: Regnery Publishing 7811 Montrose Road • Potomac, MD 20854

Or for even faster service call 1-888-219-4747. Tell them you are calling about the Gary Aldrich gift offer.

Please send a gift copy of *Unlimited Access* to those listed below:

Name: _____

Address: _____ City, State, Zip: _____

Gift From _____ I prefer to remain anonymous _____

• •

Name: _____

Address: _____ City, State, Zip: _____

Gift From _____ I prefer to remain anonymous _____

• •

Name: _____

Address: _____ City, State, Zip: _____

Gift From _____ I prefer to remain anonymous _____

• •

Name: _____

Address: _____ City, State, Zip: _____

Gift From _____ I prefer to remain anonymous _____

• •

Special Bonus: This copy FREE!!! (with four paid orders above)

Name: _____

Address: _____ City, State, Zip: _____

Gift From _____ I prefer to remain anonymous _____

Use Order Coupon on Reverse or call: 1-888-219-4747

The Book of Virtues —
In a time where smut, violence, and immorality pervade the media, this inspiring collection of fables, poetry, stories, and other readings is a lesson in morality, and a must-read for our nations families! This #1 best-seller by Ronald Reagan's Secretary of Education will provide a solid foundation of morality for you and your family.

Item #3884   Retail $30.00

The New Age Movement and the Biblical Worldview — What makes the New Age movement so dangerous to your family? Dr. John Newport uncovers every area of this many-sided movement and explains the need for Christians to understand the New Age threat and how it differs from Christianity.

Item #4915   Retail $35.00

A History of the American People — In a single sweeping volume (1,136 pages): the American story in full - as it's never been told before. Paul Johnson's conservative outlook reverses a half-century of liberal myth-making on everything from America's founding principles to the achievements of Ronald Reagan.

Item #4840   Retail $35.00

The Coming Conflict With China — Bernstein and Munro present overwhelming documentary evidence that communist China has targeted the U.S. as its chief global adversary and is aggressively pursuing a well-mapped plan for achieving dominance. Chilling reading in the light of recent history.

Item #4573   Retail $23.00

A Familiar Exposition of the Constitution of the United States — In this exclusive Conservative Book Club edition, Justice Joseph Story opens a brilliant window into the thinking of the Founders and introduces a new generation to this unsurpassed work of American constitutional interpretation.

Item #4712   Club Exclusive $24.95

The Great Betrayal — Poised to announce his candidacy for the Republican presidential nomination in 2000, Pat Buchanan has refined his message on trade and economic nationalism. Agree with him or not, this is a must read for the grass roots conservative.

Item #4860   Retail $22.95

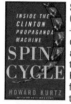

Spin Cycle: Inside the Clinton Propaganda Machine — Is this liberal journalist part of the "vast right-wing conspiracy" or is he just telling the truth about the Clinton White House? Howard Kurtz, reporter for the Washington Post, gives the first behind-the-scenes account of the Clinton White House as it attempts to package and control the news by manipulating, misleading, and intimidating the press.

Item #4906   Retail $25.00

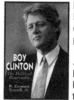

Coolidge — Silent Cal, the President most admired by Ronald Reagan, most trivialized by historians and most misunderstood by modern Americans. Now, the real story of the man and his presidency is told in an amazing new biography.

Item #4964   Retail $35.00

Boy Clinton — Blockbuster expose by the publisher of *The American Spectator*. R. Emmett Tyrrell has unearthed the truth about the real Bill Clinton — including facts that have never been revealed before.

Item #4367P   Retail $14.95

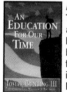

An Education for Our Time — Josiah Bunting attacks the modern higher education system by constructing a fictional story about the ideal university. As President of this new university, Bunting lays out a curriculum based on classical teaching, dedicated to instilling young Americans with virtue and knowledge.

Item #5028   Retail $24.95

Nearer, My God — Explore conservatism's Christian soul in William F. Buckley's moving autobiography of faith. "The greatest conservative figure of our age relentlessly probes the ultimate question: God. And gives us a stirring, at times deeply personal defense of his Catholic faith." — *Charles Colson*

Item #4780   Retail $24.95

Hollywood Party — Author Kenneth L. Billingsley uncovers the true face of Hollywood Communism and reveals how the Party — through the muscle of trade unionists, the intellect of celebrity writers, and the facade of glamorous movie stars — nearly came to dominate America's first mass medium.

Item #5075   Retail $25.00

The Politics of Bad Faith — 1960s radical turned conservative writer, David Horowitz, reveals how the American political Left is quietly, but relentlessly waging a new "cold war" on the nation. Liberals and Clinton-style "centrists" are undermining our founding principles in the guise of "social justice."

Item #5074   Retail $25.00

The Conservative Leadership Series — Created exclusively for members, this series brings you the founding works of modern conservatism in collectors quality hard cover editions. Beginning with the three titles pictured and continuing through Kirk and Buckley the Conservative Leadership Series will span more than a century of conservative thought. These and upcoming volumes deserve a prominent position in your personal library.

The Best of Burke	Item #4595	Club Exclusive $27.95
The Theory of Moral Sentiments	Item #8001	Club Exclusive $27.95
The Wealth of Nations	Item #4965	Club Exclusive $27.95

Books That Matter. Books

In 1964 America was walking down Lyndon Johnson's path to a socialist "Great Society." In the midst of the growth of big government spending a few bold voices appeared and challenged the liberal elites and their impractical policies. That same year the Conservative Book Club was born. Thirty-five years later we still bring you the books that will make a difference in battling liberal ideas now, and into the next millennium. Join the fight by choosing your first three books today.

The Strange Death of Vincent Foster — With remarkable first-hand research, investigative journalist Christopher Ruddy details the disturbing inconsistencies surrounding Foster's alleged suicide. "A persuasive case that the American public has not been told the complete facts about the case." —*William S. Sessions, Former Director, FBI*

Item #4711   Retail $25.00

The Millennium Bug — January 1, 2000: you have no electricity, your bank has no record of your account, and the police are unable to respond to calls for help. Learn about the causes and issues surrounding this biggest crisis in the *information age* and prepare yourself for the inevitable chaos.

Item #4881   Retail $25.00

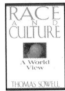

High Crimes and Misdemeanors — Ann Coulter, a legal affairs correspondent for *Human Events*, outlines the 6 categories of impeachable conduct and demonstrates how Bill Clinton has violated all of them since 1993. This hard-hitting work takes the reader through the web of lies that the Clinton administration rests on.

Item #4923   Retail $24.95

Saving Childhood — Protect your children from the national assault on their innocence. Parents and authors Michael and Diane Medved take you through the four major sources of this assault: the media, schools, peers, and parents. Learn how to see the subtle influences that poison your child's innocence.

Item #5011   Retail $24.00

The Impeachment of William J. Clinton - A masterful work by R. Emmett Tyrrell showing how Clinton could be impeached within a few months. It will leave you wondering not if it will ever happen, but when! "A riveting novel that may yet play out in real life." — *Robert Novak*

Item # 4757   Retail $24.95

Race and Culture — If a white man wrote this book, the liberals would lynch him. Find out why, after more than a decade of research, Thomas Sowell came to the conclusion that some cultures are better - yes BETTER - than others.

Item #4079   Retail $25.00

Unlimited Access — Former FBI Special Agent Gary Aldrich takes you inside a counter-culture White House and shows how Clinton and his cronies dismantled security protocols to allow drug users, drug dealers, gun runners and foreign campaign donors full access. This updated, quality paperback edition includes three new chapters.

Item #5048   Retail $15.95

Ronald Reagan: How an Ordinary Man Became an Extraordinary Leader — Dinesh D'Souza presents a vivid portrait of the man himself, revealing the moral sources of his vision and leadership. "Move over, President Clinton, and make room for a real leader!" —*Rush Limbaugh*

Item #4751   Retail $25.00

Conquests and Cultures — Thomas Sowell takes his controversial views a step further, daring to argue: The best thing that ever happened to some cultures was to suffer military conquest by another.

Item #4880   Retail $35.00

Worth Reading...Since 1964